Indifferent

To Mary & Charlie

Cass Cassidy

Cass Cassidy

Published by David (Cass) Cassidy
Publishing partner: Paragon Publishing, Rothersthorpe
© David Cassidy 2016

ISBN 978-1-78222-459-4

Book design, layout and production management by Into Print
www.intoprint.net
+44 (0)1604 832149
Printed and bound in UK and USA by Lightning Source

Contents

In the beginning there was nothing...

Temptation Led to Sin...

Cast out of Eden, Adam and Eve had three sons:

Cain, Abel and Seth.

Cain killed Abel and fled to the East
where he was sheltered by a band of fallen angels:

The Watchers.

These Watchers helped Cain's descendants
build a great industrial civilization.

Cain's cities spread wickedness
devouring the World.

Only the descendants of Seth
defend and protect what is left of Creation.

To-day, the last of Seth's line became a man.

Countries, worked and lived in:-

Saudi Arabia.
Nigeria, West Africa.
Ghana, West Africa.
Scotland. North Sea. [Oil-Rig Hook-Ups]
Uganda, East Africa.
Central America. Belize.
Turkish Republic [Northern Cyprus]

Voluntary work after retirement in 1994:-

1994-1995: Botswana Central Africa. [Kalahari Desert with the San People]
1996-1999: South Africa [After the collapse of Apartheid]
2001-2002: Ecuador.
2002-2003: Bangladesh.

Which reminds me of the old adage by **J.R.R. Tolkien:**

> "NOT ALL
> WHO WANDER
> ARE LOST"

This story was inspired by events and is dedicated to my grandchildren:
Leilah Peligren.
Cameron Peligren.
Sean Cassidy
Emma Cassidy.

Previous books published by Paragon Publising that complete this Trilogy:

"Gaba Road" 2012.
Non-Fiction Story of our life in Uganda 1980-1984, just after the Uganda-Tanzanian War and how the people of Uganda continued to suffer during that period.

"Blind Man in Africa" 2014.
Non-Fiction Story about life in Saudi Arabia, Norway, Nigeria, and Ghana between 1971-1978, and the daily survival of the people of these countries.

Preamble

"Indifferent", is the First book of a trilogy about the life of the writer, which he eventually shared with his wife Kathleen Cassidy [Nee Kathleen McAuley] and their three children Linda Ann, Lorna Theresa and Mark McNeill.

This is a non-fiction story about the writer who was born in one of the poorer areas of Edinburgh the capital city of Scotland. The story will take you from Edinburgh to the picturesque city of Trieste in Italy where the writer goes to do his Compulsory National Service in the British Army. Whilst in Trieste he wins accolades for his well-groomed appearance, stature and driving skills. His achievements are shattered when he faces a Court Martial and ends up spending a considerable time incarcerated in a military prison administered and run by psychopathic, malicious and evil military staff.

Eventually the writer is liberated, demobbed from the army and returns home to his parents and siblings in Edinburgh. Eventually he meets a lovely Irish girl and they are married. He is now determined to make something of himself and with the support of his treasured wife they begin their quest for a better quality and standard of life for themselves and eventually, their three children.

This is an interesting story which should arouse your curiosity because of its varied locations and many characters, some colourful and cheerful, others sad and vulnerable and several, malicious and evil.

This book "Indifferent" is the first book of a trilogy and covers the period between 1934 / 1968.

The Second book of the trilogy is "Blind Man in Africa" which covers the period between 1971 /1978 and will take you too England, Saudi Arabia, Norway, Nigeria and Ghana in West Africa. The book, "Blind Man in Africa" is attention-grabbing and out of the ordinary.

The Third book of the trilogy is "Gaba Road" which covers the period between 1980 / 1984 and will take you to Uganda and Kenya in East Africa. This book, is remarkably exciting, stimulating, breathtaking and a cant put down page turner..

Cass Cassidy

Indifferent: 1

On the eighth of April 1934 at number 7 Middle Arthur Place, one of the working class areas of Edinburgh the capital city of Scotland; my mother Evangelina Matilda Cassidy better known to our dad and neighbours as *Millie,* gave birth to her fourth child. It was another boy and I, David Cassidy was born. My Mum already had three children. Cathy, my sister who was the eldest and was born in 1927. My two elder brothers, Hector, who was named after our dad and was born in 1928 and Hugh who was named after our granddad, was born in 1932.

I was three years old when my sister Rachel was born in 1937 and six years old when my other wee sister Margaret was born in 1940. I had just left school at fifteen when my younger brother James was born in 1949. I was piggy in the middle of a family of seven, three siblings older than me and three siblings younger than me. However being piggy in the middle was to turn to be advantageous for me because I was allowed to be the first member of our family to take up a very low paid apprenticeship as a heating engineer.

Unfortunately, later on in life both my younger sisters Rachel and Margaret, and my younger brother James all proved to be untrustworthy, manipulative and dishonest, therefore unworthy of any further mention in this narrative.

Our dad, Hector McNeill Cassidy was born in Old Kilpatrick in Glasgow in 1901, but his ancestors were originally from Eire and had emigrated in the 1800s to the Scottish Isles and eventually merged with the McNeill Clan of Bara. According to my dad's birth certificate, my grandparents signed their names with an X, indicating that perhaps they could not read or write the English. My mother, whose maiden name was Evangelina Matilda Vast, was born in Edinburgh in 1904 and married my father in 1926. My grandmother died before my dad married my mother and the cause of my grandmothers early death is unknown to this day and was never discussed. My grandfather was still alive when I was born and I remember that he only had one arm. Nobody seemed to know how he lost his arm. In spite of this handicap, apparently he was a very resolute individual who would get involved in a fight at the drop of a hat. It was said that he would knock his adversary out cold with a smack from the stump of what was left of his right arm. Rumour had it that when in a fighting mood, especially when he lived in Glasgow; it would take two or three policemen to arrest him and strap him to the barrow that would wheel him to the police station cells.

At one time [before I was born] our dad was a semi-professional bare fisted fighter who fought in the booths in Glasgow. There were no Marquess of Queensbury rules in those bare knuckle fights; it was the last man standing that won the few shillings prize money. Both my dad and my grandfather were only about five feet five inches tall. My dad was a quiet reserved man who was physically and mentally strong. It was said that during his booth fighting days he was so hungry for money that he fought like a gladiator. However, by the time he had gathered what he had removed of his street clothes after winning a fight, my grandfather who was also his manager had already collected the winnings and was in the nearest bar spending it. Our dad was a stocky man with a strong-looking physique and in spite of his booth fighting days he had good-looking facial features.

When he married my mum in 1926, he was a military man in the Cavalry Armoured Division. I remember seeing a photograph of him in his uniform wearing all his highly polished brown leathers and he looked very impressive, just like a movie star. It was horses that pulled the cannons in those days and as a result, he always had a great respect for horses. I witnessed him once knocking our local coalman to the ground and threatening to thrash him because he was mistreating his old Clydesdale carthorse. Apparently my dad was involved in a terrible accident during his military career. He was cleaning his rifle one day and was unaware that he had a single bullet in the breach. He accidentally shot the soldier sitting on the next bed. The soldier survived and a full investigation by the army cleared my dad of any offence; however he was discharged with discredit. All this happened long before I was born. Cathy, my eldest sister was their only child at that time. The story is that my dad found it extremely difficult to exonerate himself for nearly killing a fellow soldier and being dismissed from the Cavalry Armoured Division.

I remember our dad having many jobs; he was a coal carrier, carrying 1cwt bags of coal up tenement buildings that were six / eight stories high. I remember him coming home in the evening as black as his coal. My mum would boil water in a kettle over the coal fire as we had no electricity, only gas mantles for the lighting. She would gently wash the bleeding scars on his broad shoulders. He was also a Carter that drove a horse drawn cart delivering goods and parcels to shops throughout Edinburgh. When Hugh, my big brother and I were on our summer holidays from school, he used to take us to work with him. He would leave for work very early in the morning on his bicycle as he had to collect his horse from the stable and rig up its harness and hook it up to it's huge long cart. Then he would have to get the cart loaded up by the dispatch people before heading off to deliver his load for that day. He would pre-arrange a time and place for us to meet him and it was always around 0900 hours in the morning and as close to home as possible so as we did not have to pay for tram- car fares. We would sit on the cart and be driven all around Edinburgh, even along the grand majestic and famous Princes Street. The highlight of the day was always when we would stop for our ten-o-clock in the morning tea break. He would take us into a typical working mans cafe which were always full of other carters

10

with big mugs of tea and huge bacon rolls. We were the only kids that appeared to be in these cafes. I remember us being so happy and feeling very grown-up and proud. For lunch, we would carry sandwiches that our mum had made up for the three of us because our dad didn't have enough cash to purchase more mugs of tea and bacon sandwiches.

Dad always had the same huge horse that he called Sandy. Sandy was a mare, but he called her Sandy because that was her beautiful colour and I do believe that she had a liking for that name because she always responded to it. He treated that horse as an equal, like a person and an individual He would talk to her all day; I swear to God that, that horse knew when our dad was talking to her. When he was talking to Sandy, her ears would continually move backwards and forwards and he would always introduce us to her when we joined them first thing in the morning. We would be allowed to stroke her huge chest as dad talked to her while gently patting her head and ever so gently stroking her tender mouth and nose. As we stroked, dad would be speaking to her and she would shiver her huge front legs and chest muscles as if to let us know that it was nice, as if thanking all three of us for being kind to her and informing us that she liked us too. Dad finished his working days with the Edinburgh Council as a sort of odd job man. I have no idea why he left Sandy his horse that he used to speak to, perhaps he thought he was getting too old to be driving a huge horse drawn cart through Edinburgh's chaotic traffic, especially the screeching and screaming tram cars that always appeared to frighten the cart horses.

During the summer school holidays, he would take Hugh and I camping nearly every weekend. We would cycle for hours past Dalkeith and as far as Pathead and set up camp near Tyne water which is a tributary of the river Tyne. Alternatively we would go towards the Pentlands Hills to Juniper Green or Currie. Often we would set up our camp at Balerno which would allow us to swim in the reservoir. Other locations were Roslin and Penicuik. Our dad took us anywhere and everywhere. Often, we were allowed to invite one friend each, providing they had bicycles and could provide their own provisions. Dad and Hugh had their own bicycles and I would sit on the rear of my dad's bicycle. He had reinforced the small tray for carrying goods that was situated behind his saddle seat and directly above the rear wheel. Dad was an expert at building bicycles out of any scrap bicycles he could pick up from waste bins and scrap yards. No fancy tents and sleeping bags for us. It was strong canvas waterproof tarpaulins that he would borrow from his horse drawn cart, one for a roof and one for the floor. We would all sleep fully clothed and always pitched our tarpaulins in a wooded area adjacent to a water stream or river. On arrival at the site he had chosen, we were sent to collect dry fire wood while he rigged-up the "Tarps" to small trees for cover from any inclement weather. Then we would go for walks to survey the land around us. The highlight would be in the evening when the fire was lit for our evening meal. Our diet was kept very simple. We would have one small frying pan for heating the beans over the timber fire. On a special weekend, we had a few fried eggs with our beans with slices of bread that were toasted over the timber fire. Tea was brewed in empty syrup or treacle tins with broken match sticks or twigs floating on top of the water we had drawn from the nearby stream to prevent the smoke from the fire impregnating the water for our tea. We would sit around the fire in the evening after our meal just talking and laughing late into the night. At times our dad would entertain us by playing the spoons. This was a technique where he would put two large spoons together in his right hand and play tunes by clicking them together and smacking the spoons against his knees, elbows and left hand. He had a natural ability for making music because he also played the mouth organ and the accordion. When it was time for bed dad would douse the fire out with water and inform us that it was time to rest and get some sleep. In the morning he would always be up and about before us and be sitting at a new timber fire smoking his woodbine cigarette and drinking a new brew of tea. If we had camped near a village and he had some spare cash, he would send Hugh for some freshly made hot rolls for our Sunday morning breakfast. After cycling or walking around our new area we would have our beans and eggs for lunch. After Sunday lunch we would dismantle our camp site and head back home. It was an incredibly fantastic experience. We only had a few friends that owned bicycles therefore choosing who would join us on these camping trips was never a problem. However I do believe that it was more personal and reassuring when there was just the three of us.

My mum must have spent a great deal of her young life being pregnant and the remainder of her time doing all that she could to keep us kids clothed and fed. She spent most of her life looking after her seven children. She was a very proud women who cherished her family and was often melancholy if she could not provide enough for us. My eldest sister Cathy and brother Hector could never make arrangements to meet their grown up friends during the week days because every Monday morning without fail, their good clothes would go directly into the pawnshop and remain there until pay day on the Friday night or Saturday morning. In spite of all that our mother had to endure, I can't ever remember her complaining. My mother's maiden name was Vass. Like my granddad's missing arm and my missing grandmother, no one ever thought of asking her about her extraordinary maiden name and where it came from.

*Guy-Fawkes night was always a serious time for conflict
because we were all stealing each others timber debris
as each individual street aspired to have the biggest bone-fire*

The Nine of us, my parents and seven children all lived in a two-room house on the South Side of Edinburgh. It consisted of a kitchen / dining room, where our parents slept in a double bed in an alcove and one bedroom where all us kids slept. In spite of this, we regarded ourselves as being posh because our house was a main door house and not a flat in the surrounding six storey tenement buildings. We had our own private toilet, not communal like the other families who had to share a toilet with four or five other families. However, we had no bathroom, no hot water and no electricity. We had to wash ourselves in the small black sink in the kitchen / dining room that was also used to wash the dishes and pots and pans. We had no refrigerator, freezer, cooker or TV and all my mother had to cook on and to provide hot water, was the coal fire. We kids all slept in the one bedroom, the girls in one bed and the boys in the other. On winter nights, the coats that we wore to keep us warm outside, doubled up as blankets on our bed at night. We would sit up at night listening to the rats running amok under the floor boards and behind the skirting boards. We would often have to throw a shoes at the odd huge rat that had managed to venture into our bedroom. We had no idea that we were poor because everyone around us was equally poor, with some poorer than others. That was until I went to school and witnessed how smartly dressed the other kids from other parts of the area were. That's when I realized that everyone from Arthur Street, West Arthur Place, Middle Arthur Place and East Arthur Place were poor and as I said previously, some poorer than others. Each street had its own private gangs but there was never any serious rivalry. The build up to Guy Fawkes night was always a serious time for conflicts because we would all be stealing each other's collection of timber debris as each street aspired to have the largest and best bone-fire.

I was soon to become a wee tough guy like my granddad and would fight anybody or everybody at the drop of a hat, except that I had two arms to fight with. Perhaps that was because I had red hair, freckles and wore a cheap pair of steel rimmed glasses. My dad had an old army kit bag stuffed full of paper and it hung from our bedroom door frame and it was used as a punch bag. Dad taught all us boys how and where to hit this punch bag as if it was a person. His philosophy was that it was without purpose or beneficial to ever consider running away from a bully or a fight. As far as he was concerned, it was better to put up a fight and even take a beating than to run away. If you put up a fight, the bully will think twice about bullying you ever again. That bully would prefer to go elsewhere and harass someone else that hopefully not put up a fight and will succumb to his bullying tactics.

My dad was a Catholic and my mother a Presbyterian. They were married in St Margaret's church in Prospect Terrace at the bottom of Arthur street which was a Presbyterian church, therefore we all went to non-catholic schools. I remember coming home from school one day to find my mother in tears, very upset and concerned. Apparently a priest had called to the house and had interrogated my mum, which was common practice in those days. The priest had suggested that because our mother and father had not married in a Catholic Church and we; Cathy, Hector, Hugh and myself were not going to catholic school's. We were all bastards! I remember thinking that if our dad had been at home, he would have thrown the priest out off our house.

Actually, at number 7 Middle Arthur Place, there were not nine of us there were ten. We had a huge cat called Tam and like our dads horse Sandy, Tam was a queen [female]. Tam had a litter of kittens every six months and our dad would drown the entire litter as soon as possible because neither we or Tam the cat could afford to feed them. Big Tam was kept and fed for one reason and one reason only and that was to kill any rat that ever ventured into our house and there were often a few. Big Tam was one crazy cat, she must have been the only cat in the entire world that chased and fought dogs. The minute she spied a dog or dogs, she would run at them and leap up onto their backs. I once saw her leap into the middle of a dog fight and scatter them both.

After a bout of measles at the age of six I developed a squint in my right eye. My mum immediately arranged for me to see an eye specialist. I was admitted to the Edinburgh Royal Infirmary E.N.T. department. An operation was carried out on what they said was my lazy eye and the squint was corrected. However, from that day on I had to wear glasses and of course the only glasses my parent's could afford were the free N.H.S. type that were cheap and very nasty looking. They had a thin wire frame with round lenses which identified them immediately as the free cheap nasty N.H.S. eye glasses. What, with my red hair, freckles and four-eyes, I was easy prey for bullies and others that liked to intimidate people like me. Unfortunately for them, this only made me more aggressive, if that was possible. When I was eight years old, I picked up a dead fish that was lying at the edge of the Caledonian Canal to take home for our cat, big Tam. This was going to be a luxury for the cat because she never ever got fish and lived on our scrap food of mince and tatties, soup, porridge, broken biscuits and bread. Perhaps that was why she could fight and beat-up-dogs. From the carcass of the dead fish I picked up a parasite through a scratch in my wrist, it eventually developed into meningitis which is a serious and often fatal illness. Apparently I was knocking on deaths door for a substantial time whilst I was in hospital and fortunately for me, no one answered the door. Because I was absent from school for a considerable time, when it was time for me to return to school, our family doctor wanted to send me to a school for handicapped children. My Mum went berserk because this 'Duncan Street School' was infamous and had its own special buses that collected all the children that lived in that Edinburgh

14

area. We kids from around the South Side area used to laugh and make fun of the kids on those buses. However I did return to my old school at South Bridge and was soon fighting everyone that called me carrot head, cock-eyes or four-eyes. Unfortunately, we all suffered.

When I was eleven years old, I moved to James Clerk's Secondary school which is situated on the edge of The Kings Park, as it was named then. We Arthur Street kids may have lived in a slum area but we had the biggest and most beautiful playground in all off Scotland, perhaps Britain; maybe even in the entire world. The Arthur Street slums were adjacent to this fantastic park complete with its own three lakes. It has its own extinct volcano named 'Arthur Seat' and the 'Crags' which is a solid rock face a mile long and fifty to sixty feet high and surrounded by miles of rolling pastures. Most of us kids could all climb these 'Crags' before we left school. Our playground even had its own Palace. Hollyrood Palace which dates back to the 12th century and sits inside the Kings Park directly opposite the 'Crags'. Hollyrood Palace was founded as a monastery in 1128 and was closely associated with Scotland's turbulent past including being the home of Mary Queen of Scots between 1561 and 1567. It is still the official residence of the monarchy when they visit Edinburgh and is the setting for State ceremonies and official entertaining.

One lovely summer day during our summer holidays from school I was sitting on my bed repairing my torn trousers. I was about ten years old. Cathy my elder sister arrived home from work and told me that she needed to use the scissors that I was using. Cathy was in the kitchen with our mum and kept persistently calling out for the scissors. Without thinking and seeing that my elder sister was harassing me and because both the bedroom and kitchen doors were wide open, I picked up the scissors and threw them into the kitchen. The scissors hurled through the air, through the two open doors and only stopped after they had embedded themselves in Cathy's right arm. When she screamed and I realized what had happened, I ran and crawled underneath the big double bed. As it turned out my mum had ran out of the house to get help. Mr Bertram our next-door neighbour hastily escorted my Mum and Cathy with the scissors still embedded in her arm up to the Deaconess Hospital which was situated at the Pleasance, which thank goodness was only a fifteen minute brisk walk away from Arthur Street. In the meantime I remained in my hiding place until my dad arrived home from work. He dragged me out from underneath the bed but not before he had banged his head a few times against the huge iron bed base, which made him even angrier. I received the thrashing that I obviously deserved.

I got my first job at eleven years old, delivering milk to the toffs that lived in Morningside, which was the posh side of Edinburgh. My two elder brothers, Hector and Hugh were already working there and that was probably one of the reasons that I got the job. We started work at five-o-clock in the morning so we had to leave Arthur Street at around four-o-clock in the morning as it was an hours walk through the Meadows to get to the Morningside milk shop. We finished our milk rounds at around seven-o-clock and were back home by eight, just in time to get ready for school at nine-o-clock. We loved it; the winter month's were a bit tough walking through the snow. Our shoes normally had holes in the soles and the cardboard that we put in to protect our feet once wet, would disintegrate therefore exposing our feet to the cold wet snow. We didn't complain, we were the lucky ones because we had a job, we were earning a few pennies and drinking free milk.

When Cathie the eldest in our family was fourteen years old and would have left school in 1941, it must have been a celebrated occasion for my parents because she would have commenced work immediately and would be earning a few shilling's that would increase my mums weekly household income. Then when our elder brother Hector left school in 1942, when he was fourteen years old, he started working at McEwen's Brewery which would further increase my mums household income. Hector worked with the coopers who made the beer barrels and the timber boxes for carrying the beer bottles. As a result he was able to pick-up some joinery and other useful skills. He also had access to free timber and at Christmas times he would make toys for us. The toys were good because apparently he was given lots of advice and assistance from the coopers. We may have been poor financially but we were rich in other ways. The Cassidy's were known for having good, reliable bicycles which our dad had built from various bits and parts and pieces that he had collected from waste bins and scrap yards. We also had the best go-karts in the South Side that were made off timber platforms fitted across four pram wheels. Hector supplied and made the timber platforms. Our dad would collect the wheels off discarded prams and fit them. Our snow sledges were famous because of their elegance and rapid speed sliding through the snow. Once more Hector had them made at work. Steel rims, used by the coopers to wrap around the beer barrels were fitted to our snow sledges that hurled us speedily through the snow. We often ended up at the Deaconess Hospital for stitches to various parts of our bodies after being hurled off our speeding snow sledges, or tumbling off our extremely fast go-karts.

I remember when I was around twelve years old having these weird dreams about the birds and the bee's. I had heard about a girl who lived in Arthur Street who for a few sweetie coupons would give you a hug and a kiss, depending on how many sweetie coupons you had to give her. She was a few years older than me and I discovered that she knew a lot more about the birds and the bees than I ever imagined. The only thing that I knew about bees were the ones we used to catch in our empty jam jars by guiding them into the empty jar with the jar lid. I have to say that we always let them go free after a few hours. As far as the birds were concerned, the only birds that I knew off were the pigeons around Arthur Street. Some people kept them in big boxes outside their windows or in big boxes on the roofs. I started removing some of the sweetie coupons from the ration books that my mother kept hidden in what she thought was her secret hiding place that I was also aware of. Mum used to sell our sweetie and clothing coupons to other neighbours that were not as poor as we were. However, she eventually discovered that some of her precious sweet's coupons were missing and all hell was let loose. These sweet and clothes coupons were a source of income for mum, therefore it was a very serious and immoral act. From that day on, my devious *birds and bees* meeting's with the girl from Arthur Street were over. I was never popular with girls anyway because as I have said previously, I had red hair, freckles and wore cheap wire framed N.H.S glasses. When we played kick-the-can in the street, the girls would all wait to see where my friends, John Nixon, Henry Fallon or the Forsyth brothers would all run too and hide, then all the girls would follow them. I always found myself hiding in some stairwell on my very own. It used to hurt, but I would never let it show and would just get into a fight to ease my hurt, anger, and pride

By the age of thirteen I had left the milk delivery job at Morningside and was now earning more money working in a very posh butcher's shop called Brechin Brothers in Newington; another posh area in Edinburgh very near Morningside. I worked in the shop for two hours after school Monday to Friday, cleaning the shop floors and washing the mincing and sausage machines. Saturday, with the use of one of the butcher shops bicycles I would deliver the butcher meat parcels to the customers who mostly lived around Newington and Morningside. I truly loved working in Brechin Brother's of Newington. I used to go straight to the shop direct from school and normally running all the way. Saturdays were magic; sitting on my huge delivery bike with its big metal basket fixed over the front wheel filled with parcels of butcher's meat. I just felt so important cycling along Clerk Street among all the tram cars and motor vehicles. The shops two beautiful cashier girls were always very nice and kind to me. I will never forget how special they made me feel. It was a very large and popular shop with at least five butcher's working in the shop front serving the customers. Another six working in the back shop butchering the animal carcasses and four more butcher's in the basement making mince, sausages, black pudding and killing and plucking the live chickens. The last thing I had to do every evening once the shop was closed was to sweep the shop front floors and remove all the dirty sawdust then sprinkle new clean sawdust ready for the shop opening in the morning. It was an art and I had to learn how to sprinkle the sawdust from the bucket so that it covered the entire floor area in an even layer without lumps or humps. During special

17

holidays and especially Xmas and New-Year, I worked all day on the Sunday's helping making mince, sausage's black pudding, and learning how to kill and pluck chickens. Every weekend I not only went home with my wages, I went home with a huge brown parcel filled with sausages, black pudding, mince and huge lumps of dripping fat, all for free.

My eldest brother Hector was the first to leave home. As soon as he was seventeen he joined the Royal Air Force Cadets and would spend the next twenty-five years in the R.A.F. Hector was a very good-looking young man and his nickname was handsome. It was a school teacher that fashioned his nickname. One day in class at James Clerk secondary school, Hector was looking out of the window admiring the view of the 'Crags' and the 'Arthur Seat' extinct volcano in the Kings Park. To get his attention the teacher shouted out. "Hey, handsome, would you mind joining us". The nickname stuck to him like glue. From that day on, even when his friends called at the house they would ask. "Is handsome coming out?". I remember missing handsome a lot, but it had its advantage because Hugh and I had more room in the bed! When Hugh left school he worked on the railway as a stoker who shovelled the coal into the steam engine furnaces. As soon as he was eighteen he had to leave home also and go and do his compulsory National Service in the Army. I remember missing Hugh as well because we were also very close and did a lot of crazy, wonderful things together.

Cathy, our eldest sister always appeared to be the only one that had to assist our mum with the housework chores and looking after the youngest members of the family. She appeared to have to work day and night and never ever appeared to have time for a social life. She was taken for granted by us all, probably because she was the oldest and a girl. I remember around 1949/1950 our mum appeared to be unable to cope. Apparently our mother was suffering from severe depression. Pre and Post Natal Depression was unheard off and not acceptable in the 1950's, particularly around the slums in Arthur Street. Cathy was left to handle all the problems, and she was only twenty-two years old herself. Hector was in England somewhere in the R.A.F. Hugh had just left home to do his National Service and was also somewhere in England. I was fifteen years old and had just left school and was working full time. My two other sisters would be twelve and nine-years old and a younger brother that had just been born. Our mum, suffering from serious depression was unable to cope with a one year baby, therefore the everyday chores and other demands were all left for twenty two year old Cathy to solve. She worked full time all day in a printers factory until she had an accident when her hair was caught in a machine. She then worked in a factory that produced ceiling- wax and eventually in a tea- packing factory. In the evening when she arrived home after completing a full day's work there were many chores waiting for her. Often a pile of dirty nappies that had to be washed because there were no disposable nappies in those days and even if there were, we could never have afforded them. The weekends must have been the worst for Cathie because she would be left to look after the new baby and that would include washing, dressing and making the powdered hot milk to feed him. She would be involved in all the cooking and all the other domestic chores. Cathy was to spend the next seven or eight years working full time and on arriving home in the evening to become involved in the house chores which involved cleaning, cooking and washing. During this time, Cathie would spend all her hard earned pocket money buying the new baby nice, decent clothes.

Before Hugh left for the army he had bought himself a toothbrush and he allowed me to also use it, in fact we shared it. We used to brush our teeth with the soot from the coal fire chimney by pushing the toothbrush up the chimney, then brushing our teeth with the coal black soot. I suppose it was not a case of the soot making our teeth snow-white, it probably just made our gums black, therefore making our teeth look snow-white. Cathy also had a toothbrush but she never used the soot from the chimney. Cathy used a red toothpaste that was in a round flat tin. Hugh and I could never ever find her toothbrush or toothpaste and we searched everywhere in the house. We eventually agreed that perhaps Cathie took them to work with her because she knew that if we found the toothpaste we would use it.

As soon as I was fourteen I left James Clerk school, but not before my art teacher had given me a note requesting my parents to come and speak with him. My mum, who was still unwell at the time was the only person available so she went to school with me to find out what he wanted. I knew I was good at art and I liked it very much because I was always top of the class at Art and would get 90 out of 100 nearly every time there was an exam. The art teacher informed my mother that I was a natural artist and should be sent to Art College and that he would make all the necessary financial arrangements. My mother promptly explained to him that we were a large family and it was necessary for me to start work immediately and earn the much needed money as soon as possible. Therefore forced by economic necessity, I could not go to art college. I was indifferent to that fact because Brechin Brother's had already offered me a full time job as soon as I left school, if I was interested.

Indifferent: 2

In 1948 when I was fourteen years old and with no qualifications to speak off, I started full time employment immediately with Brechin Brothers. I was a full time message and odd job boy. I now had my own personal bicycle, as there were a few other part time message boys. Any spare time that I had I would I spend it cleaning and maintaining my bicycle. My dad had taught me all there was too know about looking after bikes.

After six months delivering meat parcels, mincing meat, making sausages, black puddings and cleaning and scuffing the butcher blocks, the shop manager invited me into his office one day. He explained that he wanted me to commence my training as a fully qualified butcher. He further explained that this would entail day release school and some night school. I had never ever thought about being a butcher and frankly, I don't think I could be involved in carving up all these carcasses of cows, sheep, lambs and pigs that were delivered to our huge shop practically every single day. He obviously observed my indifference and suggested that I consider it and discuss it with my parents. My parents were indifferent and only concerned if this would incur a reduction in my present salary.

I made my own decision and after a few days I approached the manager and informed him that I did not want to be a butcher. I told him that I liked going around on my bicycle and that I liked being outside and wanted to remain being the delivery boy and assisting the butchers. He was a very gentle old man and suggested that I was too bright and clever to be wasting my time being a butcher delivery boy. He further explained why I should have a trade and how important it was that I should become a qualified tradesman. This Brechin Brothers butcher shop at Newington was a very large and distinguished shop located in the upper class side of town. My manager further explained that most of his customers were business people and asked me to consider very carefully what trade I thought that I would prefer to be trained and qualified in. He mentioned the possibility of being a motor mechanic, electrician, plumber, heating engineering, printer or painter. He further suggested that which ever trade I decided on, he would speak with his customers and recommend me as a good candidate for an apprenticeship. I felt that I had no other choice but to agree to his suggestions. After further discussions with my parents and my big sister Cathy, it was agreed that I should take the opportunity of an apprenticeship. It was a massive decision because I was certainly going to be earning less money and lose my weekly free food parcel every weekend, but my parents and Cathy agreed. Handsome my eldest brother was now in the Royal Air Force and Hugh had just been drafted into the Army to do his compulsory Military National Service.

First year apprentices in the 1950's were paid pea-nuts and a lot less than I was earning as a messenger boy, without even considering my free food parcel, this decision was a huge financial set-back. I was unsure which trade I wanted to do an apprenticeship for. It was now December, so we, my parents, Cathy and myself decided that I should remain working with Brechin Brothers until after Christmas and New Year because I would receive a lot of gratuity from my customers and continue to receive my free weekly food parcels over the Christmas and New year period. This would also give me time to consider which trade I wished to do an apprenticeship for. I discussed it with my boss and he was delighted.

I eventually decided I wanted to be a Heating Engineer and as promised, my Brechin Brothers manager arranged it. On January 1949, I started my five year apprenticeship as a Plumber / Heating Engineer with J.& R. Adams & Son an established business located at Surgeons Hall. I was just under Fifteen years old when I started my meagre paid apprenticeship and first thing we all missed was the weekend food parcels. Surgeons Hall Edinburgh was only a twenty five minute walk away from Middle Arthur Place, therefore there was no transport costs involved in commuting to and from work. Adams & Son employed eight tradesmen and three apprentices including myself. I will never forget one off my first job's. The boss's son, Jock took me down into this huge under- ground cellar where there were dozens of old baths, toilets, wash hand basins, sinks, urinals, wash tubs, old boilers, radiators and miles of scrap copper, lead and steel pipes. On the roof of this huge cellar there was a large metal trap door that opened up into the street at the rear of the workshop. All this waste material had been tipped down into this cellar through this huge trap door after the completion of each and every major job.

He told me to go through every broken and smashed item and remove the lead pipes, copper pipes and brass taps. I was to remove every item of valued scrap and heap them all in separate bundles. I was down that cellar for weeks at times. I was often vomiting when I got some excrete from the old toilets on my clothes, shoes and hands. This was my first experience as an apprentice heating engineer / plumber and I was already regretting it. I had no idea that I was going to see other peoples excrement let alone get it on my clothes and hands. Often, but not very often, one of the other older apprentice's would be sent down to assist me. I was being ever so careful removing the lead and copper pipes or brass water taps. He would remove them faster and easier with a huge sledge hammer.

Old man Adams was at the retirement age and the perfect old gentleman. He lived with his wife in a bungalow at the top of Liberton Brae on the outskirts of town. His son Jock Adams was an ex-rugby player who at one time had been given a trial for Scotland. He was over six feet tall and built like a large bull and behaved like one. He was an extremely ill-tempered man, therefore a very unpopular person in the workplace. His wife, who was also huge in stature and volume, was a cranky bitch and a despicable snob. I remember one time I was sent with one of the tradesmen to Jock Adams house in Spottiswood Crescent in the posh Marchment area. They had just had a new double bed delivered complete with metal frame and spring base. Angus, one of the tradesmen that was sent to assemble it decided to take me with him. Not only did Angus assemble the bed, apparently he had been instructed to built four brick pillars around the metal spring base frame for additional support. Apparently, the existing bed had halved in two while both Jock and his wife were still in it. The tradesmen in the shop reckoned that they were having sex and that both of them were rolling about like two huge ball bearings when suddenly and without warning the entire bed collapsed dropping both of them in a heap of raw flesh onto the floor.

The first year of my apprenticeship was good and exciting but financially our family suffered somewhat. During the second year of my apprenticeship, things began to improve because Hugh my big brother had returned home after completing his compulsory eighteen months Military National Service and was soon back at work as a coal stoker on the steam engines on the railway and bringing home wages. During our spare time in the evening Hugh would tell me all about England. He had been a driver in the Royal Army Service Corp, [R.A.S.C] during his national service. He was an ambulance driver and he would explain to me in detail about having to drive through London, sometimes in an emergency. We had a long bench in the kitchen that sat in front of our coal fire. In the middle of the bench there was a small hole in it. Hugh would put the poker for poking the fire into the hole and pretend it was a gear-stick and spend hours teaching me how to change-gear when driving. He taught me how to change gear double clutch style. Gear-boxes in the 50s were not synchronized therefore it was necessary to double-de-clutch. I could drive even before I sat inside my first vehicle. It was so good having Hugh home again. I had missed him so much.

During my second year of my apprenticeship I had spent most of my time with engineer Angus. He was a very exacting tradesman and just like a surgeon. Engineer Angus insisted that all his tools were spread out on a ground sheet and they had to be in precision. All screw drivers together, pliers and wrenches, soldering irons had to be beside the flux and solder. At the end of each day, I had to wipe and clean every tool and wrap them all up again in the clean ground sheet. Angus was always immaculately dressed with highly polished boots that could be used mirrors. His general appearance like his work was to perfection. Angus McCloud was always given the most prestigious jobs therefore I was very fortunate to be Angus's apprentice. I was learning fast and how to be a first class tradesman, in addition, I liked Angus McCloud. On one particular job I spent nearly six months working with Angus McCloud in the Adelphi Hotel in Cockburn Street upgrading their central heating system. I remember learning an awful lot on that particular job, thanks to Angus. I also got to know his wife, they had an apartment in Clerk Street where we often called in for a quick cup of tea. They were a very nice couple. They had no children and I often wondered why? Because they would have been wonderful parents.

At the beginning of my third year Jock Adams had me doing jobs on my own. It was not much fun because it was all uninteresting and undemanding work As an apprentice I was exempt from having to do my compulsory Military National Service in the armed forces until such as I was a qualified heating engineer/ plumber. Unfortunately, I would still have to do my eighteen months Military Service one I was qualified. However, J.R. Adams & Son would have to re-employ me for at least a minimum of twelve month after I had completed my National Military Service. It was during my third year apprenticeship that a new tradesman by the name of Willie Hamilton was re- employed. He had served his apprenticeship with J.R. Adams & Son and left to do his compulsory Military National Service. Willie Hamilton was a breath of-fresh air. He was about twenty four years old and did not appreciate or indeed succumb to big Jock Adams attitude. Willie Hamilton was a very bronzed good looking guy who had just spent eighteen months in the army stationed in Egypt. He would turn up for work in the most amazing wonderful clothes. His jeans, shirts and shoes were all expensive designer model wear. Big Jock was always protesting about his style of dress by informing him. "Hamilton, this is not a fashion show, we are all here to work". All the other tradesmen including Willie Hamilton would smile, then Hamilton would reply. "That's not a problem Mr Adams. I am here to work and I have just spent eighteen months with people telling me what to do, how to do it and what to wear. Therefore I would appreciate it if you would just back off some". Big Jock Adams would storm out of the workshop like an enraged bull.

I had made friends with four guys from East Arthur Place. Jordon, Conoboy, Fordy and Mitch. Joe Jordon and Conoboy were both apprentice plumbers. Fordy was an apprentice roof Slater and Mitch was an apprentice coach builder. Most weekends we would go dancing to the Excelsior dance hall or the Clan House. The Clan House was our favourite as we had found a wee pub in Fountainbridge that would serve us beer in the Jug Bar. Of course, this was against the law as we were all still seventeen years old, therefore underage. In Scotland in the 1950's women were not allowed in bars and so if they wanted a drink, even if they were with their husbands, they had to go into a wee separate room called the Jug Bar. The five of us would crowd into the tiny Jug Bar and the bar man would serve us a few pints of beers each.

23

One Saturday night after we had all left the Clan House dance hall in Fountainbridge, I met up with a few of the lads from Middle Arthur Place who were still hanging around Bells the grocer shop at the corner of Arthur Street. My friends from East Arthur Place, Mitch, Fordy, Conoboy and Jordon had already wandered on and away towards their homes. I am not to sure how or what actually happened but I got into a dispute with one of the Middle Arthur Place guy's, a very tall lad named Anthony Bald. Before I was aware of it he had pulled a knife and stabbed me in the stomach. Everyone including Anthony Bald scattered and ran. I managed to get along the street to our house whilst holding both my hands on my stomach to stem the flow of blood. My Dad wrapped a cloth around my wound and promptly walked me up to the Deaconess Hospital which was a twenty minute brisk walk away from our house. Apparently they had to pump my stomach to get the beer out before they could stitch me up. As it turned out I only required a few stitches. I had told my parents and the hospital that the entire incident was an accident therefore nothing was made of it and the incident was never ever mentioned again. That's the way it was in the 1950's, well in the South Side of Edinburgh anyway. The fact that I was only seventeen and had been drinking beer was as big a disaster, if not bigger than the actual stabbing. My parents, especially my mother went ballistic, I had never seen my mother so angry and emotional. She was in tears and I was unsure if she was crying because I had been drinking beer, or because I had been stabbed!!

I was doing well at work and was still being sent out on jobs on my own, unfortunately, it was mostly plumbing jobs. I was not that keen on the plumbing side of my training, I was only interested in heating-engineering, however the jobs I was being sent were in posh houses around the Marchment area and that was always a wee bonus as it was pleasant work. I was sent on few jobs with Willie Hamilton who unlike Angus was a very unorthodox tradesman. I learned nothing from Willie except how to chat up females, how to dress and how to be cool. I caught Willie having sex a few times with female customers. If we went to a house where a youngish attractive female answered the door Willie's face would sparkle and if that female was willing and most of them were, I was usually sent on a fools errand. If we went on a job near Fountainbridge where Willie lived with his parents in a big posh house, we would always call into his house for a tea or coffee break. I discovered that Willie was an only child and his parents appeared to be very affluent. Willie would take me into his vast bedroom which was larger that our entire two roomed house in Middle Arthur Place. He had walk in wardrobes that were as big as our only bedroom. He would show me a collection of suits, shirts, ties and shoes. Willie was good to me, and anytime we went to his house I always went home with a parcel. A shirts, a jacket or a pair of trousers, all good designer clothes that he had got tired off. I paid for them

24

in instalments but nothing like what they were worth and Willie was never over anxious to be paid. The only reason I could afford this pleasant self indulgency was because my mother was very good and would let me keep 50% of my silly wages when I needed it.

Lea was a very beautiful half Asian girl, her dark hair and features without any doubt gave her that mysterious oriental look.

I now had two suits of clothing, courtesy of an account with Burrton's the Taylor, actually everybody in the South Side of Edinburgh had accounts with *Happy Burrton's*, as it was known. When I had left school and started working in Brechin Brothers the butchers, I had thrown my cheap nasty wire eye glasses into the rubbish bin and had become a lot more confident about myself and my appearance. Meeting and working with Willie Hamilton also had a lot of influence in my new found self assurance. I was at a dance hall one Wednesday night on the other side of town and spotted this stunning looking Asian girl who was dancing with another girl. When the dance finished my eyes followed the beautiful Asian girl and her female dancing partner. The next dance was announced and it was a slow fox-trot. Mitch, Fordy, Conoboy and Jordon were all soon on the floor dancing with the girls that they had invited to dance. My eyes had never left the Asian beauty. My heart missed a beat as a guy took her female friend onto the floor to dance. I could not believe my eyes that this guy had not asked the gorgeous Asian girl to dance? I suddenly found myself like a robot heading towards her and asking her. "Would you like to dance?". This beautiful girl looked at me and smiled. "Thank you, yes I would". I could not believe my luck, it was a slow dance, the lights had been dimmed and everyone else around us were dancing very close together and hugging each other. I was afraid to hold her to close, afraid that I would upset her. After the dance had ended we thanked each other and departed. I watched her go away and eventually join her girlfriend. I suffered as I watched other guy's get her up to dance and was so angry with myself for being such a coward. I waited in pain and pounced on her when the first opportunity arrived and asked her to dance with me again. My heart missed a few beats this time when she agreed. When the dance finished I immediately asked her if I could take her for a coffee and she replied. "Yes, that would be nice, please let me go and tell my girl friend where I will be". She hesitated and said. "Please come, let me introduce you to her". We held hands as she guided me through the crowd's to find her girl friend. After the introductions I asked her girl friend to join us and was shocked and saddened when she accepted my invitation. I was finding the coffee break with two girls just too much for me to

25

cope with and was more than happy when I was once more dancing alone with my Asian beauty. I eventually asked her if I could walk her home and honestly thought I was going to die when my heart missed a few beats this time when she smiled and said. "Yes, I would like that"

This beautiful Asian girls could have lived 1000 miles away and I still would have walked her home. Her name was Lea, her mother was Chinese and her father was a Scot. They lived in a posh house on Hollyrood Road, the road that leads to Hollyrood Palace. Lea was born in Edinburgh and was presently training to be a fashion designer. Hollyrood Road was a twenty minutes walk away from Middle Arthur Place taking the short-cut down Arthur Street and along Prospect Terrace. I told her that I lived in the Pleasance, I did not have the heart to tell her that I lived in the Arthur Street slums, as she had probably heard about them. Her girl friend Joyce, also lived in Hollyrood Road and I ended up walking both off them home. Joyce worked in the offices of Younger's Brewery also located on Hollyrood Road. That night and after Joyce had finally left Lea and I alone we hugged and kissed each other. I am sure I would have still been there if it had not been for her mother calling out her name and suggesting that it was time for bed. We agreed to meet in the same dance hall next Friday night. That night I floated home to Middle Arthur Place, it was the first time in my life that I had ever floated and I liked it, I liked it very much indeed.

From then on I met Lea every Friday and Saturday night at that dance hall. We danced and laughed all night and hugged each other at every slow waltz. We even modified the fox-trot into a very slow hugging dance. Lea asked me one night when we were kissing each other good night. "Why do your friends all call you Cass when your name is David?" "It's short for Cassidy and that's what we all do. Mitch's real name is John Mitchell, Joe's full name is Joseph Jordon, Fordy's real name is Patrick Ford that's how it works and that's what we do". Lea was silent for a few seconds, then suggested. "Oh, that's not fair, I like David, can I call you David?". I replied. "If you call me David in front of my friends they will just all laugh and then make a fool of me". "All right, I will call you Cass, but when we are on our own like now, can I call you David?". "If you wish, but why would you want to talk when we are on our own?" Lea burst out laughing, then enquired. "Do you all come from the Pleasance?" "Well, yes round about there". I decided that I had to change the subject, however there was no need. Lea's mother shouted her name in a whisper and suggested that it was time for bed. When that happened Lea would leave almost instantly after a quick kiss, usually on one of my cheeks.

I started meeting Lea every Sunday afternoon outside her house. We would walk up the Royal Mile and down the Bridges into Princess Street then into Princess Street Gardens. When I was on my own with Mitch, Joe, Conoboy and

26

Fordy they would often all start singing. *~When China boy, meets China girl.~* .It was a very popular song around that time but it did not bother me, we just all laughed. As far as I was concerned Lea was a beautiful Scot's girl, tall slim and very attractive and always very well dressed. She was dark skinned and as far as I was concerned she was tanned and looked fantastic. Lea was half Asian and her beauty and skin texture without any doubt gave her the hint of being oriental. We had planned to meet as usual on the Friday night at the dance hall but I was suddenly taken ill with Tonsillitis.

I was seventeen years old and my doctor decided that my Tonsils had to be removed immediately. I was admitted into the Deaconess Hospital where they cut my throat to remove my Tonsils. After the operation I was in so much pain that I just wanted to die. I could not speak, eat, drink or even swallow my own saliva without suffering immensely. To make matters worse, if that was possible, the ward sister decided that she was going to make me, speak, eat, drink and get involved in recreation work. My mother had brought me a small writing pad to allow us to communicate by writing words down on the pad. After a week in hospital I told my mother in writing that I wanted out and that I wanted to go home. My mother spoke to the ward sister who was furious and accused me off behaving like a spoilt immature child. After a short silence, she vanished and eventually returned with a clip board and made me sign some papers to confirm that I had not been discharged and that I was discharging myself. My Mum, who was also not too pleased about al this fuss walked home with me to Middle Arthur Place in complete silence and I have to say that I have never ever felt so rejected in my entire life. I went straight to bed in our communal bedroom and just wanted to die in peace.

I have no idea how long I lay in that bed suffering, however eventually I was able to drink eat and make small conversation. One evening around seven-o-clock, my mother entered the bedroom and informed me that there were two girls at the door that wished to speak with me. I was both surprised and shocked, and eventually enquired. "What are you talking about?". "Two girls are at the door, they are asking for you, they want to speak to you". "Why? Who are they?" My mother left the bedroom and returned after a few minutes and informed me. "Its a girl named Lea and her friend Joyce". I was speechless but managed to control my distress and shame and said to my mother. "Tell them No. Tell them I can't see them. Just tell them No". My mother looked surprised and hurt then suggested. "The girl Lea say's she knows you and she wishes to speak to you". I instantly replied as I tried to crawl under the bed sheets. "I said No. I don't want to see them. I can't see them, so please tell them to go away". "Okay, I'll tell them your sleeping". "No. Don't tell them that, they will only come back. Just tell them I don't want to see them". I listened to my mother talking with them.

Then after a while the front door closed. My mother returned to the bedroom ranting on about how I could have spoken to them, how they looked like two nice girls then enquired. "Do you know them?" Before I could reply she further enquired. "Why could you not speak to them, they looked like two nice respectable lassies". I was not listening, I was shocked and bewildered, how the hell did Lea find out where I lived. Now she knows that I lied. Now she knows that I live in the Arthur Street slums. Oh my God I thought, now I will never ever be able to face her again. I asked my mother to go and close the bedroom door as I wanted to go to sleep, when in fact I really wanted to disappear.

Three day's later, I was able to get my body with its depressed mind, broken heart and ripped throat up and out of bed. That evening I visited Mitch in East Arthur Place, he explained to me how Lea had approached them in the dance hall and asked them what had happened to me and why I had stopped coming to the dance hall. When they explained that I had been in hospital but was now recovering at home, Lea had asked them for my address. Of course, none of my friends had any knowledge that I had lied to Lea about my address.

I returned to work and never ever went back to that Westfield Dance Hall where I had met Lea. I was tempted many times to go and wait outside her house in Hollyrood Road and try to explain to her why I had lied. Try to explain to her how I was afraid to tell her that I lived in the slums of Arthur Street because she may have been shocked and would have nothing to do with people like me. Try to explain to her that even if she accepted me, perhaps her parents would forbid her to ever see me again. Try to explain to her how ashamed and terrified I was that night when she called to see me. Try to explain to her how I was too ashamed to let her see me lying in my impoverished bedroom bed in my humble house. Perhaps I should have listened to my mother when she was ranting on. Maybe I should have let Lea see me in my poverty, if she had felt the way I did about her, perhaps she would have understood and accepted my poverty. I will never know.

A few weeks later at the Clan House dance hall in Fountainbridge one Saturday night, I met this girl Ann and walked her home to Gilmerton. Ann was a wee bit common and very sure of herself, not vulgar in any way and she always wore very trendy fashionable clothes. I suppose because she was also a good-looking girl she was just a wee bit over confident. We had not yet gone out together to the cinema or anything like that and were still only meeting each other at the Clan House dance Hall on the Saturday night. One Wednesday night, Jordon, Mitch, Conoboy, Fordy and myself decided to go to the Clan House. Actually Jordon, Conoboy and myself were all playing truant, because Wednesday nights were our night school nights and this was very unusual for Jordon because he was a very enthusiastic apprentice and never ever missed day or night school. That night in question there was a sudden whispering buzz, that some members of the notorious *Valdor-Boys* gang were in the dance hall. The *Valdor-Boys* were an infamous tough bunch of guys that dominated the South Side of Edinburgh. At full strength there were normally a dozen of them and apparently they were pretty brutal and violent when involved in a conflict. According to the stories, they normally outnumbered any adversary and they all wore the same *Teddy-Boy* suits with string ties and thick sole beetle crusher shoes. I was having a slow dance with Ann and as usual the lights were dimmed and like all the other couples we had our arms wrapped around each other. This guy tapped me on the shoulder, which normally indicated that he wanted me to allow him to dance with my partner. I was a wee bit surprised and apprehensive because slow dances were not normally *excuse-me dances*, therefore I was unsure what to do. My mind was made up for me when he boorishly edged me out of the way. I was walking off the floor when I heard Ann protesting. "No, I'm sorry I don't want to dance with you". I immediately turned back and as Ann was backing off, this guy was grabbing at her. I shouted. " Hey, leave her alone". As he still had his back to me I grabbed one of his arms. He swiftly turned around and lashed out at me with his free arm but missed me. My first reaction was to back off slightly away from him. As he was still slightly off balance, I ran at him and pushed him so violently that he was propelled backwards and very swiftly he staggered off the dance floor and vanished out of- sight. A few of the couples dancing close to us were disturbed and gave me some obscure looks. I noticed a couple of bouncers pushing their way through the crowd. I was about to make myself scarce when Ann grabbed my hand, so I immediately commenced dancing with her. The incident appeared to have happened so fast and furious that it was over before too many people became involved. I was shocked when Ann explained to me that the guy that started this conflict was not only an ex-boyfriend, he was also a member of the *Valdor-Boys!! Gang!!*

I realized immediately that I could be in trouble and nearly jumped out of my shoes when someone touched my arm. It was Mitch one of my friends. He asked me. "Were you involved in that fight?" I instantly replied. "There was no fight". Mitch was smiling now and said. " You had better go and explain that to the bouncers and the *Valdor-Boy* that they have just thrown out of the dance hall". The band had started up for the next dance and the dance floor was once more moving with gyrating dancers. Mitch, who was our non-elected leader suggested that we should get out of here before the remaining *Valdor-Boys* find out that I was involved. Without hesitation I told Ann that I had to go. Within ten minutes, Mitch, Jordon, Conoboy, Fordy and myself were heading for the exit door. Ann suddenly appeared and touched my arm, I suggested that I would see her on Saturday, here in the dance hall. She whispered. "Be Careful".

As we reached the exit door, I spotted the guy that had started this problem standing outside the dance hall in Grove Street. I whispered to Mitch that he was the guy that had started all this shit. Mitch suggested that there were a lot more off them and that we should walk away and try and get some space between us. The five of us walked up Grove Street and onto Fountainbridge. Just before we got to the junction of Lothian Road, Jordon confirmed that we were being followed. Mitch wanted to know how many and two or three of us all turned around simultaneously and someone said. "Seven".

We all seemed to stop simultaneously and look backwards in the direction of the seven *Valdor-Boy's* all striding towards us. Mitch suggested that we should continue walking but before we had time to consider what to do, the seven *Valdor-Boy's* were charging towards us! It must have been coming on for eleven-o-clock at night. It was dark and the streets were deserted, perhaps that's why they decided to attack us! However, we stood our ground and spread ourselves out wide, even off the pavement and onto the road. I do believe that the *Valdor-Boys* expected us to run, therefore we immediately had an early advantage.

It was an immediate chaotic unruly carnage. People were punching and kick-ing each other, others that were already on the ground were rolling around on the road. We were soon to find out that the *Valdor-Boy's* were surprised at our decision to fight them because they normally chase people, catch them and then give them a good kicking. On this occasion, not only did we not run away, we were taking them on and by all accounts we were hurting them physically and mentally. I noticed that two off them appeared to be backing off as if to get ready to run away and one off them looked like the guy that had started all this. I ran at him once more but on this occasion it was me that was pummelled to the ground and it appeared that two of them commenced kicking the hell out off me whilst I was on the ground. Before I could roll myself into the foetus position I had received a few kicks and one off them was in my face. As quickly as the kicking had started it stopped as two off my own guys were now smacking them around. Once more I was upright and it appeared that the *Valdor-Boy's* were in retreat and one off them that was running away was the person that started all this and one off the guy's that had kicked the hell out of me when I was on the ground. Jordon was running after him and I immediately was hot on Jordon's heels. Jordon caught up with him first and pushed him from behind causing him to crash face first onto the road. We both stood over him panting for breath. I kicked him in the hip and shouted. "Get up". He was looking up at us whilst sort of backing away using his arms and legs but still sitting on the ground. I shouted again. "Get up". As soon as he was on his feet I pummelled and punched him back onto the ground. He refused to get up. I noticed a few metal rubbish bins stacked against the wall. I sauntered over and removed one off the lids and asked Jordon to help me. We lifted him off the ground and tipped him headfirst into the empty bin, however as we were walking away the bin fell onto its side. It was only when we were wandering back down Fountainbridge that Jordon told me that I had blood all over my mouth and chin, I ran the back of my hand across my face and it was covered in blood. We soon met up with Mitch, Conoboy and Fordy and it was confirmed that the other *Valdor-Boy's* had capitulated and wandered away.

My parents were upset and very angry when I eventually got home. After examining me, my dad confirmed that at least four of my front teeth were all bent backward into my mouth and bleeding. A dentist confirmed that five my front teeth would have to be removed and a stainless-steel plate with five synthetic teeth would be fabricated to replace them. I was therefore out of the circuit for a few weeks until this special metal denture plate was made and fitted.

I did eventually meet up with Ann again and we started seeing each other and spending all day together every Sunday. Of course once she had heard the full story, I was her hero. Ann wanted me to meet her parents and I really was not that interested however I did eventually agree to go for lunch one Sunday. Everything was going fine after I had been introduced to her parents and younger brother. That was until during the lunch, every time I lifted up my cup to have a sip of my tea, the saucer remained attached to the bottom of the cup! I of course instantly and as discreetly as possible very quickly replaced both the cup with the saucer attached to it back onto the table. I actually thought that perhaps something was accidentally holding them together! I tried once more and was so embarrassed to find that the saucer was still stuck fast to the cup. I tried very hard to remain cool and even discreetly tried to separate the cup from the saucer whilst they were both sitting on the table in front of me, without any success! I was getting very agitated and had no idea what the hell I should do until Ann's father and her wee brother both burst out laughing! Ann's father admitted that it was a deliberate prank. Her mother smiled and removed the spurious cup and saucer and replaced them with a genuine cup of tea sitting on an actual seperate saucer. I was furious and actually found it impossible to look at any of them, especially Ann. I knew that I had to get the hell out of this house as soon as possible. I excused myself from the table, Ann and her mother apologised for the prank because obviously they were now aware that I was not impressed. I left the house with Ann following me and ignored her stupid father when he made some comment about being pleased to meet me. Once outside in the staircase, I questioned Ann and asked her if she was aware that her father had set me up with his stupid prank. She denied that she knew anything about it and apologised profusely. I remained silent for a few moments then turned around and leapt down the stairs two at a time leaving Ann in the silence. I avoided the

Clan House for a few weeks but eventually met up with Ann again but we just greeted each other with a dry but courteous smile.

I never ever seemed to have much luck with girls. On another occasion I was very friendly with a girl that lived in Arthur Street, Mary Majoribanks. We were at a New Year party in Arthur Street where a gang of us were partying. It was a good fun social gathering and we had a few cases of beer. Mary started talking to the gang about us and what we would get up too at times and she was continually laughing and giggling about it. I was furious and after attempting a few times to get her to change the subject because I thought that she was making a fool of both of us, I eventually tipped what was left of the glass of beer that I had in my hand over her head, left the house and went home. So, it was not a surprise to me that when I was eighteen years old, I was still a virgin.

Indifferent: 3

On the fifth of November 1952, My dad opened our front door leading out onto the street and the heat from the bonfire in Middle Arthur Place hit us both like a blast from a furnace. The reason why the heat was so intense is because the bonfire was blazing in the middle of the cul-de-sac street directly opposite the front door to our house. My dad hesitated, then ran his hand over the front of our door before he closed it. I assumed that he was feeling for blisters, but said nothing to me or the gang of people that were gathered around the blazing fire. It was nine-o-clock in the evening and my Dad was walking with me to the Edinburgh Waverly Railway Station. I was booked on the ten-o-clock train to London's Kings Cross Railway Station. I was eighteen and seven months old and was going off to do my eighteen months compulsory national service in the Royal Army Service Corp, [R.A.S.C.]

As an apprentice, I was exempt from this compulsory National Service until such time as I was a qualified tradesman. However, when I received the letter from the government informing me to report for my medical, instead of writing to inform them that I was serving an apprenticeship and giving them all the necessary information and details, I arranged a date for my medical. I had told no one about my decision, not my mother, father, brothers or sisters or even J & R Adams & Son. The doctor at the medical centre held my testicles in his hands and told me to cough, I did and was immediately classed as, A1.

I will never ever know why I decided to do this. My parents, and other members of my family had sacrificed a lot to allow me to enter into the five year very low paid apprenticeship and unknown to me I was in the process of blowing it all away. Jock Adam's, the boss's son went berserk when he became aware that I had decided to go into the army and finish my national service, before completing my apprenticeship. His father, Mr. Adams senior wanted to contact the government agents and inform them that I had made a mistake, as I was serving a five year apprenticeship as a Heating engineer/plumber and was therefore exempt National Service until such time as my apprenticeship was complete. I would have nothing to do with it, I had made up my mind that I wanted to get this damn military service over and done with now and not when I was twenty one years old and ready to start a new life. Jock Adam's eventually informed me that if I go ahead and do this, J.R. Adams & Son would have no obligation by law to allow me to continue with my apprenticeship on completion of my National Service. I was shocked and had never ever considered that they could, or would do this. I was always of the opinion that I could do my Military Service, then return to finish my apprenticeship. Now it appeared that I was wrong. I had tried to explain to big Jock Adams, that I was not aware of that and tried to apologise for any inconvenience I had caused. Big Jock Adams was of the opinion that it was too late now because my commitment to doing my Military Service now had been accepted and confirmed that I would not be welcomed back to complete my apprenticeship. I was devastated and decided not to inform my parents, or anyone of the dreadful error I had made.

The Aberdeen to London Kings Cross train eventually pulled into the Waverly Station Edinburgh. I was surprised, and shocked when I realized that the train was full to capacity and that people were already standing. They were steam- trains in those days and I had a ten -hour journey to London King's Cross facing me and it looked like I would be standing all the way. Just before I boarded the train my dad tapped me on the shoulder and said. "Look after yourself and you'll be okay. You had better get onto the train and find yourself a wee a corner". I sauntered very slowly and very unsure of myself towards the train and when I turned around for the last wave, my dad had already gone. The train appeared to be full of military people, Navy, Air Force and Army personnel. What I was unaware of as the train pulled out of Edinburgh was that there were many more people going to join this train at other scheduled stops in England who would also be going to Aldershot to join the Armed Forces for the first time. I could not even get into a carriage, therefore had to spend the entire ten hour journey huddled up in the small area corridor between two carriages. It was noisy, cold and extremely uncomfortable. This was the first time in my life that I had experienced a train journey and I was soon to discover that not only was I crushed in-between to carriages, I was also squashed against a toilet door. Some of the passengers who were drinking and getting inebriated disturbed us people all night when using the toilets. At one time I thought I was going to get trampled to death by the drunks or die of hypothermia and was also beginning to realize that perhaps I should have continued with the remaining two and half years to complete my apprenticeship.

Around seven thirty the next morning the fetid and now filthy steam train pulled into London King's Cross Station. Of course, we were the first passengers off the train. There were military people in uniform running up and down the platform shouting out all sorts of information and or orders. I approached a guy in an Army uniform and handed him my telegram, he quickly read it then handed it back to me and shouted. "Okay boy, outside under the arch to the right you will see some military vehicles, go there and wait and don't move". I was tired, cold, exhausted, hungry and a wee bit apprehensive, so I made no response except that I had the feeling that this guy shouting at me must think I'm deaf, or perhaps he is deaf. Under the arch to the right there were three large army trucks covered over by heavy canvas tarpaulins. The first thing I thought about was,

Oh they would be great for camping !. All the tail gates were down exposing long bench type seats running the length of both sides of the vehicles. It must have been an hour before at least forty of us young non-military people were gathering around and near the two trucks and everyone appeared to be unwilling or afraid to communicate with each other so we all remained silent. There were more soldiers in a small group all gathered together near the front of the vehicles, I assumed they were the drivers and they all appeared to be smoking and smiling at us! or perhaps they were laughing! It was another hour before approximately fifty of us were all horded into the rear of the trucks like cattle complete with our suitcases and bag packs. We were then driven through London and eventually into the countryside. The soldiers that accompanied us civilians on the long bench seats in the rear of the vehicle completely ignored us.

Aldershot was made-up of what appeared to me to be many large military camps. After we were all told to get out of the vehicles we were lined up and shouted at as if we were all stone deaf. The soldiers that were screaming and shouting at us all appeared to be waiting for our vehicles to arrive. These soldiers then made us all run down this road, and I remember thinking, *why are we running*! We all ran for at least fifteen minutes until we were stopped outside these long low huts. Within seconds we were all chased in single file into the huts. The one I was chased into had lines of single beds in neat rows on both sides of the long room. I was stopped in the middle and on the right hand side beside a bed that was going to be my very own bed for the first time in my life.

That afternoon other military people in uniforms forced us to run to a huge dining hall for lunch. After lunch other military people in uniform forced us to run to a huge warehouses where we were issued with green underwear, hairy uniforms, overcoat's, boots, socks and a beret. This running around went on all day until eventually these other military people in uniform told us to get to bed. As they left the long room, they switched all the lights off leaving the twenty of us that were in this room standing beside our beds in complete darkness. I very soon realized that I had made the biggest mistake in my life by leaving behind Middle Arthur Place and J & R Adams & Son in Edinburgh.

It must have been five-o-clock in the morning when I was rudely awakened by people shouting and screaming. Then without warning I hit the floor with a silent thud. I was shocked, bewildered and suddenly became very angry when I realized that my bed had been tipped over onto its side. I leaped to my feet and immediately clenched my fists in preparation to fight, defend myself and attack. No one paid any attention to me. The shouting and screaming continued, then I noticed that a few other beds had been tipped onto their side. People were standing around rubbing their eyes. I counted at least four soldiers in uniform moving around the room screaming abuse at everyone. They even appeared to be screaming and shouting abuse at each other. It was weird, we soon discovered that they were telling us to get washed, showered and dressed, but it was nearly impossible to comprehend exactly what they were saying because of the shouting and screaming.

After breakfast, the first four or five portioned cooked breakfast I had ever had in my life, we were all running again and on this occasion it was to a hut where a group of people armed with hair clippers and scissors were about to savage our hair and scalps. When eventually I had time to have a look at the rest of the civilians who were with me and were now dressed in their issued military uniforms, I was shocked. They all looked like scary scarecrows that would have frightened the devil himself. Most of the uniforms were too large for the person that was wearing them, including the berets. The greatcoats were so big, they looked like capes that hung over ones shoulder and touched the snow covered ground and before I had time to think we were all running around a huge snow covered parade ground like a flock of ostrich, but probably much faster. However unlike the Ostrich, we were all very ungainly and running as if we were all demented or inebriated.

In spite of the fact that we were now all members of the Royal Army Service Corp, it was weeks before we sat in our first vehicles and began learning how to drive. We spent weeks running around in circles and marching all over freezing frost covered gigantic parade grounds. Then eventually we were introduced to our first huge Bedford military vehicles. My first driving instructor immediately asked me if I had driven before? I could hardly tell him that I had spent weeks with my big brother Hugh double-de-clutching with the poker in the hole in the bench in front of my mothers kitchen fire in No 7 Middle Arthur Place Edinburgh. However I did pass my driving test with flying colours on my first test driving through the town of Salisbury in a huge Bedford truck, I was now a qualified driver in the Royal Army Service Corp.

There were two things that bothered me a lot in the barrack room that I shared with another nineteen soldiers. I was the only Scot and the only person not to have a photograph of a girlfriend on the inside of the metal wardrobe door. The pictures of some of their girlfriends reminded me of Lea and It brought back memories that made me wish that I had went to look for her at the Westfield dance hall, or had gone to Hollyrood Road to find her and ask her forgive me.

During our six weeks military training we spent most of our time being marched around a parade square with a .303 rifle on ones shoulder. We were taught how to use the rifle and how to stab people to death with a bayonet that fitted neatly after a twist onto the end of ones rifle. Finally the day arrived when a squad of us were loaded once more onto a troop carrying vehicle that would take us on the first stage of our journey to our posting. On this occasion we were not carrying suitcase's or haversacks, we were all carrying kit-bags. I was beginning to think that this man's army was not only to do with training one to defend ones country when under attack from ones enemy, It was also a class distinction hierarchy. We were a huge group of people all from the same country, but in this man's army it was obvious that we would never ever be treated as equals. The officers had total power and authority over the non-commissioned officers such as sergeants majors, sergeants, corporals and foot soldiers. These non-commissioned officers are brain washed by the hierarchy to maintain total control of the foot soldiers including their train of thoughts and expressions.

*During these fourteen days I was mentally and physically
exhausted and completely abandoned, as I was the only prisoner.*

I had spent six weeks with many other people and we had all suffered some form of degradation and despair, some more than others. We had all shared the same humiliation and pain during this so called training, therefore we all had something in common. However, there were only a dozen or so of these people that I had trained with sitting in the rear of this vehicle with me on our way to Italy where we had been posted. The other's were strangers and the only thing we had in common was that they had also just completed their six weeks training and were probably separated from the people that they had just spent six weeks with. This mans army philosophy appeared to be devoted to making the foot soldiers existence as uncomfortable and despondent as humanly possible. We were driven to a sea port, some people said it was Dover, others said it was Ramsgate. On the docks we met up with another squad that apparently were infantry soldiers. Eventually with a couple of officer and non-commissioned officers in charge, we all boarded a vessel that looked like an old cargo boat. Apparently we were heading across the English Channel to a place called, The Hook of Holland. It was the week before Xmas, it was freezing cold and the weather was awful. We were all eventually herded on board this old cargo boat and allocated hammocks below deck. This was all extremely strange and unusual for me. I was eighteen years old and had only recently made my first train journey from Edinburgh to London. Slept in a bed on my own for the first time in my life and eaten a breakfast every morning that I had no idea existed. Now it appears that I am going to sleep in a hammock on a ship that was crossing the English Channel to take me to a strange country named Italy. I was truly overwhelmed, apprehensive and very discontented. When we awoke in the morning we were still berthed in the docks, apparently the weather was too severe for us to make the crossing. We eventually set of later that day and another fleet of army vehicles were waiting for us at the Hook-of-Holland. There were about sixty of us, twenty from the R.A.S.C. others were infantry soldiers. We were driven to a railway station, given packed lunches and marched and pushed onto a train. Rumour had it that we were heading to a place in Italy named Trieste. I had no idea where Italy was never mind this city named Trieste. I was told that Trieste was a city in Italy and located on the Adriatic coast.

The train journey was long and tedious and we received no other food except the packed lunches that we had received before we boarded the train. We were on the train for twenty four hours travelling through some strange and mysterious countries which I discovered much later were Germany and Austria then eventually into Italy. In Italy, more army vehicles delivered us all to various camps. We R.A.S.C. personnel were delivered to the 65 Coy barracks on the outskirts of Trieste city town centre. The company was made up off approximately two hundred of us. During the first two weeks we were driving three ton Bedford trucks around the country-side accompanied by drivers that had been stationed in Trieste for a considerable time. We were being familiarized with driving on the right hand side of the road. Then on the third week we were driving through Trieste city itself. I found driving around in the country-side boring, however driving through Trieste city was an experience that I will never forget because it was so scary, especially driving a large three ton Bedford truck with these tiny little vehicles and moped scooters squirming all around you. I was sure that at some time, my huge three ton Bedford truck was going to crush and mangle one of these crazy Italian drivers that continually zigzagged through the traffic.

I was eventually put on my first guard duty and I swear to God I thought I was going to die of monotony. My first real driving assignment was driving a water tanker. I would fill it with water first thing every morning. Then I would be given a map reference and sent to some remote mountain range to deliver the water to some infantry soldiers that were involved in what the military people called schemes, i.e. Mock Wars. I have to say that the journey to these remote areas through the mountains were both breathtaking and frightening but exceptionally stunning and extremely isolated. It was usually the regiment with a huge plume in their berets, the Yorkshire Fusiliers and these poor guys were out there for weeks at a time, sleeping in tents and eating camp food out off their billy-cans, yet in a way, I envied them. I ended up delivering water to one particular squad on a daily basis therefore I got to know a few of them quite well. One day they asked me if I could get them some beer out of one of the village bars that I obviously pass on my way to their camp. Without thinking and without any hesitation, I readily agreed.

The next day on my way to the Fusiliers to deliver their drinking water, I stopped at a local bar and bought a dozen small bottles of beer. I was aware that what I was I about to do was not exactly acceptable to military regulations or procedure, but what the hell's harm can a few beers do shared among a few Fusiliers. I carefully loaded them into the two rubber buckets that I had lashed to the back of my water tanker. I had already rigged up two pieces of rope to the underside of the manhole on the tanker. I tied the two buckets to the rope's and lowered the buckets with the bottles of beer into the cool water to keep them out of sight and keep the beer cool. When I arrived at the field camp and after reporting to the duty officer, the guys that had requested the beer very soon made contact with me and I very discreetly and swiftly handed over the beers and collected my Lira. They could not wait to get their hands on their beer and the bottles of beer were empty in one swallow. I was suddenly the most important and popular guy in this mock war. We had a scare at one time when one of their sergeants appeared on the scene wondering why I was taking so long in pumping the drinking water supply into their field tanks. I jumped to attention, apologised profusely and immediately went about pumping the water from my tanker into their temporary field water tanks. Before I departed that day, the soldiers were begging me to double my delivery. I had to explain to them that I only had the two buckets and that If I got caught, I could be in serious trouble. However, I promised them that tomorrow I will fill both buckets but not any more than the two buckets can hold. I further insisted that I collect all the empty bottles to ensure that there is no evidence lying around. On my return journey to the camp I was able to increase my beer delivery from twelve to twenty as I managed to get ten of the small bottles of beer in each bucket. On my next run, some of these stupid infantry soldiers failed to return my empty bottles and I had to leave with only seventeen. They promised me that they would retrieve the missing three and bury them. The next day as I drove into the field camp I was stopped by an officer and a sergeant and was instructed to get out of the vehicle. The sergeant immediately climbed into the cab and commenced searching it. He then climbed all over my water tanker and eventually lifted the manhole lid. Of course the ropes were now exposed and eventually the two buckets full of beer were hauled up and out of the water. My tanker off water was emptied into their field water tanks. I was escorted back to my own barracks with the officer being driven in a land rover in front of me and the sergeant sitting beside me in my water tanker. As it had turned out, the three empty beer bottles had been discovered by an officer scattered on the grass adjacent to the tents. The field camp commander immediately ordered a full investigation. Of course me and my water tanker were caught red-handed. I was accused and charged with various different misdemeanours and one felony. I was found not guilty of the felony, but guilty of all other charges and sentenced to fourteen days in the prison cells in our barracks guard house. I remember thinking, *Oh my God, would I have been put in front of a firing squad if I had been found guilty of the*

Felony!! During these fourteen days in the guard room cells, I had to scrub the guard house floors and outside ground areas every day. I had to scrub and repaint all the white painted stones around the grass verges in the entire camp. During these fourteen days I was mentally and physically exhausted and completely abandoned, as I was the only prisoner.

On my release, I spent my first seven evenings scrubbing huge pots and pans in the kitchen until midnight every evening. I never got my water tanker back and was now driving a Bedford three ton vehicle delivering rations to hotels in Trieste where British military officers were billeted. That's when I realized that there were hundreds of British military officers living in four and five star hotels in absolute luxury in Trieste. That's when I found out why the British army had thousands of troops in Italy. Apparently, President Josep Broz Tito of Yugoslavia [*Now Slovenia, Croatia, Bosnia, Serbia, Montenegro, Kosovo & Macedonia*] after World War II, [1939-1945] had threatened to raid and occupy Italy. Britain immediately sent in troops to dissuade Tito and apparently these troops remained there until Toto's death in 1980.

Eventually after doing these hotel delivery runs for nearly six months and because I was constantly driving all over the very busy beautiful city of Trieste, I was upgraded to a B4 driver. Owing to the fact that I was now recognised as being an excellent driver, I was eventually transferred to the learning school. This involved me driving one of the troop carrying vehicle's that was used to familiarize new recruits and others to drive on the right hand side of the road. I personally found the promotion wearisome and an insult to my integrity because It was not as if these drivers could not drive, they were all qualified drivers but had not driven on the right hand side of the road. I normally had at least six drivers to train and familiarise on how to drive on the right hand side of the road. Five of them would sit on the benches in the back, with one of them driving the vehicle with me sitting in the co-driver seat beside him. The procedure was, I would take them up into the hills that surround the beautiful city of Trieste. Each trainee driver, with me sitting in the co-driver seat beside him would be allowed to drive the vehicle around the secluded hillsides for an hour or so, then I would organize and supervise a change of driver. After a couple of week of everyone of them driving around the empty roads up in the hills, I would introduce them into driving around the edge of the city, then eventually into the city and let them have turns each driving the vehicle through the very busy city centre of Trieste.

One week while driving around up in the hills, it was severely hot therefore tediously boring. I instructed the driver that was driving to stop the vehicle. I suggested and explained to the six drivers that I wanted two of them to sit up front as I was going to sit in the back with the other four drivers. I explained that I wanted one of them to drive for half an hour, then change drivers and after he had driven for half an hour they should stop the vehicle and hand the vehicle over to another two drivers and so on and so forth. They all understood exactly what I meant so I gave them my watch and handed the vehicle over to the first pair of drivers. I have to say that they all looked rather pleased and excited, however, I did remind them that I was still in charge. and not far away as I was just relaxing in the back of the vehicle where it was much cooler. I climbed into the back of the vehicle with the other four drivers and immediately commandeered one of the long bench seats for myself and stretched out on my back. Everything appeared to be going as I had planned. After what appeared to be an hour the vehicle stopped, to change drivers. After a further hour or so the vehicle stopped again and the two drivers changed over for the other two drivers. After another hour I realized that it must be nearing lunch time. When the next pair was about to change over I checked the time on the watch and decided it was time for me to take us and the vehicle back to camp for our lunch.

After lunch we were once more back up into the hills and I eventually handed my watch and vehicle back to the six drivers. By the expression on their faces, it appeared that they were all very happy and agreeable with my plan. So once more I was stretched out on my back in the coolness of the rear of the vehicle. On this occasion I had taken one of my small packs with me with a few clothes in it for a pillow. I must have fallen asleep because I was suddenly awakened when I hit the floor of the vehicle with a thud when it appeared to have suddenly stopped with a bang. I leapt over the tail gate and was shocked to find that we were stopped right outside our company parking lot where the vehicle had smashed into the double gate post. The duty guard and one of the platoon sergeants were both surprised and shocked when they caught a glimpse of me leaping out of the rear of my vehicle. The very vehicle that I was in charge off. The sergeant suffered a double jolt when he spotted the two learner drivers sitting in the front of the huge vehicle. As it had transpired, the stupid L drivers driving the vehicle had decided because it was close to finishing time they would surprise me by driving the vehicle back to camp on their own. Of course the nearer they got to the camp and I had not attempted to stop or reprimand them, they both thought that I was in favour of this crazy stunt. They had no idea that I was sound asleep.

Once more I was on a charge and the next morning I was sentenced to fourteen days prison that was to be served once more in our guard room prison cells. This was my second time in five months that I had been charged and sent to our prison cells in the camp. On both these occasions I was the only prisoner and I have to say that it never bothered me too much. I was kept too busy to even think about it and so traumatized at the end of the day that I slept like a dead man would. Five-o-clock sharp in the morning I was awakened by the guards and marched at the double to the ablution for a cold shower and shave then spent the rest of the early morning cleaning the entire guard room in preparation for the regimental police taking over at Seven-o-clock. At Six-thirty I was double quick marched back across the square by the guards to the kitchen to collect my breakfast. The kitchen staff would have my breakfast spread out on a large tray. With the large tray in my hands, I was double marched back to my cell and by the time one reaches the cell, there is not much on the tray worth eating or drinking. After breakfast I would be marched back to the kitchen cookhouse with my tray and kitchen utensils then back to the cells to begin my chores which normally commenced at Seven-o-clock when the regimental police took control of the cells and guard-room. I would then be working non-stop scrubbing the stone floors of the cells, guard rooms and all the white painted stones that surrounded the entire area, that was except for breaks for my lunch and evening meal. Nine-o-clock in the evening after I had assisted the guards to collect their suppers from the kitchen, I was once more locked up for the night until Five-o-clock sharp the next morning.

One time during the night or very early in the morning, I was suddenly awakened when guards opened my cell gate. I wondered what the hell was going on when they swiftly pushed someone into my cell then without a single word they hurriedly locked the cell gate again. I was more surprised and inquisitive when the person they had pushed into my cell didn't attempt to move or speak so I slowly unfolded myself from my bunk and stood upright then suddenly realized even in the dark that it was a female!! I was shocked when I recognised that she was one of the prostitutes that normally hang around the rear of the barracks!! I was now interested, even tempted!! Closer inspection however confirmed that she was intoxicated and had been sick down the front of her clothes. In the stillness of the darkness, I could hear someone sniggering at the cell entrance gate. I realized then that it could only be one of the duty guards that was trying to take the p*** out of me. I knew all the duty guards because they were just ordinary soldiers and drivers like myself doing their turn of guard duty. The duty guard commander is normally a non commissioned officer and he must have been temporarily absent or changing the guards down at the outside parking compound. I shouted. "Hey, get her out off here you b*******. If you don't, I swear to god, I'm going to start screaming and shouting and the commanding officer or orderly officer will appear and then all of you will be here in the cells with me". Within a few minutes two of the guards were opening the cell gates with their bunch of keys and suggesting that they thought they were doing me a favour. As they were removing the girl I shouted at them. "Go f*** yourselves".

Eventually my fourteen days were over. It was pretty tough going being locked up in the local guard house so it was nice to be back in my uniform and driving again. I had a pleasant surprise awaiting me because during my time in the guardroom cells a few fellow Scots had joined our company. Three from Glasgow and one from Aberdeen. Up until then I had been quite friendly with a guy from Bristol, a tall guy named Willie Hansen. Within days Willie Hansen and myself were sharing a table in the dining room with the Scot from Aberdeen, another tall guy named Falconer, Bill Falconer. The three Glasgow guys were friendly enough, but appeared to prefer to spend most of their time together when not on duty. Eventually I was back driving one of the huge troop carrying vehicles which involved taking the Fusilier Infantry regiment to the hills and mountains where they got involved in their mock battles. On one occasion their mock war was with an American Infantry regiment that was also stationed in Trieste. These imitation wars as I have stated could go on for several weeks. Fortunately I was not always required to remain with them permanently. I would often have to spend a night or so with them when they knew that certain troop had to be moved around, thank goodness that was not too often.

I had discovered that the reason we British troops were in Trieste was because Tito, the communist leader of Yugoslavia had intentions of invading Italy in order to have control and access to the port of Trieste and the Adriatic Sea. Trieste is the largest port on the Adriatic coast. Apparently it was formerly held by Austria, annexed by Italy after the first world war; created a free territory after the second world war, then eventually was returned to Italy. Tito was of the opinion that Yugoslavia had every right to have access to the port of Trieste and was prepared to take it from Italy and most certainly would have if it had not been for the American and British troops protecting it. When I was not driving the infantry troops around the hills when they were having their imitation wars with themselves or the Yanks, I was delivering food rations and booze to hotels that the British army had commandeered for the military officers with their families and other senior civil servants.

Whilst up in the remote isolated hills with the Yorkshire Infantry troops and one had to remain with them, it was bloody awful. The food was dreadful, there was not enough water to have a wash and we drivers had to sleep for days on end fully clothed in the cabins or in the rear of our vehicles because we were often awakened during the night with officers screaming at us to prepare to move their troops out. Of course our huge vehicles were draped in giant camouflage netting which could take a considerable time to untangle and remove. After the troops had all been loaded onto the vehicles we would drive for a few miles in complete darkness down remote tracks. I felt truly sorry for the poor infantry troops that were sitting inside the rear of my vehicle dressed in full battle kit and getting knocked and battered all over the place. At times and after only driving for half an hour or so we were suddenly stopped and the troops were ordered to quickly disembark. After dropping our tail gates we would stand aside and watch these poor infantry guys disappearing into the bleak darkness of the Italian hills. It was not over for us either, we were ordered to scrum-up and refit our complicated camouflage nettings.

On one occasion, it was after midnight and I was trying to get some sleep whilst lying in the rear of my vehicle when without any warning I was ordered to prepare to move out. In my wisdom and instead of completely removing my camouflage netting, which was the norm. I instructed my co-driver that we would just roll the netting up at both sides of the vehicle up past the wheels and secure them. The front and rear netting, we would roll-up to roof level, then secure them. Driving down the roads and remote tracks around two-o-clock in the morning with a truck load of Yorkshire Infantry Fusiliers all dressed up and ready for battle, I noticed that my huge vehicle engine was overheating. I had to stop immediately. Armed with my torch and before I got around to inspecting my engine, I noticed that my camouflaged netting had dropped loose and was now well and truly wrapped around my wheels and transmission. After explaining to the troops that we had a wee engine problem, my co driver and I crawled underneath our vehicle armed with torches, an axe and a bayonet to cut loose the tough rugged camouflage netting. A platoon officer arrived in his land rover and was soon screaming and demanding to know why we had stopped. Under the circumstances and with flashlights now searching all across and over my stationery vehicle and the camouflage netting being fully exposed. It was impossible to pretend that it was a mechanical fault. The young officer went berserk and accused me of sabotaging his mission and went on about everyone being taken prisoners or killed. I honestly thought that at one time he was going to shoot me. When he eventually calmed down, I suggested that he could assist us by having a few of the infantry men with their bayonets help us cut the camouflage netting off the transmission. With at least eight of us chopping away at the now ruined camouflage netting we were soon once more on our way. I was extremely lucky that no one became aware of my negligence. I can only assume that the officer was only interested in getting his soldiers back into the battle field to be too concerned about why! or how! the netting was tangled around the transmission? Or, perhaps like myself, he was just wanted to get back to his barracks for a comfortable bowl-movement, shower, shave, decent food and a clean soft bed.

When I eventually got back to my barracks, my face was covered in spots, the ones with big yellow heads. I had not seen my face in a mirror for over two weeks. I looked bloody awful and It took me an hour to burst all these dreadful huge spots full of suppuration and contaminated blood. I decided that I wanted no more to do with playing soldiers in these bloody phoney imitation wars.

Indifferent: 4

I had now been in the Royal Army Service Corp for one year and with 65 Coy in Trieste for ten months. I had been upgraded to a class A driver which meant that I was now driving one of 65 Coy's three Humber saloon staff cars. It felt a wee bit privileged to be given the responsibility of driving one of these magnificent cars. It also made me feel important when gliding through the beautiful city of Trieste driving this huge luxury car. However, the down side was that some of these high ranking military officers would have me driving them around Trieste until after midnight or sitting in the car outside 5 star hotels until the wee hours in the morning waiting to take them back home to their own hotels. There were only three of us staff car drivers and we all suffered the same fate. I still just wanted to get the hell out of this man's army and back to Edinburgh and complete my apprenticeship, if that was going to be possible.

I knew that I was one of the best drivers in 65 Coy and that I was also one of the smartest and tidiest, because that was the reputation I had. Not one driver in the entire company ever wanted to be selected for guard duty along side me. When the guard duty list was posted there were always nine soldiers listed for guard duty on that particular night, but only eight were required. The guard commander who would be a non-commissioned officer, i.e. a sergeant or full corporal would parade his nine guards in front of the duty officer for inspection. The smartest turned out guard would receive the officers *Baton*. [It was a token gesture] The guard who received the officers *Baton,* would be excused / released from that nights guard duty. This entire procedure was to encourage all soldiers to be well-groomed enough to win the officers *Baton* and be excused the all night guard duty. It was a rare occasions if I did not receive the officers *Baton*. Therefore I very rarely had to do an all night guard duty. In spite of my good fortunes, I was aware of the fact that I had got myself into trouble a couple of times and had to pay the price of confinement and heavy work duty in our barracks prison cells a couple of times for two silly misdemeanours.

I was having a problem with my right eye as it was beginning to wander at certain times especially after I had been driving for a considerable time. It was obviously due to stress and I would end up with a temporary squint and the only cure was rest or sleep. I eventually had to go to the optician and he prescribed and issued me with a pair of army issue dreadful wire framed glasses that reminded me of my younger days and I just could not and would not wear them. Falconer, Hansen and I spent most of our spare time together after duty, that is of course if I was still not driving some high ranking officer around Trieste or sitting in my car outside some five star hotel waiting for him to decide where he wanted me to take him next. Willie Hansen for some unknown reason was always trying to fix me up with his younger sister by suggesting that I should meet up with her because she was a lovely girl. He appeared to be of the opinion that we were made for each other. I was always embarrassed, especially when he went on about it in front of Falconer. He eventually showed me a picture off her and I have to admit, she was an attractive girl. At one time he even admitted that she was not a virgin and when I obviously showed my concern and shock at such an admission, he suggested that he only mentioned that because he did not want me to be disappointed. It was a bit ironic, here was Hansen offering me his sisters body and apologising to me because she was not a virgin and I was a nineteen year old virgin. On the other hand, perhaps Hansen had worked that out because I was the only driver that did not have a photograph of a girl friend on the doors of my lockers. That of course was because I did not have a girl friend and even when Hansen insisted that I keep the photograph of his sister and put it on my locker, I indignantly refused, removed it and insisted that he takes it away.

Bill Falconer was a tall Aberdonian from the 'Granite City' of Aberdeen. He had jet black hair and like the Granite City, he was tough guy and unyielding. With his dark features, jet black hair and Italian sun tan, he always looked good! He always warranted a second glance from the Italian females any time we were down town Trieste and most of these females were beauties. Bill Falconer worked in the docks in the huge port in Aberdeen, whilst Willie Hansen was a truck driver in Bristol city. They could not understand why I was in the army; with me being a trainee Heating Engineer. Even when I tried to explain that I had decided to break my apprenticeship temporary in order to get this compulsory National Service over with, they couldn't understand it. I have to admit, that I was now as puzzled as they were and now regretted my stupid decision.

The three of us applied and received a twenty-four hour pass for the Saturday night to allow us to do a bit of sight-seeing around Trieste. We had no idea what we intended to do, because we most certainly did not have enough money [Lira] to afford to stay overnight in a hotel in Trieste, but at least we wouldn't have to rush back to the barracks before midnight. Unfortunately, Hansen and his vehicle were sent up into the hills with the fighting Fusiliers on another mock war. Falconer and I waited until late on the Saturday afternoon, but alas it appeared that Hansen had been taken a prisoner off war or had gone *AWOL*. We had all been looking forward to this so Falconer and I decided to proceed with our plan and on the Saturday afternoon we headed for down town Trieste.

I was awakened by Falconer climbing out of bed,
he appeared to have been trapped against the wall and
the beauty, Maria was sleeping in-between us!

We were extremely fortunate as our barracks was only a few bus stop's away from the centre of the beautiful city of Trieste. We had all tried to save as much Lira as possible to allow us to have a good time. Falconer and I casually wandered around the city that was certainly not a stranger to us as we had been driving through and around it now for over a year. We headed for the sea front as it was always cool around there and after a few cold white Vino Bianca's we went back up into the city centre. We were both dressed in our civilian clothes as we both had passes that gave us permission to wear civy clothes. We toured all the local busy noisy bars, eating a few local ham split-rolls washed down with more local Vino Bianca wine. We were having a great time and toasted nearly every second drink to our friend, Big Willie Hansen who was lost somewhere up in the hills with the Yorkshire Fusiliers and their military opponents.

We were both sitting in this large nearly empty bar just after midnight deciding that perhaps it was time to start heading back to our barracks when three beautiful girls wandered in. One of them could not keep her eyes off Falconer and of course Falconer being blessed with such distinctive qualities, self confidence and having drank a few large wines eventually wandered over to their table. He eventually returned to our table and asked me how much Lira I had left. Without question I commenced counting my money and told him how much I had, then asked him why he wanted to know. As it turned out, the three beauties were prostitutes, I have to say that I was shocked because these girls were absolutely stunning, especially the one that fancied Falconer. They were a wee bit older than us, I would say around twenty five years old. They were dressed and looked like movie stars. After counting our duel finances, Falconer suggested that between us we were just short of enough Lira for one of us to spend the night with Falconer's stunning looking admirer. We were now both slightly inebriated and therefore not exactly fully comprehensive or in a position to make realistic practical decisions. Falconer suggested a plan and although I was not entirely in favour of his plan, I eventually agreed to it.

Falconer would convince the beauty to accept the Lira that he would offer her for him to spend the night with her at her apartment. As soon as they left the bar and were walking home to her apartment, I was to discreetly follow them. As soon as they were both safely in her apartment, Falconer would discreetly allow me also to enter. Falconer was convinced that he could charm the beauty into accommodating both of us for the night, for less than the price of one. I had still been a wee bit apprehensive until Falconer promised me that he would not hand over our Lira; until such time as they were inside her apartment and that she lived alone. It was only when the beauty and Falconer left the bar, that I realized that the beauty was also slightly inebriated and had obviously agreed to Falconer's proposal.

As planned, I followed them by sliding along the wide quiet roads as close to the buildings as possible. They eventually entered a building in what looked like a very posh area, however when I reached the entrance, the door was locked. I looked around and discovered brass type buttons on both sides of the entrance door. After waiting a few minutes, I pressed one of the buttons but nothing happened. I pressed another one, then a few more until there was this buzzing noise at the door. I pushed it and it opened. I could hear voices and people talking so I remained quiet and very still. The entrance was very elegant and all around and beneath me appeared to be white marble tiles. I did not move until the voices stopped and all was quiet, then I very slowly commenced climbing the beautiful white marble circular staircase. On the first landing there were two very nice ornamental carved timber entrance doors at each end of the landing; which I assumed were the entrance to two apartments. I looked around and upwards and there appeared to be another three landings, but, there was no sign of Falconer. That's when the first doubt's started entering my puzzled head. In spite of my doubt's, I continued to climb to the next landing and continued climbing until I reached the fourth and top landing. My best friend Falconer was nowhere to be seen. I was now very upset and extremely angry. I could not believe that Falconer could take my Lira and deceive like this!

On my way back down I stopped and listened at every apartment entrance door. I heard nothing. On the last landing, I noticed that one of the entrance doors was slightly ajar, so I crept towards it and listened and instantly heard Falconers Scottish accent, he was obviously talking to the beauty. I very slowly pushed the door open and pushed it gently behind me but keeping it ajar. There were two other doors in this large hallway so I gently whispered quietly. *"Falconer, Falconer"*. Eventually, Falconer and the Italian beauty were both standing in one of the open doors. The beauty gave a sigh that sounded like *Mama Mia* and Falconer immediately put his arms around her whispering. "It's okay *Maria*, he's my friend, it's not a problem". He was kissing the girl on her cheek and arms as he lead her back in through the open door. I meekly followed them into this huge lounge. Falconer asked me if I had locked the door. I immediately returned to the entrance door and closed it. When I returned to the lounge, Falconer and the beauty, *Maria* were sitting holding hands. Falconer confirmed to me that he had convinced the lovely *Maria* that it was okay and that I should make myself at home. I have to say that I felt very uncomfortable and extremely embarrassed when Falconer after a few minutes suggested that we should all! go to bed.

I was awakened in the morning by Falconer climbing out of the bed. He appeared to have been trapped against the wall and the beauty, *Maria* was sleeping in-between us. Falconer, who was also naked, vanished into the lounge leaving me alone with *Maria* the naked beauty lying beside me. I thought Falconer had gone to the Loo, however he soon reappeared fully clothed and whispered to me. "Cass, come on, let's go. Its time to go, don't waken her. Come on". Very hesitantly, I crawled out of the bed, the beauty stirred, turned over and faced the wall. My clothes were lying in a heap on the floor where I had obviously dropped them. I gathered them and joined Falconer in the lounge. I thought I saw him closing a drawer so I asked him. "What are you doing, what's wrong?" Falconer put the fingers of his right hand up to his lips and whispered. "Shoo, come on, lets go".

He was away and out of the door before I could make any response. My watch indicated that it was only five thirty in the morning, Sunday morning. Walking back towards our barracks Falconer suggested that we should look for a bar or cafe that's open and have a coffee and a Prosciutto Panini [ham filled-roll]. "We have no Lira". I reminded him. Grinning like a Cheshire cat, Falconer pulled a fistful of Italian Lira out of one of his pockets. "Where did you get that?". I asked. He was still smiling whilst counting it, then said. "It's the Lira we paid the prostitute, I found it in a drawer in the lounge, also this stuff". He held up various pieces of jewellery! I stopped, looked at him and I swear, if looks could kill, he would have died instantly. I said. "You dirty b****** Falconer, how could you do such a filthy thing like stealing that girls money and her jewellery? Oh Jesus Christ, I don't believe this". Falconer was still smiling and replied. "Come on, it's not her money, it's ours. This is yours". He was handing me some Lira. I shook my head and shouted. "I don't want anything to do with that money". Still smiling, he replied. "No problem Cass, only I was hoping that maybe you would buy some of this jewellery from me for Hanson's wee sister?". He was still smiling as he was putting the money and jewellery back into his pocket. I reiterated. "You're f****** sick Falconer and please, don't try to take the piss out off me. We walked in silence for a good few minutes, me slightly behind Falconer. Without any warning, he suddenly turned and pointed at me. "I warn you Cass, if you spread this around the camp I will give you such a beating that you may never recover from". I stopped dead in my track and pointed at him. "Perhaps you can Falconer, but I promise you this, if you try, you will carry scars for the rest of your miserable life and regret the day that you ever met-up with me". Falconer grinned and walked on, he did not respond, he just walked on. I followed, then stopped. I was so angry about the money and his threat of giving me a beating I shouted to him. "Hey, Falconer, let's get this over with. let's find a quiet place and maybe you can start beating me up, come on, let's do it now". He was silent for a few seconds then said. "You're f****** crazy Cassidy, let's get back to camp and let's just keep all this crap to ourselves. We walked all the way back to our camp in a single file. Me two or three paces behind Falconer. I was still raging with anger and considered running and leaping onto his back in an effort to knock him to the ground and beat the shit out of him. He had ruined what should have been a most memorable weekend for me.

We avoided each other for days and even Hanson enquired a few times, what had happened during our twenty-four-hour pass. Both Falconer and I always suggested that nothing had happened, but I knew different. I was no longer a nineteen year old virgin! and Bill Falconer had nearly ruined everything! However the fact is, if it had not been for Falconer's suave looks and personality, I would still be chaste!

Indifferent: 5

Being a staff car driver was a very prestigious assignment and I didn't have to marched a quarter of a mile every morning to the huge R.A.S.C. car park depot like all the other drivers had to do in order to reach their vehicles. Our three Humber vehicle staff car's were parked in a corner under cover in our barracks. We three drivers also had special concession's with the kitchen and were allowed to sit down for a meal at any given time.

Always being impeccably dressed was easy for me because that's what I wanted, I did it for me and not for the army. When I say impeccably, I mean as far as was ethically possible in these dreadful army uniforms. They were made from a rough crude hairy material, khaki in colour and not exactly made to measure. These extremely unpleasant uniforms appeared to be made in two sizes only, and that was large and extra large. The black beret was only made in one size and that was extra large and had to be worn at the most bizarre angle over ones head. The American soldiers that were stationed in Trieste all wore light blue gabardine uniforms with pleasant looking braided caps and they did not have to wear these stupid canvas leg gaiters that we had to wear.

I had spent months scraping, scratching and shaving my dreadful hairy uniform with razor blades in order to remove all the excess hairy khaki coloured material. I did this in order to make the brownish-yellowish khaki hairy material smoother and lighter. Once I had achieved that, it was now possible to press sharper creases in my trousers and jacket sleeves with an electrical heated iron. This allowed me to feel a wee bit more respectable looking. I also spent months plunging my huge oversized stupid beret into boiling water then into cold water in an effort to shrink it. That was also a great success as my beret now sat on top of my head and not like a tent hanging over it. I pressed special creases into the sleeves of my uniform jacket and the creases on my trousers legs were as sharp as scalpels. The toe caps of my boots were spit- polished to such a shine that they could be used as mirrors. I inserted small metal chains to weigh and push down my trouser bottoms so that they hung perfectly even over the top of my stupid canvas gaiters. I was as sharp as a razor. I have to say that my big brother Hugh who had just been demobbed from the army prior to me going in, had given me lots of hints and advice.

Our Company Sergeant Major had taken a liking to me simply because I was always impeccably turned out and dressed. That was in spite of the fact that I had broken a few rules and had spent a few weeks in his prison cells in his barracks. He would often pull me out of Company Parades and use me as a model and suggest that he expected all drivers to be turned out in a similar state and code of dress. Obviously to some of the rag-tag drivers, I was not very popular, however that was not my concern, as I have said previously, I did not dress to please the army or the Sergeant Major, I dressed to please myself. I now only had another six months to do to complete my eighteen months National Service then I would be demobbed and be able to return home to Edinburgh and hopefully complete my apprenticeship and become a fully qualified Heating Engineer.

Two of my regular military officers that qualified for the use my chauffer driven Humber staff car were Padres. One was a Roman Catholic priest and the other was a Church of England minister. I would spend an entire day driving one these officers to various barracks around Trieste. The Catholic Priest one day and the Church of England Minister some other day and more than often, to the same military barracks. They were both only Major's and the lowest ranking officers I had ever chauffeured. I would also take them to various conferences and meetings, therefore I got to know both of them rather well and the distinguishing difference between these two officers was immeasurable. The Church of England minister insisted on sitting up front beside me in the front passenger seat and when we arrived at our destination and before leaving the vehicle he would insist on giving me some money [Lira] to go to the camp NAFFI, and treat myself to a sandwich and cup of tea. He would further insist that I remain in the NAFFI until such time as he would come and collect me when it was time to leave.

The Roman Catholic priest insisted that I always opened the rear door of the vehicle for him whenever he was entering or leaving the vehicle. On a few occasions when he instructed me to drive him to a specific location that I was unaware of and I would have to check my directory, he would imply that I was *incompetent and irritatingly wasting his time!* Whenever we reached our designated location, he would suggest that I should not sit around idle and that I should wash or polish the vehicle. This was in spite of the fact that these staff cars were permanently gleaming. On such occasions and during his *'incompetent and irritatingly wasting his time'* remarks, I would completely ignored him. However, I could never ever stray very far away from the vehicle for even a second or two or go to the NAFFI for a break. I did on one occasion have to go to the Loo and on returning found him standing waiting beside the car. In spite of the fact that I apologised profusely and explained where I had been, he went berserk and accused me of being idle, incompetent and unreliable.

In spite of the priest's dreadful and in my opinion racist demeanour, I became very friendly with his pretty Italian female secretary, *Anjelica,* who spoke very good English. We also had one thing in common, we both disliked the priest. I was getting to a point where I intended to ask *Anjelica* out on a date. Perhaps that was because I had a wee bit more confidence now that I was no longer a nineteen year old virgin! and I was getting a wee bit *demob happy* because I was soon to be a civilian again. The priest had a small office in the hotel that he was a resident and when I arrived at his hotel at eight-o-clock sharp in the morning, I had to report direct to his office. If he was not in his office, which was the norm, *Anjelica* would phone his room and I was usually instructed to wait in my vehicle. I would hang around for a few minutes talking to *Anjelica,* that's how I knew that *Anjelica* also disliked him and that she had a wee soft spot for me! because *Anjelica* knew that the priest disliked me.

One morning I arrived as usual at eight-o-clock and wandered into his hotel office. *Anjelica* had also just arrived, phoned his room immediately. The instructions were the usual, I was to wait in my car. Before I left I asked *Anjelica* if I could meet her some Saturday afternoon and we could go for a stroll by the harbour and perhaps have a coffee or a glass of vino. Without any dithering or hesitation she smiled and replied. "That would be nice, yes". I explained that I would have to wait to ensure that it was a weekend that I was sure of being free, as I often had to work some weekends. So it was agreed. I was delighted and overjoyed as I returned to my car to wait for Major Rees, the ghastly priest. Eventually an hour or so later he arrived. I leapt out of my car as usual, bid him good morning and promptly opened the rear vehicle door to allow him to enter my car. He made no response, which was the norm, therefore I assumed that he was in another one of his moods and because as far as I was concerned, he was an ignorant b******. We visited a huge magnificent chapel, then a few shops and were back at the hotel just after midday. He instructed me to be back sharp at one-o-clock as he had an important meeting.

I headed back to our barracks which was approximately a fifteen minutes drive and actually had lunch with Hansen and Falconer for the first time in weeks as I was always late for lunch. On my return to the hotel I wandered into the priest's office and was shocked when *Anjelica* informed me that Major Rees had left. She explained. "He has gone to the Hotel Impero down the road where he has a meeting. He is furious and said that you were late. Before he left he phoned your Company and requested a dispatch rider to report to him at the Impero Hotel where he has gone to the meeting". *Anjelica* looked very concerned. I checked my watch. It was seven/eight minutes past one. I must have been a few minutes late! *Anjelica* continued. "You must to go to the hotel quickly, You know the Hotel Impero, it's just a few doors down the road". "Yes I know it, I had better go". I suggested as I ran out of the office and hotel to my car. I had to do a U turn to get back to the Hotel Impero. I parked my car directly in front of the Impero hotel main entrance door. We staff car drivers had special Italian Government VIP passes to park almost anywhere and everywhere.

*"This is you're last chance driver, if you appear in front
of me again you are going to have to spend some time in San-Giusto"*
[A notorious military prison known locally as 'del Castello di San Giusto]

I had only been sitting there for about fifteen minutes when one of our dispatch riders from 65 Coy arrived on his motor-bike. As soon as he stopped and removed his helmet, I recognised him. He was a corporal from my own 65 R.A.S.C. Company. As he was about to enter the hotel he stopped and walked back over to my Humber so I immediately stepped out of my car. The corporal asked me. "Are you Major Rees the priests driver ?" "Yes corporal" Was my instant reply. "Is there a problem?" He enquired. "Not to my knowledge corporal". Without another word the corporal walked very briskly into the hotel. He returned within half hour with a large brown envelope in his possession and asked me. "Were you late in reporting for duty?" I hesitated somewhat, then eventually replied. "Perhaps, I could have been a few minutes late corporal". He waved the brown envelope in the air and said. "He is charging you". He jumped on his motor-bike and roared off. I sat in my car for nearly four hour's, then just after five-o-clock that afternoon the priest stepped out of the hotel. I jumped out of the car opened his door and he climbed in. Once back in my car and sitting behind the steering wheel I requested. "Where to sir?". "My hotel, where else". Was his abrupt reply. After a two minute drive to his own hotel, I leapt out of my car and opened the rear door for him. He climbed out and walked away into his hotel without uttering a single word. I thought, *you sanctimonious b******.* Back at the barracks as I was parking my staff car, my platoon sergeant approached me and asked me what had happened. I explained in detail. After a protracted silence he informed me. "Prepare yourself for orders in the morning, however I'll try and have a word with the Sergeant Major before he takes you in front of the C.O". "Thanks Sarg". Was all I could think of to say. "Don't thank me! I can't promise you anything". Was his reply.

The next morning I was double marched in front of our Commanding Officer by the Coy Sergeant Major. The R.A.S.C. 65 Coy Commanding Officer was consulting a letter that was in front of him on his desk, then he looked up at me. "Have you any idea what this letter from Major Rees say's". "No Sir". "He charges you with default, failure to exercise your duty and being Idle. What do you have to say driver?". "Sir I was late at being discharged from my duty to have my lunch and a minute or two late at arriving back at the Major's office after lunch". The C.O looked at the Sergeant Major, then as if talking to himself said. "I find this entire affair rather Indifferent". The C.O. then nodded his head at the Sergeant Major who immediately marched me back outside and ordered me to stand easy. The Sergeant Major swiftly returned to the C.O's office. After nine ten minutes, the Sergeant Major re-appeared and marched me back into the C.O's office. I was found guilty of being negligent. Demoted from staff car duty and sentenced to fourteen days after duty labour in the kitchen. Before being marched out of the office, the C.O informed me. "This is your last chance driver, if you appear before me again you are going to have to spend some time up in San Gesto". [A notorious Army Prison known locally as the 'del Castello di San Giusto']

I was now back to driving a three ton truck around Trieste. Compared to driving my elegant Humber staff car, it was demeaning. When I was driving my Humber salon staff car I was parking in front of most of the five star hotels in the city of Trieste. Now I was driving my cumbersome three ton truck to the trades-men's entrance at the rear of these hotels delivering all type of goods and various foodstuff. I never did get a chance to make a date with the villain Priest's secretary, *Anjelica*. The fourteen days labour duty after normal working hours involved me working in our barrack's kitchen from 1700 hours until midnight during the week and all day Saturday and Sunday, scrubbing pots, pans and floors and preparing tons of vegetables. I did realise and appreciate that I had been pretty lucky that I not been slammed back into the barrack's prison cell's again after that b****** priest had charged me. I had heard through the grapevine that both my platoon sergeant and the Coy Sergeant Major had pleaded on my behalf. This *San Gesto* was a mili-tary prison that sat on top off a hill on the outside of Trieste. It is an old castle and now a notorious prison run by the Military Corrective Establishment [M.C.E.] This military prison had a reputation off being a frightful place and run by some loathsome M.C.E. prison officers.

One particular day my wonky eye was very bad. When I had a look in one of my wing mirrors, my eyeball had wandered away over to the far corner of my eye and was sitting adjacent to my nose as if it was trying to escape. When I eventu-ally got back to our company barracks enclosed car park around four-o-clock, I deliberately made a point of parking my truck away in a secluded corner in the car park. I sneaked out of the car park without signing myself in or logging my log book and went straight up to the barracks. Once inside the barracks I went direct to my room to rest on top of my bed. I knew that I had to rest this wonky eye of mine to stop it from escaping and assist it to return to its desig-nated location and function. I must have dozed off to sleep because the next thing I remember was being awakened by someone nudging me. When I looked up it was my platoon sergeant and a corporal. The corporal ordered me to get up and stand to attention. The sergeant demanded to know what the hell I was doing in the barracks and in bed. I tried to explained about my eye, however at this time it had wandered back to normal. I was put on a charge for not handing in my log book at the parking lot, neglecting my duty and going absent without permission.

Apparently another driver by the name of Bowles had arrived in the car park lot just after me and as he was logging in his log book, he was given another assignment. He immediately registered a complaint and enquired why driver Cassidy had not been given the assignment. *Of course, driver Cassidy had not logged in his log book yet and instead, had sneaked off to the barracks.* Bowles had been informed that driver Cassidy had not yet finished duty and that was when Bowles pointed-out that my truck was parked over in the far corner of the parking lot. I was in now deep trouble.

In the mess hall that evening I spotted driver Bowles so I wandered over to his table and asked him. "Why, did you have to tell the dispatch office that my truck was in the compound?". "Because it was! and you were first in and you should have got that other assignment, not me" Was his instant reply. He was of course correct but I still felt that he had betrayed me, so I replied angrily. "Jesus Christ you stupid idiot, have any idea what you have done? You are responsible for having me put on at least two charges". "That's not my problem". Was his instant response and to add insult to injury, he appeared to be enjoying this bravado attitude in front of his friends that he was sitting at the table with. I just lost it and stormily replied. "You stupid b*******, I'm going to make it part off your problem". I quickly skipped around the table and made a grab for him! I had no idea that Falconer had followed me. Falconer grabbed me by the waist and dragged me away then pushed me back to the table where we had been sitting at with Hansen. Falconer pointed at me and whispered loudly. "Are you crazy?, are you going to thump that creep in front off fifty / sixty, spectators. All witness's. You have to cool it and if you have to thump him, do it when you get him on his own". I was shaking with anger whilst big Hansen was nodding his head in agreement with what Falconer had said. When we were eventually leaving the mess-hall, Bowles and the others at his table were all laughing. I thought to myself, *I'll get you, you bloody creep!!*

It was impossible for me to sleep, just thinking about Bowles, the charges and the possibility that the C.O. was going to throw the book at me tomorrow. It was after one-o-clock in the morning when I discretely got out of bed and tip-toed down the corridor still only wearing my vest and underpants. I stopped outside Bowles billet room. All the billet rooms had six people sleeping in them. I had already checked out where Bowles bed was so I very gently and slowly opened the door and left it ajar. I tip-toed up to the side of his bed and whispered. "Bowles, Bowles, wake up". He stirred and turned over. "Who, what is it?" He asked, then he very slowly sat up in the darkness. I remained silent and slammed my right clenched into his face. He squealed like the pig that he was. I pulled him from his bed and slammed another couple of clenched right fist into the side of his face. As I turned to leave, all the other five people in the

56

billet room now appeared to be awake!! This was not what I had planned or expected to happen, I was planning to be back into my own billet and into bed before anyone else had been disturbed. As I stepped out off Bowles billet into the main corridor and closed the door, some of the electric lights in some of the other billets were now being switched on and someone opened a billet door adjacent to my own billet and stepped out into the corridor. I panicked and ran the opposite way and found myself standing at the top of the main wide sweeping staircase. Before I knew it, I was heading away from the scene and running down the staircase barefooted and wearing only a pair of shorts and vest. At the bottom, I ran towards the closed N.A.F.F.I. canteen bar and sat down at one of the empty table's to think about what I should do next!

I suddenly heard someone shout. "Call out the guards?". After a protracted silence I heard the heavy boots of the guards pounding up the staircase. After another ten fifteen minutes, I heard the heavy boots pounding down the marble staircase. I got myself into a corner, pulled a few tables and chairs around me and sat down on the cold floor. Two of the guards came running into the empty isolated N.A.F.F.I. They wandered around then ran away back towards the entrance to the building and the staircase. There was a hell of shouting and loud talking going on and it seemed to last forever. After an hour or so, it went quiet. I waited another fifteen minutes or so then headed back towards the stairway and my billet. As I was walking up the staircase, a voice shouted out. "Halt soldier. Stay exactly where you are soldier". I looked upwards to where the order appeared to have come from. A group of soldiers, some with rifles were gazing down at me from the landing above. Someone shouted. "Advance towards us soldier slowly". I was then confronted with an officer a sergeant and four guards. The officer was the first to address me. "Where have you been soldier?". I remember trying to think what to say, then sort of whispered aloud. "I lost some money earlier this evening and I couldn't sleep because I was upset. I thought that I may have dropped the money in the N.A.F.F.I. which was the last place I had been so I went down to have a look". The sergeant screamed at me. "Sir, you will address the officer as Sir". The sergeant then moved very close to my right hand side. The officer informed me. "You are in a state off undress soldier, why?" "I didn't expect to see anyone". Was my instant reply, then the sergeant without warning screamed into my ear. "Sir, you answer Sir, you will address the officer as Sir". His mouth was so close to my face that I could feel his hot breath on my ear drum. The officer, who appeared to be ignoring the sergeant, asked me. "Do you know that a soldier has been assaulted in his billet on this landing this morning?" Before I could reply he continued. "Why on earth are you wandering around improperly dressed at this ungodly hour in the morning soldier?" "I told you". Before I could continue, I shuddered in shock as the sergeant once more burned my ear drum with his screaming. "Sir, you will answer the officer as Sir, soldier". His face was so close to me that I could feel his saliva on the lob off my right ear. The officer continued. "What do you know about this assault?". I remember hesitating, then replied. "I know nothing about an assault". Then once more my right hand side ear-drum nearly burst as this stupid sergeant screamed. "Sir, Sir, you will address the officer as Sir, you stupid imbecile". I asked the officer to tell the sergeant to stop screaming into my ear. The officer ignored me and asked. "Is that blood on the back of your hand?" The officer was now pointing to my right hand. I was shocked and automatically very quickly covered my right hand with my left hand and instantly decided not too respond. The screaming from the sergeant made me twitch once more as he shrieked. "You will answer the officer you wretched creature, do you understand?". I really have no idea why or exactly what made me react. Perhaps it was because it was obvious that I was in serious trouble. Also the continuous screaming in my ear drum was seriously affecting my train of thoughts! I suddenly and very quickly stepped sideways and away from the sergeant and the officer and slammed my right handed fist into the sergeant's face. The punch smashed into the side off his face with such surprise and ferocity that his head twisted away from me pulling his body with it. He staggered backwards, slipped and hit the marble tiled floor with a silent thud and appeared to slide across the highly polished smooth floor surface. The officer and four guards were so surprised and shocked that for a few seconds there was an eerie silence. Then the officer let an *'oh my God'* sort of vociferation then shouted. "Arrest this soldier, arrest him immediately. Arrest him"!! *All Hell !!* was suddenly let loose!! All four guards pointed their rifles at me. The officer un-holstered his pistol and also pointed it in my direction. The officer then instructed one of the guards to assist the sergeant then proceeded to make the other three guards form a circle around me. The three guards and the officer escorted me down the spiral staircase and across the square to the prison cell's. One of the guards after he had locked the cell gate whispered to me. "Oh Christ Cass, what have you done? I'll get a message to Falconer and Hansen. Oh Christ Cass this is a f****** mess!"

Next morning, I was escorted to my billet by the regimental police to get dressed and then escorted back to my cell for a shower and eventually breakfast. Later on in the morning the regimental police marched me over to the Coy Regimental Sergeant Major. I was only in front of our Commanding Officer for three seconds when he informed me that I was to be tried by a Court Martial. I was doubled back to my cell where the Coy Regimental Sergeant Major explained that the military police would now be taking over. He looked rueful as he told me to. "Stand easy soldier". He further explained that I would be held in custody in San Gesto Military Prison until my Court Martial. He then asked me. "Do you have any question's soldier?" I hesitated for a minute then asked. "How long before my Court Martial sir". "It could be a month, it could be longer. You are initially being charged with assaulting a non-commissioned officer which is a very serious offence. Very serious indeed. Apparently there could be other charges of assault and other misdemeanours. You are now in some serious trouble soldier".

Indifferent: 6

The four military policemen that picked me up from the guard room cells in their land rover to escort me to *San Gesto Prison,* were vicious individuals who appeared to enjoy treating me unfairly and with unwarranted disrespect. Although I was handcuffed and surrounded by the four of them, they harassed me verbally and physically continuously. When I was attempting to climb into the rear of their long-base land-rover they pushed me from behind causing me to tumble onto the metal floor and they left me crumbled up there during the half hour journey to the military prison. The two that sat in the rear of the vehicle beside me pushed the toes of their boots into various delicate parts of my body as I lay prostrated on the land-rover floor. On arrival at the *San Gesto Prison* they dragged me out of the land-rover like I was the carcass of some animal. I was hurt and angry and perhaps it was fortuitous that I was in handcuffs because I most definitely would have attempted to try to retaliate in some way.

I was soon to discover that the four brutal military policemen were celestial angels compared to the sadistic *San Gesto* prison staff. The *San Gesto* prison officers and the military policemen that delivered me to them were signing pieces of paper for me like I was some insane criminal or a parcel of goods. In spite of the fact that I was still handcuffed and had never been out of the sight of these four military policemen since they had searched and handcuffed me in my barracks cells, I was rigorously and viciously searched by the *San-Gesto* prison staff. When the handcuffs were eventually removed, I was flanked by four of the sturdy prison officers and marched at the double through four huge metal security gates and into a prison square. Then without a pause I entered the prison itself and was soon being made to run extremely fast down a steep circular worn-out winding staircase with steps that were barely wide enough to accommodate the length of my size nine military boots. Prison staff members were screaming at me to go faster, which was impossible and eventually I stumbled against the circular wall and nearly crashed down onto the worn-out thousand years old stone steps. At the bottom I was eventually pushed into this small empty room that was barely wide enough to accommodate the five of us. I was ordered to and eventually stripped naked and was very roughly man-handled. Each and every one of these treacherous officers took turns each peering into my ears, under my arms, between my toes and into my mouth. The final insult was when one of them deliberately and painstakingly pulled on a pair of plastic gloves and ordered to me to bend over. For a few seconds I froze and without uttering a single word, I shook my head indicating *No!* I was so naive that I thought by not verbally saying *No*, I could not be accused of disobeying a direct order. The officer wearing the plastic gloves screamed at me. "Prisoner, bend over"! Once more remaining silent I shook my head indicating *No*. Without warning one of the other officers rushed at me and within seconds was kneeling in front of me while another two grabbed me and pushed me over the top of his broad back. One of them pulled and stretched my arms firmly on the stone floor in front of me while the other, who was now behind me had hold of both my legs and appeared to spread eagle them apart. I was so shocked and dumbfounded that I could do not even scream when I felt this object being forced up and into my anus and being rotated within me. They left me naked on the floor face down and to my amazement, I was too embarrassed to be angry or attempt to lift myself up off the cold stone floor. I remained transfixed face down on the floor until someone threw the plastic gloves onto the floor just in front of my head. Someone touched me with his boot or something on my leg then screamed at me to get dressed. Obviously I was still devastated and not moving fast enough because all four of the officers were now screaming at me to. "Move it"!

They bundled and chased me back up the steep narrow circular worn stone staircase and back outside into a square that was engulfed in the bright Trieste sunshine. This small parade square was surrounded by a twelve foot high wall that was draped on top with bundles of barbed wire. I was double marched across the square and back through one of the ten foot high gates and into another wee room with only a table and chair in it. One of the officers opened a drawer in the table and removed what looked like a pair of hair clippers. He then casually asked the other three officers who's turn it was. I was pushed into the chair with my back to three of them. Someone collected the clippers and after a few seconds silence the sound of an electric appliance started up then I felt the clippers cutting up the back of my neck onto the top of my head. I tried to pull away but was instantly restrained and they laughingly continued to rip away at my head and hair. It was so painful that I continually tried to break free but was brutally restrained. I was eventually marched at the double back across the small parade square and that's when I saw my first inmate. He was marching time in the middle of the square with his full pack-on his back. Two other prison staff members were screaming orders at him. I was trotting in front of two of the four screws that were maltreating me when one of them caught up with me and screamed. "March time on the spot prisoner". It was at this time that I realized that my head was bleeding when a drop of blood seemed to drip of the end of my nose onto the ground. I was suddenly shaken out of my thoughts when the screw standing beside me screamed. "Prisoner forward double march". I was rushed down the circular set of a thousand year old worn-out steps for at least three ground levels until I was stopped to march time on the spot in front of a cell gate. When the cell gate was unlocked I was marched into the cell still running until I nearly ran through the dungeon wall and was told to march time. I only stopped 'marching time' when I heard the metal cell gate being locked and the four screws walking away.

It was a cell with six beds. One bed was empty and the other five were made up as if they were on show in an exhibition in art gallery. At the top of the beds there was a square that consisted of two bed sheets and two blankets. A third blanket was wrapped around them holding the near perfect square together. The sequence set inside the square consisted of a blanket, a sheet, a blanket, a sheet. One in particular was a perfect square but the four others were mediocre. Two brilliant shining metal mess cans had been placed in front of the blanket/ sheet square box. Then a shining tin plate had been placed in the centre of the bed. Military webbing such as large packs and small packs including their straps, belts and gaiters that had been scrubbed clean and free of it's khaki coloured blanco [A substance used for rubbing onto military webbing especially prior to inspection] were all laid out on the bed as if for critical examination. Finally at the bottom of the beds there was a shaving brush, toothbrush, shaving soap and toothpaste, also all laid out as if in an exhibition. One particular bed was perfect. Everything was just exact and detailed. One bed looked as if it had been disturbed and had no webbing on it. The other three beds were in various stages of order and looked indifferent. My isolation and survey of the beds were suddenly disturbed by shouting and the clattering and sliding of heavy boots on the short steep dangerous and precarious circular staircase. I walked to the cell gate just as some inmates appeared at the bottom of staircase. A screw chasing them spotted me! and immediately screamed at the inmates who were all now visible. "March time". I jumped back out of view and he screamed. "Stand tooooo prisoner". Even over the clatter of the inmates crashing their big army issued boots onto the ancient stone floors, I could hear him walking towards the cell door. Then he screamed again. "Prisoner, stand by the cell gate". I suddenly recognised the screws accent, it was Scottish. I guessed, Glasgow and I actually felt somewhat relieved, even comforted at hearing the Scottish accent. Then I was brought to reality again with the rattling of metal against the steel metal cell gates and the Scottish accent again screamed. "Prisoner stand by the cell gate". It was only then that I realized that he was still screaming at me. I moved ever so slowly towards the cell gate and the second I was in range of his vision, the Scottish accent sergeant screamed. "Stand to attention you moron. What are you doing creeping around like a cockroach?" "I am a new arrival sir". Was my extremely uncertain reply. He screamed. "Don't address me as sir you moron. You will address me as Staff. Don't you ever stand around idle prisoner. Double march time on the spot". I started marching time on the spot where I stood and thudding my great heavy army boots onto the stone cell floor. He screamed.

62

"That's not double marching time you imbecile. "Move it". Left right, left right, left right" His rapid timing was so fast I could hardly keep up with it. Outside the cell the bunch of inmates who were facing me were also marching time on the spot with their huge army boots crashing down fast and furiously onto the stone floor. It was sheer madness and the clatter was insanely deafening and not a single individual was moving, we were all being treated as if we were retards.

I was nineteen years old, in a foreign country that I had briefly heard of and now I find myself locked-up in this hell hole surrounded by prison officers who all appear to be insane, extremely dangerous and move around like riot mobs. I had never known fear like this and realized that I was in serious trouble. In the pit of my stomach for the first time in my life I felt insecure and desperate. Somehow, someone had taken away my freedom and my life as I previously knew it. I continued thumping my boots onto this ancient dungeon stone cell floor and wondered why the floor was not disintegrating. I was looking at the other inmates thumping and crashing their huge studded boots onto the stone floor and somehow I couldn't hear the noise that should be emanating from them. I wanted to stop marching time in order to find out if I was deaf, or just going mad. However, under the circumstances I decided that would not be a very good idea because this was a nut house run by lunatics. We were all in this prison, me inside a prison cell facing outside and marching time, outside the cell were a gang of insane prison officers and a half-a dozen inmates facing towards the cell and they were all marching time. It looked to me that if this cell door is eventually opened and one of these insane hysterical prison officers suddenly screams *Forward March'* there is going to be a terrible crash of bodies, minds and boots.

Another screw with a large bunch of keys arrived and he immediately commenced screaming. "Left right, left right, left right. Halt, stand easy". I had no idea who he was screaming at or what I should do, but I halted anyway. As it turned out, all off us inmates made the same decision and halted. The instant silence was eerie. The screw with the bunch of keys had opened the cell door and was now facing me and yelled. "Not you, you bloody fool, left right, left right, left right, left turn" I immediately commenced marching time only and didn't move because I just did not understand what all this madness was all about. Then he screamed at me. "You bloody imbecile, left turn". I turned left and was now facing in towards the inside of the cell, then the screaming continued. "Left right, left right, quick march, left right, left right, left turn, left right, left right". I was moving like a machine and not really paying much attention to what this lunatic was still screaming at me. All I was doing was avoiding crashing into the beds that were at each side of me and marched on until I was about to crash into the dungeon wall at the end of the cell then he screamed. "March time, left right, left right". I was now standing inches away from the dungeon wall marching time on the spot. Then above the clatter of my own boots hitting the stone floor, I heard the clobber of the other inmates boots rushing into the cell. Although I could see nothing as I was facing the end of the dungeon cell wall I knew that I was not deaf or insane, well not yet!

Whilst I was still marching on the spot, the other prisoners appeared to be running and sliding around and smashing into the metal framed beds. One of the prison officers was now screaming. "Move it, you lazy slobs, move it" The other prisoners then all seemed to run out of the cell. A sergeant was suddenly standing at my right hand side and screamed. "Left right, left right. Halt, stand easy" I took a chance and decided that this lunatic was barking his orders at me. I was in luck, because when I stopped marching time he shouted at me. "You the new intake?" "Yes sir". I replied. "Don't sir me you bloody fool. You will address me as staff and don't look at me unless you have permission. Look ahead. Have you been issued with any kit?". "No staff". Then I heard the other inmates now running and sliding back into the cell and then a staff member screamed. "Stand by the cell gate. Move it, move it". Then someone screamed at me. "That goes for you to you imbecile! Move it, move it". Everyone appeared to be scattering towards the cell gate with boots skidding and sliding on the stone floor, I turned and ran after them not knowing if that was what I was suppose do. I counted only four other inmates lined up at the cell gate. They all had tin plates, mugs and plastic knives and forks in their hands and were all standing rigidly to attention and in a line one behind the other facing the open cell gate so I joined the end of the line. The prison officer in front of us was joined by another and I noticed that he was the one with the Scottish accent. Suddenly there was another clattering and skidding of boots as it appeared that other inmates were being screamed at and chased down the circular stone staircase. As the clattering of boots descended down the staircase the screaming orders grew louder. "Move it, move it, move it". It was a solitary prisoner, the inmate that I had passed on the square when I had first entered this nut house. As he turned to run towards the cell he skidded and went down in a heap in front off us all. The screw with the Scottish accent was now standing over him and within seconds was screaming at this pathetic crumbled boy spread eagled on the floor. "Move it, move it you fool. Get up, get up. Quickly, move it you stupid imbecile, move it". That's when I realized that we inmates were all *imbeciles,* not just me! The poor boy was obviously hurt and suffering but clawed his way up the nearest wall. The screw that had been chasing him down the stairs was also now screeching at him. "Move it you fool, move it. He ran past us into the cell with the screw with the Scot's accent hot on his heels still bawling. "Move it, move it, move it".

I had only observed five other prisoners and yet I had witnessed at least eight

64

prison officers and everyone of them had the rank of a sergeant and as far as I was concerned, they were all *MAD*. Eventually the inmate that had slid and had hit the stone floor with a thud had now joined the line and was now standing behind me with his tin plate, mug and plastic knife, fork and spoon he looked like a wee boy and younger than me. The six of us were chased up the ancient circular stone staircase by the four screws all taking turns at screaming at us to "Move it". We all scampered up what I counted must have been at least three landings until we reached the main ground level. In this main hallway/chamber there was a spiral metal staircase complete with metal handrails that went twisting upward to another landing. The inmate leading us went straight for it and without hesitation pounded up and around the twisting metal stairs. The four screws were still taking it turns to scream at us to *"Move it"*. This spiral staircase opened into a large kitchen and dining area. The entire area was spotless with modern stainless steel equipment everywhere including dining tables and chairs. One at a time the prisoners all stepped forward their food served by the chefs, that was until it was my turn. The screw with the Scottish accent told me to stand aside. Once the other five prisoners had their food plated and placed on their trays, they were all allowed to sit down in the dining area.

I was finding it difficult looking at the image of myself in the mirror whilst shaving, I looked like a scarecrow with the small turfs of hair that was left protruding out of my scarred bald head.

The screw with the Scot's accent handed me a tray with a plastic knife, fork and spoon on it. A soup plate filled to the brim and nearly overflowing was placed on my tray. I was also served a main course and pudding and both plates were also filled to the brim and nearly overflowing. The screw with the Scot's accent told me. "You will move it, when I give you the order". He wandered off slightly, then without warning screamed. "Attention prisoner. By the right, double quick march. Left right, left right, left right. Move it, move it, move it". I hesitated and glanced down at my tray. The fellow Scot screw ran at my side and howled at me. "Move it you damn fool, you are disobeying a direct order. Move it. Left right, left right, left right". I was marching / running towards the tables whilst the food was spilling onto and over my tray until the Scots screw ordered. "Halt". I instantly stopped and was thankful for that until another screw wandered over to me and shouted. "You are in isolation and until further notice you will dine on your own and in your prison cell, do you understand prisoner?" Before I could respond my fellow Scot the screw hollered. "Isolation prisoner. Quick march". I looked towards the metal spiral staircase, walked quickly towards it reached the top and automatically hesitated, then stopped.

The screw, not the Scot, who was now standing directly behind me appeared to go berserk and screamed. "Move it prisoner at the double. One two, one two, one two, move it, move it". I very cautiously stepped onto the first metal step on the circular staircase and started descending completely ignoring the screaming screws orders whilst trying to concentrate on my tray. However this lunatic was following me and screaming into the back off my head. I was not a quarter of the way down when my soup plate skidded on the soup that had already spilled and slid off the tray and went into orbit. Once the soup plate went, my entire balancing act was gone. The main dish was next to go into orbit. The only plate remaining on the tray was the pudding. The soup and main dish plate had clattered and banged all the way down the spiral staircase and hit the stone floor at the bottom with a terrible clatter. By the time I eventually reached the bottom the tray was empty and the insane screw were still screaming abuses at me. What remained of the food was splattered all the way down the metal staircase and all over the stone floor. I was rushed around by another sergeant because the one that had chased me all the way down the spiral metal staircase and the one with the Scot's accent had both vanished. I was soon collecting a bucket, wash cloth and scrubbing brush. I spent the next few hour's scrubbing and cleaning the kitchen floors, the spiral metal staircase and the entire stone floor beneath the spiral staircase. When I was finished, I was rushed back down to the cell and locked up.

After the screw locked the cell gate and told me to stand easy, I entered the cell where the beds were. Four of the other five cell inmates were all sitting on the floor adjacent to their beds and they all looked as young as me and in a state of distress. The squared of blankets and bed sheets, shining mess tins, military webbing and other articles that appeared to be on show were still all placed neatly on their beds. The other inmate was lying stretched out on the mattress of the empty bed. He sat up and suggested to me. "I believe this bed now belongs to you? Welcome to hell, also known as 'San Gesto' brother". He sprang to his feet and indicated by a gesture of both his hands to the mattress, suggesting that I should take over. The other four inmates who appeared to be in shock did not seem to have the energy or the mental capacity to speak, or even look in my direction. The first thing I noticed about the smart articulate inmate that had greeted me was that he was older than the rest of us and must have been in his mid twenties. The second thing that I noticed was that he had a white band on his left lapel of his army issue khaki shirt. I sat on the mattress and dropped my head into both my cupped hands.

"May I join you brother?". I looked up. The articulate inmate was standing beside my bed. I didn't reply, but did indicate that he could, so he immediately sat on the edge of my mattress and introduced himself. "My name is Richard brother and how long are we going to have the privilege off your company?". After a protracted silence, I replied. "Richard, I have no idea". I lifted the palm of my right hand towards him, indicating; please leave me alone, but he continued. "I understand brother, we will speak another time, however I think you should know that the lunch time caper is a deliberate plan. No new inmate ever gets to eat their first meal. No one". He moved stealthily away and back to his bed, and like the others, squatted down on the cold stone floor. The complete silence in the cell was short lived, as someone screamed. "Stand by your cell gate. Move, move it, move it".

I was taken away on my own by a sergeant that I had never set eyes on before and I have to say that I was concerned about this. I had already witnessed the obvious authority and power these people had and the lack of empathy they showed towards us vulnerable inmates. It was surreal the amount of power they appeared to have over us. It also appeared that they had the authority and were capable of beating us senseless, just for the hell of it. However my concerns were in vain, he marched me around at the double to pick up blankets, sheets, tin plates, plastic knifes forks and spoons. We also visited a small shop where I was issued a toothbrush, toothpaste, shaving cream, shaving brush and face soap. The other five inmates in my cell were all being marched at the double around the square doing rifle drill. The hullabaloo from the three screws that were screaming out the orders was obscene, ridiculous and unnecessary. I was still unsure where the rest of the inmates were and was curious and always looking and listening for them. Eventually, all six of us were chased into a large shower room and that was the first time I realized that my head had been cut in several places when these sadist's had cropped my hair. To add insult to injury, what was left of my hair was a few tiny clutches dotted over my scarred bald head. We were all rushed back into our cell whilst our bodies were still wet under our clothes and double marched back up to the kitchen at the top of the infamous spiral staircase. In this instance, I was allowed to follow the others into the dining area and sit at a table.

After washing up our utensils and returning to our cell, we were eventually marched at the double back up the incredible abominable century old circular stone staircase into a recreation room. It had a table tennis table, a small library, playing cards, a couple of modern tables, two arm chairs and a sofa. This was the first time I encountered a sergeant Major by the name of Green. I remember thinking that he must be the ugliest person I had ever seen in my life, even uglier than me with my badly scarred bald head. He was perhaps around thirty five years old and looked like a pig with glasses. The only difference that I could think off was that a pigs teeth were probably cleaner because his teeth were black and yellow. I was to find out much later why he hated human beings, especially young army soldiers. He had an eighteen year old daughter that some young soldier had made pregnant. Apparently to make matters worse, she had no idea which one it was. I was pleasantly surprised and shocked when I learned that we were all allowed one cigarette per person, per night. Four of us were marched outside onto the small parade ground for our nightly cigarette. We each received a single cigarette from the [pig] sergeant major Green, then he lit each one of our cigarettes with a lighter and immediately started shouting. "Come on get smoking, puff, puff, puff. Come on get puffing, puff, puff, puff". The four cigarettes that were not even half finished were systematically taken from us and pushed down the drain cover that we were all standing adjacent too and briskly double marched back into the recreation room by the pig, sergeant major Green.

On my first night in the cell, I was shocked to find that the only prisoners to get into their beds were articulate Richard and myself because the other four inmates slept on the floor. Articulate Richard explained to me that they were afraid to unwrap their blankets and sheet squares because they could never get them together again in time for inspection in the morning inspection. He also explained that if you fail the morning inspection you are put on a charge and severely punished. He also suggested that I should enjoy my sleep because It will most probably be my first and last in a bed! Apparently all the screws were aware of this sadistic event and it probably made them sleep sounder at night knowing that they were still inflicting pain on their vulnerable inmates whilst they all slept soundly.

Aristocrat Richard, as I had decided to nickname him sat up late into the night chatting with me and he was indeed a wealth of information. He was three months into a six month prison sentence, after a court - martial. He had been a lieutenant officer in the Fusiliers guards and had been accused, charged, court-martial and found guilty of being a Bolshevik communist and inciting troops to resist company orders. They had photographs of him in the NAAFI and in local bars in Trieste city standing on tables giving the Marxist salute. When he was found guilty he was reduced to the ranks, given a dishonourable discharge and sentenced to six months prison in San Gesto. He was obviously an educated young man, aged around twenty five / twenty six. He was tall and lean with fair hair and a fair complexion. An attractive young man, very active and very much alive. He certainly frightened me that night when he informed me that I could be sentenced to at least a year at my Court- Martial after I had informed that I was being charged for assaulting a non commissioned officer. He also informed me that I would be dispatched to Germany to the huge military prison there because San Gesto prison in Trieste Italy only incarcerate inmates for a maximum of six months. Any soldier in Trieste sentenced to longer periods had to be sent back to Germany.

That night I had very little sleep, my bald head was very tender and sore where these lunatics had ripped the hair from my scalp with a set of clippers. Plus the thought of a year in prison kept me awake most of the night. The morning arrived like a bullet from a gun when a screw was suddenly rattling something against the bars of the cell gate whilst screaming. "Stand by the gate, stand by the gate, move it, move it, move it". Aristocrat Richard had warned me about this procedure that took place every morning at five thirty and had also explained that the last man in the line up at the door every morning was charged with being idle. After the six off us had lined up at the gate to identify ourselves and be identified by the two screws, the poor guy that had skidded and fell down on the stone floor last night, was last. He was the idle one! and he was charged with being idle and he would be made to suffer more than we would for the rest of this miserable day. We were rushed in the same single line back to our beds to collect our soap and shaving gear etc. Even washing and shaving in this mad house was harassment time. The two screws present just walked among our six naked bodies screaming abuse at us. Shouting into our ears from a very short distance of inches away. "Move it, move it, come on you lazy louts, move it, move it". I found it very difficult to look at my own image in the mirror whilst shaving. I looked like a scarecrow with small turfs of straw for hair protruding from my bald head. I looked that ugly that my own mother would not have recognised me, or would have preferred not to.

Breakfast was okay for me because it was thick porridge with thick slices of bread and a mug of hot thick tea made with tea leaves. Richard told me that in military prisons they trebled the amount of bromide they put in your tea. I had no idea what he was talking about until he further explained. "Bromide is a sedative to give you a soothing platitude, especially towards sex". Richard suggested that it would take him maybe another six months once he is released before he will be able to get an erection. He also suggested that if things go bad at my trial, I may never ever get an erection again in my entire life. In spite of Aristocrat Richard's doom and gloom attitude towards my outcome at my trial, we did became very close friends. There was a very good reasons for that because all the other prisoners that where incarcerated in San Gesto were only with us for seven days, or so. They arrived and were very soon gone after sleeping on the stone floor for a few days. Most off them were charged for being lazy because they were last in the line-up first thing in the morning in spite of the fact that someone! had to be last! It was a stupid sadistic principle and to add insult to injury, the majority of these young soldiers were from middle class backgrounds and were unable to cope with the overall barbarity.

Richard was absolutely correct, I did have a big problem preparing all my kit and spreading it out on my bed every morning for inspection. I did get charged plenty of times because I failed the morning inspection and therefore had to spend a couple of nights sleeping on the floor. However with the help of Aristocratic Richards expertise and in spite of the limited time we had in the morning before the full inspection. I eventually became capable enough to spread out all the kit on my bed to a standard that was good enough to pass the extremely thorough inspection. Therefore I was soon able to remove it all at night and have the use of my bed to sleep in. Richard had also explained to me that I was not in the true sense a prisoner, not until I was tried and found guilty. He explained that I was entitled to smoke as many cigarettes as I wanted too, providing I had cash to purchase them and that I was not on duty. He also confirmed that I should have a white band indicating that I was a trustee inmate simply because I was still not guilty of any crime. He had earned his white band as a trusted prisoner but I was entitled to one because I was not yet a prisoner. He advised me not to confront the ugly pig sergeant major Green, or the mad commandant Major Carter. He advised me to speak with a certain staff sergeant major named Holburn, a staff member that I had never yet met. Richard had also confirmed to me that there was a total of eleven staff members, eight sergeants, two sergeant majors and a crazy Commandant. He also confirmed that the other inmates I was constantly looking for did not exist. The six number inmates that I had encountered when I was first imprisoned was the total number of prisoners in the entire prison. It was difficult at first for me to accept that there were more prison staff than there were prisoners, it was no wonder that they could afford to take turns each in making our lives as miserable as possible. On a few occasions the total number of inmates fell to four, Richard, myself and two others. However there always appeared to be a steady intake of young soldiers being imprisoned for seven to fourteen days and too often, these young soldiers were pathetic individuals that should have been sent to recreation centres, but most certainly not to San Gesto.

I had now been in San Gesto for just over three weeks. After two weeks the military police picked me up and after handcuffing me escorted me back to my barracks where I was handed over to our regimental police and placed in the barrack cells. The first thing that the regimental police asked was what had happened to my head and who had done that too me. Eventually I was paraded in front of my Commanding Officer who very quickly briefed me about my pending court-martial. I personally found the entire procedure nothing but bull-shit. I wanted to complain about the severe treatment I was being exposed to in San Gesto. I wanted to enquire why I was being held in San Gesto and not in our own prison cells in our own barracks. I wanted to enquire how long will I have to wait until my court-martial. I was not allowed to *Speak!!!* I was very swiftly marched out off my Commanding officers office and taken back to the cells in our barracks guard room and temporarily locked in a cell until the military police returned to collected me. At least whilst in my barrack guard room cell for an hour or so I was allowed to feel like a human being again. I was able to talk to our regimental police guys who of course were known to me and were just ordinary drivers like myself who had been promoted. They of course were very interested to know what was happening to me and what it was like in San Gesto. They were shocked after I had told them how much I was being mistreated. I also got the chance to enquire about my friends, Hansen and Falconer and suggested that they should try and find out if they can come and give me quick visit. Unfortunately for me before I got any news about Falconer and Hansen the military police arrived and returned me too San Gesto. After the military policemen removed my handcuffs and handed me over to the San Gesto staff, three of the sergeants strip-searched me again including my anus! I do believe that the strip and search procedure was a farce and just another excuse to intimidate and hurt me physically and mentally. What on earth would they be looking for in my ears, mouth, under my arms, between my toes and legs and up my A***!

Staff sergeant Holburn was a six foot four inch giant, an English man from Portsmouth and the only screw that treated us humanly. I had taken the advice from Aristocrat Richard and spoke with staff sergeant Holburn and within a few days I had a white band and was given the right to request a cigarette whenever I was not on duty. He had also explained to me that I am still receiving my weekly army pay and will do so until my court-martial, then and only then will my salary be reviewed. The cost of any goods I request including toiletry goods will be deducted from my salary My request for an additional cigarette mostly fell on deaf ears, but I did manage to get a few extra smokes. However the white band was to prove to be extremely rewarding as it allowed me to go with Richard to a very private small beach that was strictly for the use of British army officers, their wives and families which was situated only on the Adriatic coast the outskirts of Trieste. We were both first taken there one Thursday morning to clean up sea-weed and other debris that had been washed onto the beach. This was in preparation for the officers and their families that may visit the beach during the weekend. It was just wonderful getting out of the prison and away from the other screaming and shouting *MAD* staff members. The remarkable thing about it was that it was staff Holburn that escorted us to the beach along with another staff member. However it was soon very obvious that staff Holburn was in charge. Staff Holburn had pre-arranged packed lunches; therefore we were on the beach all day. Richard and I could hardly believe our luck when staff Holburn suggested to us when it was time to return to San Gesto that we will have to return again on Friday morning!

Aristocrat Richard like myself, was a smoker and put me wise to the fact that most of the screws were also smokers often leave large cigarette ends lying around in their rest room and dining area, often on the floor but usually in the cigarette

71

ash trays. Owing to the fact that we inmates are responsible for cleaning these rooms and scrubbing their floors, we have access to these discarded cigarette ends. He suggested that in future, we should collect and hide these cigarette ends on our person and smuggle them back into our cell. These cigarette ends could be broken open and the tobacco collected could be rolled in toilet paper and made into a cigarette. He suggested that in future during our ablution period we must smuggle one of our razor blades back into our cell. With this razor blade we scratch loose some off the rough fibre from the bed blankets, impregnate the loose fibre with some of our liquid brasso that we have for polishing our brass buckles and buttons. We then ignite the loose ball of fibre that is impregnated with the liquid brasso by using a lighter flint and this would allow us to light up the home made cigarette. I was mesmerized and shocked when he continued to endorse more plans.

He suggested that the next time I am taken out of San Gesto and back to my barracks for another hearing about my pending court-martial, I should try to smuggle some small flints that are used to ignite lighters back into the prison. He explained how I could arrange for some of my brothers to give me the flints, then I should put them in my mouth and lodge them under my tongue. He further suggested that the screws would never find them when they strip- search me. He also suggested that owing to the fact that I was still not a prisoner, there was not a great deal that they could do to me except confiscate them and give me an extremely tough time for a few days. I have to say that during this particular period in time, I was hanging on every word that Richard had to say to me because he had done so much to help me and had made my existence in this *Hell-Hole* as acceptable as humanly possible. I promised Richard that I would think about it, but assured him that it was going to be a daunting task because I was never ever left entirely on my own and the only other people I ever get a chance to talk too was the regimental police in the guard room prison cells in my barracks and I was unsure if I could trust them!

I also explained that I thought it was possible to fool the military police when they searched but I had grave doubts about getting past the prison staff when they strip-search me. I also enlightened him that I did not have the experience or courage that he had and that I was a wee bit petrified about what the screw would do to me if I was caught. However, I did promise, that if the opportunity presents itself, I will try to do it, because It was a very clever and ingenious plot and it would be a pity if it could not come to fruition because of the lack of a tiny lighter flint. His contingency plan was that we, Richard and myself collect as many tea leaves as we can every time we have tea, dry them out then roll them up in the toilet paper which we always had access too and Eureka, we have a smoke! Although we had access to most of the ingredients, we had no flint!!

Richard and I started collecting any discarded cigarette ends that we ever had access too, but there was not a lot so we also started collecting our tea leaves. I was shocked when Richard reminded me that the screws often do snatch searches without warning and that everyone gets be strip-searched. He also informed me that the screws also often have lock-ins. That is when everyone is in their cells, they raid it, lock everyone in including themselves, then they tip and toss everything upside down and do a complete thorough search. He further explained that during the surprise individual body- search, each inmate is responsible for himself and will be punished individually if found in possession of something he should not have. In lock-ins, the entire inmates in the cell will be punished if anything is found, unless the guilty party admits his guilt. That's when he suggested in the event that our cigarette ends, tea leaves or anything else relating to our plan is ever discovered in our cell, one off must admit being the guilty person. In spite .of all this startling information I was receiving, I had made up my mind that I just had to get the flints.

In due course I was informed that I was being temporarily returned to my barracks to be paraded once more in front of my Coy Commanding officer. I immediately scribbled a note to Hansen and Falconer on toilet paper and started praying that on this occasion I would get a chance to talk to them. In the morning it was the usual perverse procedure, the military police arrived at San Gesto, signed for me, handcuffed me and escorted me to my barracks prison cells. I removed the folded piece of toilet paper with the written note to Hanson / Falconer from down the side of my right-hand boot. I knew that I was not yet, in any danger because I would only be strip-searched on my return to San Gesto prison. In the event that I do not have the opportunity to see Hanson / Falconer, I would flush the note down this cell toilet before the military police collect me to take back to San Gesto. I was talking to two of our regimental police and before I could decide if I should mention Hansen or Falconer, they were called away. After a few minutes the corporal in charge of the regimental police returned to inform me that I had two visitors, but suggested that he was unsure if I'm allowed visitors. I was shaking with anticipation and asked him. "Who are they?" "It's one of the chefs from the kitchen and one of the local female staff". Was his reply. I was speechless at first then begged him to let them in even suggesting what harm can they do and perhaps they have brought me a sandwich. He very reluctantly agreed to give them five minutes. During my staff car driving days and the time I spent on jankers working in the kitchen I got to know all the kitchen staff very well.

It was Ron the Liverpool chef and Lena one of the Italian ladies that cleared up the tables after meals that were escorted into the cell block. I had both fingers of my hands wrapped around the cell bars and Lena put one of her hands on mine. The regimental policeman shouted. "Do not touch the prisoner". He must have noticed how much he had frightened Lena because after a few seconds of complete silence he said ever so quietly. "Please". My friend Ron and Lena were so pleased to see me that I felt a wee bit humbled and suddenly realized the amazing opportunity I had in order to get my flints. Lena, who had very little English managed to ask me what had happened to my head. At that very second someone shouted on the regimental policeman. As soon as he vanished, I whispered to young Ron. "You must go to the NAFFI shop and get me a packet of lighter flints. Please it's urgent and I need them *Now!* before they take me back. Please go *Now!* and *Run!* Don't let these guy's the police know". At that very moment the regimental policeman in charge returned and asked Ron and Lena to leave. I thanked Ron and Lena for their visit and as they were leaving the cell block Ron turned around and winked at me. After they had gone the corporal in charge of our regimental police returned to my cell and informed me that he had just received a phone call from our Coy Sergeant Major informing him that there will be a delay in me being escorted on parade for the Commanding Officers Orders. *I felt that someone up there was at last, was looking after me.* As he was about to leave I told him that I had asked Ron the chef to let Hansen or Falconer know that I was in the cells. As he was leaving, he muttered something about me pushing my luck.

It felt like a life time, but it could only have been five / seven minutes before I heard Ron talking to the regimental police. Then they appeared to be arguing. I was beginning to feel that all was not going well when I heard the cell block gate being unlocked and Ron being escorted inside by one of the police. My heart was missing beats, Ron informed me that neither Hanson or Falconer were around, but he will see them at lunch time and give them my message. The policeman suggested that he must go now. I felt sick, Ron turned around and as they were both walking out of the cell block, with his right hand behind his back he tossed the tiny little package of flints towards my cell. In total silence they hit one of the bars and dropped onto the tiled floor just outside my cell. I immediately retrieved the tiny package as soon as I heard the entrance gate to the cell block being locked. The package was no more that a half-inch square. I was so scared that I had no idea what to do next. My mind was made up for me when I heard the cell block gate being unlocked again. I slipped the package into my trousers right hand pocket. Within minutes I was being escorted by the regimental police and the staff Sergeant Major up to the Commanding Officer's office, to be paraded before him for the second time.

The Commanding Officer face was expressionless when he looked up at me from the papers that were spread out on his desk. "I have been informed to advise you that you have the right to be represented by a Lawyer of your own choosing.

You can arrange the services of a lawyer from here in Italy or England. However I have to say that the Army will not be responsible for any fiscal costs. You will obviously need some time to consult your parents. Do you have any questions regarding this matter?" I remained silent for a few seconds, then explained that there was no need for me to consult my parents because it would be impossible for them to provide me with a private Lawyer. His instant response was. "So, there we have it. By law, you must be represented in court. Under these circumstances the Army will provide you with a defence lawyer at our expense. Do you have any more questions regarding this matter?" Once more I was lost for words, then asked. "How much longer will I have to wait until the court-martial sir". "Well then, that all depends on various details however I have to say that now that we have decided on the lawyer, wheels will be in motion"., Before waiting to be asked if I had any more questions, I asked. "Sir, what exactly are the charges that am I being court- martial for?" Without hesitation he angrily replied. "I am not at liberty to discuss this at this time with you. You will have the opportunity to discuss this with your lawyer, that will be all Sergeant Major". I asked. "Sir". Before I could utter another word he implied. "I warn you driver, insubordination is a very serious offence. Sergeant Major". I was instantly marched out of the office, downstairs, across the parade-ground and locked up in a cell in the guard room. I was shattered, confused and angry until I realized that I had the packet of flints in my pocket. I immediately removed the small packet from my pocket and opened it. There appeared to be five or six flints in it. I removed one and placed it in my mouth, then another two so I had three in my mouth and decided that I could handle no more. I removed the toilet paper with the message to Hanson and Falconer out of my other pocket. Removed the flints from my mouth and found that it was a wee bit difficult because they were now damp. I wrapped all the flints in the toilet paper and made as much noise as possible to get the attention of the regimental police. Within a minute or so two of the police arrived so I told them I have to get to the toilet. Once in the toilet I put three flints in my mouth and sort of uttered a few words and it felt weird, but I realized that once I leave this toilet I don't have to speak again until I am back in my cell in San Gesto. I threw the remaining flints and package into the toilet, flushed it and checked that it had all gone. I rejoined the two police that were waiting for me and I was escorted back towards the cell but never made it as the military police were waiting for me. Once they carried out a half hazard search, handcuffed me and completed the paper work, we were on our way back to San Gesto.

Back in San Gesto, after the paper work and the handcuffs were removed I was rushed into the strip-search room. One of the searchers was the screw with the Scots accent. I was now aware that his name was Gilmore and for a fellow

Scott from Glasgow he was a vicious sadistic b******. I was feeling very nervous but tried to keep cool and most important, keep my mouth closed that was until one of the screws grabbed my head and twisted it to allow him too look into my right ear, then my left ear then screamed at me to open my mouth. I now had the three tiny flints behind my front teeth and was so happy when the b****** sergeant Gilmore shouted. "Spread your legs, bend over and touch your toes" I nearly spat out the three flints from behind my teeth when someone jammed his finger! or something! up my anus and twisted it.

Richard was so proud of me when I handed him the three flints when we were eventually all locked up in our cell for the night. Actually, I was very proud of myself and that night we worked feverishly like two beavers building a dam. Richard impaled one of the tiny flints into the blunt end of a small pencil and tapped the blunt end of the pencil gently onto the stone floor to ensure that the flint was securely embedded in the wooden pencil. I started to scrape the surface of one of my blankets with the double edged razor blade and removed some of hairy fibre as Richard rolled the fibre into loose ball. There were only five inmates now and the other three new inmates were either too afraid to look at us or were to concerned about tomorrow to be interested in what we were doing. As Richard was making the home-made cigarette, I impregnated the wee fibre ball with a few drops of liquid brasso. The two of us got down on our knees at the side of my bed where the wee ball of fibre was sitting on the edge of my tin plate. We decided to let Richard proceed with the most difficult process which was igniting the ball of fibre. I held the home-made cigarette in my hand as Richard lowered the pencil against the wee ball of fibre. After a few seconds, he commenced scratching the flint that was now firmly imbedded in the pencil with the razor blade and to my amazement he actually created a spark, not every time, but occasionally. He stopped and looked despondently at me but I smiled and encouraged him to proceed, then suggested a wee bit more liquid brasso. I reached for the tin of brasso, lifted the wee ball of hairy fibre untangled it slightly and dropped another drop of brasso onto it, untangled it a wee bit more then placed it back on my tin plate. Richard re commenced scratching the flint with the razor blade and once more he occasionally created a spark and I'm sure that we both thought that it was not going to work until the fibre smoked slightly then burst into a flame. I very quickly sucked on our home-made cigarette until it was glowing and Richard dowsed the tiny flame. Richard and I smoked our first San Gesto illegal cigarette. What made it more satisfying was the fact that we had used the stupidity of the screws that had underestimated us.

That night I slept like a wee baldy headed baby.

Indifferent: 7

Apparently, the high ranking officers and their families were so pleased with the private beach that Richard and myself had cleaned up, it was now becoming a regular established procedure. Every Thursday and Friday, Richard and I were driven and escorted by sergeant major Holburn and another screw to the beach on the outskirts of Trieste to gather up and bury all the sea-weed and any other debris that had been washed up onto the beach. It was such a wonderful break getting away from the prison and its obnoxious staff. Being driven through Trieste city to an isolated beach smothered in sunshine was just pure paradise We were allowed to strip of our tops to expose our naked pale torsos to the hot sun and rake up the debris in our bare feet and even paddle up to our knees in the wash of the Adriatic sea. I owed so much to Richard because if it was not for his wise counselling I would never have been given my white band, it is little wonder that I hang on every singe word that he utters. Richard and I both knew that our deprived pitiful inmates back in San Gesto were also toiling under the same hot sunshine but for them it was Hell!! They would be fully dressed, loaded down with full packs and a heavy 303 rifle and being rushed around the parade ground by screaming staff members. They would be sweating so profusely that every item of their clothing would be saturated and clinging to their already fatigued and inapt bodies and weighing them down even further. The norm was that after just standing in the blistering sun mentally and physically abusing the inmates for half-an-hour, the two screws would get a wee bit tired and hot under the collar so they would be replaced by a fresh pair of sadistic screws and so it goes on, and even when an inmate drops exhausted, that poor soul will be made to eventually get up to be further tortured. Considering the fact that we inmates in San Gesto prison were outnumbered, because for every single inmate there were two prison wardens, therefore the cynical prison staff having nothing else to do inflicted as much suffering as possible upon each and every inmate whilst on duty.

Sergeant major Holburn would often give us a cigarette when he was having one himself after we had eaten our packed lunch. Being on this tranquil beach often gave me time to think about things, especially my pending court-martial. Presently, I only have a white band because technically speaking I am not yet a prisoner. Once my court-martial is over I will no longer have a white band therefore I would not be classed as a trustee prisoner and would not be on this beach! in fact, I may not even be in Trieste. Richard was of the opinion that I would be sent to another notorious military prison somewhere in Germany. It certainly looked as if I was in trouble. I had explained to Richard what my Commanding Officer had said to me about my defence lawyer and that the army was now going to provide one. He was very sceptical about that and even suggested that It was most unfortunate that I could not provide my own defence lawyer. When I questioned him if he had provided his own lawyer at his court-martial he appeared reluctant at first to admit that he did, then suggested that his parents had not only insisted, but had arranged it. He also suggested that if his parents had not provided and arranged his defence lawyer, his sentence would have been more exacting and that he would have been extradited to Germany. He reiterated that any military personnel in Italy sentenced to more than six months prison, is automatically extradited to a prison in Germany!

Richard had me convinced that I was going to be found guilty at my court-martial and sentenced to at least a year in prison so he hatched another plan for us. He inferred that the Yugoslavian border was only a few miles further up the road where sergeant major Holburn parks our three ton truck when we go on the detail to the officers beach. His plan was that we steal the truck and drive it over the border into comrade Tito's Yugoslavia. I was mystified at first and had no idea what the hell was talking about, then eventually I asked him. "Richard, who is Tito?. Then before he could answer, I said. "Richard, why would I want to go to Yugoslavia?". Richard looked very hard at me, then replied. "You my brother, would be a lot better off in Yugoslavia, than languishing in a prison in Germany. Tito is the head of state in Yugoslavia and he will make you most welcome. As a matter of fact, I will come with you". Richard was convinced that it was the right thing to do and it was a very doable plan indeed and by the time he was finished, I was hooked.

We discussed his plan at every opportunity especially at night. We would lie in our beds whispering to each other for hours. He had every detail planned and he was correct about the truck having no ignition keys, only a press starter button. He was positive that sergeant major Holburn never ever locked the vehicle. The access from the road down to the beach could be hazardous because of the three dozen well worn steep timber steps. It wasn't a very wide beach even when the tide was out and we spent most of our time on the beach when the tide was out. Therefore it would have to be a sharp fast sprint from the shore line to the hazardous steps. We believed that we could dodge and outrun both screws in time to reach the truck and drive it up into the mountains and through a long tunnel into Yugoslavia. The plan was that we would have to wait until both screws were as near to us both at the waters edge before we made our run. We were sure that once we started running for the truck, the two screws would never ever catch up with us and they would not be as nimble or as swift as us running up the hazardous steps to the parked vehicle. We did not underestimate the fact that they were both in good shape physically. But, they were not as young as us and we were super fit. After all back in San Gesto the screws had to take turns each at beating us up physically and mentally. I had one problem with reference to Richards plan and that was the possibility of the screws stopping another vehicle and chasing after us in a much faster little private car. Richard insisted that the road in question actually only goes to a small village and then onto the Yugoslavian border therefore there was very little traffic on this road. He was also positive that the Yugoslavian border was only a half hour away under a tunnel in the mountain and that we would be over the border before they could catch us. Richard assured me that he had been in this area many times on mock battle schemes against the American forces. He was also confident that the screws would never attempt to cross over the border into Yugoslavia dressed in British military uniforms, because If they did, they would be instantly arrested. Richard was so excited he said. "Cass, we will be treated as heroes by Tito. Two British soldiers that crossed over to the other side". I asked him. "What do you mean Richard?". "Yugoslavia is a communist regime, they will love us Cass, they will treat us very well, very well indeed, like heroes". I replied. "Is that why you are coming with me Richard? After all, you only have a couple of months to do before you are a free man". Richard smiled and replied. "Cass, I am going with you because it is so exciting and I will be free *Now,* not in a couple of months time, so brother, what do you think?" I promised Aristocratic Richard that I would certainly think about it. From then on Richard spoke about nothing else whenever he had the chance.

Apparently Josip Broz Tito, former president of Yugoslavia 1943 - 1980 was very anti British / American. After the war in 1945, the Yugoslavians thought that they automatically had an entitlement to claim Trieste and the sea-port since it was Yugoslavia troops that had fought, beaten, chased and thrown the Germans out of '*Venezia Giulia*'. That was the original name of the area in Italy where the Trieste city and the port is located and of course, Trieste city and the actual sea-port are situated on the Yugoslavia borders. However the Brits had different idea's. The resulting tension led to a mini-peace-conference led by a General Gordon. The resulting agreement was that the entire area would remain under a Military Occupation Government and of course it eventually remained part of Italy.

He would throw one of the weapons at the bare feet of a prisoner
and order him to demonstrate how one should defend oneself
if attacked.

It did not take me long to decide that I just could not spend a year locked up in some prison in Germany and if the screws there were are as sadistic as they are here, I don't think I could have handled it. I would end up maiming

79

one of them, or worse. I eventually told Richard that I would do it, we would run off to Yugoslavia. In my inner thoughts, I planned to try and sneak back into Scotland. The next time we went on the beach we watched every move that the two screws made and noted that Staff Holburn never ever locked the vehicle. We made mental notes each time they wandered down to the water front. All day we looked and watched and whispered and never took our eyes off the screws. Holburn was the one that appeared to always stay close to us at the waters edge as we collected the debris and sea-weed that had been washed up. The other screw always appeared to pace along the beach further away from us as if he knew that we were going to try an escape. It was weird. Staff Holburn gave us both a cigarette at lunch time. Then perhaps because it was extremely hot that particular day they both wandered up to the truck with their lunch boxes and with both doors wide open they sat there watching us both paddle in the hot Adriatic Sea. It was not as if we could do a runner along the beach because our small beach was a cove with steep rugged terrain on each side and of course we could not swim out to sea. The only way out of the cove was back up onto the coast road and into the vehicle. This was the first time ever that they had left us alone on the beach and went and sat in the cabin of the vehicle. Even when they returned to the beach after lunch, we had no idea if staff Holburn had locked the vehicle cabin. Eventually, it was time to return to San Gesto therefore we would have to wait until the next detail. On the way back from the beach to San Gesto prison, I felt relaxed for the first time that day and I was going back to a *Hellplace.*

Staff Gilmore, the fellow Scott appeared to have decided that he was going to single me out. One would have thought that with both of us being Scot's, he would have felt or shown some sympathy towards me, but that was not to be. Staff Gilmour had started teaching us Judo and it was compulsory. The matt that he had laid out on the stone square must have been selected by the devil himself because it only appeared to be an inch or so thick. When you were thrown onto the matt by Gilmore, every bone in your body was shaken. Gilmore had already taken a dislike to me and during these Judo lessons he would always select me to demonstrate what it was all about. During some of these lessons he would use a small timber carved knife and a baton as weapon's. He would throw one of these weapon's at the bare feet of a prisoners and invite him to demonstrate how one should defend oneself if attacked. Nine times out of ten it was thrown at my feet and he would shout. "Okay Cassidy, come, lets go, stab me". For some unknown reason, I always thought that I could get him, or would eventually get him one of the times. I actually thought that perhaps I could poke it in his eye, after all it would be an accident!. He always caught me, disarmed me then lifted me off the ground and slammed me onto the thin mat. Most times I had to be helped up

80

by Richard. A couple of times I managed to quickly roll over and leap at him full of hate and anger, only to be slammed once more into the mat. Then he would provoke me to attack him again with a huge grin on his face. At times, I wanted to cry-out in pain. I always wanted to be able to grab him and kill him, but it was no use, he was too good and strong and obviously a professional. Richard eventually convinced me to stay cool and keep away from him as he could do nothing with limp, bendy, flaccid torso.

During the hearings at my own camp with reference to my pending court-martial I was informed that the military court would provide me with a defence lawyer. One day, I was dismissed from the parade ground in San Gesto where we were getting punished during a drill with full packs and rifle under a scorching red hot sun. I had a visitor. After I was allowed to unload all my gear, I was double marched across the square and into our small recreation room. An army officer was sitting reading some papers. On hearing the screaming sergeant, he looked up at us and after dismissing the sergeant, informed me. "Ah, Cassidy, this wont take long, stand easy. I'm Major Pearson your defence lawyer, we are in court on Thursday". I was unable to respond. I was shocked. I thought that like in the movies, I would be able to sit down with my defence lawyer and discuss what we were going to do and how we were going to do it. He continued. "Well soldier, do you have nothing to say, what". On this occasion I did manage to say. "That's in two days time sir". "Yes that's correct." Once more I was unable to speak, I thought, who is this officer and what does he know about me and my crime or defence. I had never ever met him in my entire life. After a protracted silence I asked. "What do we do, I' err thought that we would spend some time discuss-ing the case against me and my defence". He stood up and very slowly walked away from me then back towards me. His hands were behind his back. Then he said. "Defence, are you mad. There is no defence, we are throwing ourselves at the mercy of the court, that's our defence, that's our only defence. The Military Police will collect you on Thursday morning. Look sharp now, Staff, Staff". The screw who had escorted me walked smartly into the room. My defence lawyer informed him. "We are finished here, you can take your prisoner away". The sergeant screamed. "Yes Sir". I was double marched out of the room and chased back on to the parade square.

That evening in our cell, Richard, for the first time since I met him was speechless after I had told him about my visitor and what he had just informed me. I further suggested to Richard that it looked like my chances of escaping were gone and because Richard could not drive, he was not going either!

Indifferent: 8

My Court-martial was an ignominious farce. Four military policemen collected me at nine o'clock sharp. My white band had been confiscated and whilst the paper-work was being completed I was handcuffed to two of the military police-men with myself in the centre. I felt nervous for the first time, in a long time. I also felt that I was being treated as if I was a serious serial killer. The three of us climbed into the rear of the long-wheel based land rover and were locked in, before the other two climbed into the front and drove out of the treble gates of *Castello di San Giusto* military prison. I had no idea where I was being taken, so I asked and was completely ignored by both of the military policemen that I was handcuffed too.

We eventually arrived at the large Fusiliers Regimental Barracks on the outskirts of Trieste city. These huge barracks were not new to me as I had been here often when I had picked up troops to deliver them to their mock-wars. We appeared to drive to the rear of the huge magnificent principal building. I was taken into a room with bench seats and the three of us sat there for at least thirty minutes in complete silence. In fact, at one time I felt that the two military escorts that I was handcuffed to were as nervous as I was. The silence was eventually broken when the other two military policemen suddenly arrived and instructed their two colleagues to remove the handcuffs and follow them. I was unceremoniously bundled into the centre of my four military escorts and brusquely marched down this impressive looking lengthily corridor.

The Court room itself was of medium size but very impressive looking. I was seated at a long table in the centre of my four military escorts. Facing us was an elevated elegant looking long bench with magnificent carvings covering the entire facade of this elongated sort of pew. I suddenly realized that the group of soldiers sitting in a large stall that looked very much like a juror box to my right were not jurors. It was the four drivers from my own company who were on guard duty that fatal night when they had arrested me. Sitting in front of them was the duty guard officer that night and the non-commissioned officer that I had punched in the face. I immediately started looking around for driver Bowles but he was nowhere to be seen and that's when I noticed the officer that had visited me in San Gesto, my defence lawyer. He appeared to be in heavy conversation with another two officers that were sitting at another lengthily table on my left hand side, this table was also facing the long elongated elevated pew. Eventually my military defence officer joined myself and the four military policemen at our table. He had still not acknowledged me.

The actual stillness in this ostentatious highly polished room was eerie, it was so still, that one could actually hear the silence. Without warning a military officer broke the eerie silence when he entered the room from somewhere behind the elevated elongated pew and instructed the room to be upstanding. Within seconds another four officers appeared and were soon seated in the elevated pew. I immediately assumed that they were the judges and wondered why there were four of them. They all appeared to remove their multi braided headwear simultaneously and commenced opening and reading the folders / files that each individual had carried with him. The court room was ordered to be seated. Eventually the court was called to order and once more we were upstanding. I was surrounded by the four military policemen as we all stood to attention and I still had no access to my military defence officer. After a few more minutes the court was ordered to be seated. I had only been seated for a few minutes when the prisoner was ordered to be upstanding. Standing alone amongst all this military bureaucracy made me feel very apprehensive and I was somewhat relieved when someone very loudly started reading out my name, rank and army number. I was asked on each occasion to confirm my name, rank and army number and on one occasion was ordered to speak up loudly. After a protracted silence, one of the officers from the table to my right commenced reading out the charges which I really did not actually understand except for the final and last charge that I physically attacked and assaulted a non-commissioned officer. Before I had time to comprehend what on earth was happening, one of the judges asked me. "How does the prisoner plead?" Before I could even consider the question, my defence lawyer leapt to his feet and replied. "We plead guilty Sir and we throw ourselves at the mercy of this honourable Court. We thank you Sir". I was shocked and frozen into silence and scarcely heard the person shouting that the court was adjourned and we were all to be upstanding, of course I was still upstanding.

After the four judges had left the court I was whisked away to the small room that I was held in when I first arrived. After what seemed like an hour or so, in fact was just over half an hour, I was taken back into court handcuffed to two of the military police escorts. The court was brought to order and we were all once more upstanding. After the four officers had returned to the pew we were all ordered to be seated. The four officers conferred for a few minutes, then ordered. "The prisoner to be upstanding". I was hauled to my feet as I was still handcuffed to two off the military policeman and I noticed that my defence lawyer also stood to attention. One of the judges read out my full name rank and army number, then hesitated. He went on to suggest that I had committed a serious crime. However, because I had pleaded guilty and saved the entire court a considerable amount of time and effort off having to call the considerable number of witnesses. This had been taken into consideration in deciding my sentence. After a few minutes silence and whispering to the officer adjacent to him he said. "You have been sentenced to Six Months Prison, to be served in San Gesto Military Detention Prison commencing from to-day. The time that you have been incarcerated whilst awaiting your court martial will not be included as part of your sentence. You will however be entitled to two months remission for good behaviour. Take the prisoner away".

I was quickly taken back to the waiting room, bewildered, confused and yet I felt good and wondering why driver Bowley was not present. I was still wondering why I was not being charged with assaulting driver Bowley when the door to the waiting room was suddenly burst open as if it had kicked open. Even the four military policemen were startled when my defence officer leapt into the room. He pointed at me and shouted. "You B******, you should have got six years, six bloody years you should have been sent away for". His face was purple as he towered over me sitting between two of the military policemen. He was still pointing his finger into my face as he was shouting this abuse at me and calling me all the bastards. Thank god I kept my cool. I just looked into his big purple fat face and whispered. "I am not a bastard and can prove it. Can you?" I thought he was going to strike me. Actually, I was wishing that he would because he was insane with anger and this was my defence lawyer. He shouted at the military policemen "Take that B****** to San Gesto prison".

I thought San Gesto was a place in hell during the month I was incarcerated while awaiting my court-martial. It got a thousand times worse after my trial, I was now a convicted prisoner. A half an hour after being handed over to the San Gesto military prison staff I was taken in front of the prison Commandant who had the rank of a major. This was the first time I had ever set eyes on this officer. Richard had warned me all about him and had suggested to me that he was psychiatrically disordered. As far as Richard was concerned that was one of the reasons why most of his staff were so ruthless and cruel. This commandant explained to me in detail how he regarded himself as being a huge tom cat and we prisoners being tiny little mice and that he and his staff could pounce on us at any given time and devour us!

I felt somehow that everyone was against me, even my friend Articulate Richard who was eventually released and returned to England. I never ever heard of Richard again and truly regret that I had not kept in touch with him. Richard had been the *pace maker* in San Gesto prison, I suppose that was because he was the longest serving prisoner and the one with the most experience. He had been the one responsible for shouting out the, *one, two three, one, two three,* whilst we were being drilled on the parade square especially when presenting arms and being drilled in general with our rifles. I was instructed to take his place. When he was released, Richard had only completed four months of his six months sentence because he had earned his two months remission. I was hoping and had made up my mind that I was going to be as fortunate as my good friend and mentor, Articulate Richard. I had a feeling that I was continually and deliberately being *set-up* by the screws and that was ever so easy for them to do. Every time I was put on a silly charge, the mad commandant did not jump on me like a huge tom cat and consume me, he did the opposite. He played with me and made me suffer by taking a day or two out of my two months remission. Within six weeks, they, the mad commandant and his insane and depraved prison officers had stolen my entire two months remission. From then on I despised the insane commandant and all his inhumane screws with a passion and as far as I was concerned it was war. I had nothing left to loose except my sanity. I was beginning to think, *if you can't beat them, join the b*******!*

One cold wet rainy unusual day I had come off the parade square with the other four prisoners and the five of us were all rushed into the shower room. Gilmore, the Scot's screw deliberately and aggressively pushed me under a cold shower. I immediately leapt out of the other side shivering. He screamed at me through the steam coming from the other hot showers to get back under the cold water. I defiantly refused. He and another staff member frog marched me naked down the well worn steps, past the cells and further down into what can only be described as a deeper dungeon. I had never ever been down into this place before and had no idea that it existed. They switched on some lights that were encased in wire cages that were fitted to the dungeon walls. I was unaware that this castle dungeon existed until now.. There appeared to be rows of solid metal cell doors on both sides of this dungeon passage-way. They unlocked one of the solid metal door's and pushed me violently into the dark rank smelling cell. I crashed into something with both my legs and it hurt. I was naked, wet, very cold, a wee bit scared and both shins of my legs were sore. After they locked the door I could hear them laughing as they left, then a small light on the roof suddenly glowed throwing weird shadows on the walls. This dungeon cell was tiny and the thing that I had crashed into was a single metal framed bed with no mattress. In one of the corner's adjacent to the solid metal door there was another metal item. This miniature cell was just a wee bit longer than the length of the single bed and allow the cell door to open and wide enough for the single bed, myself standing beside it and the metal container in the corner. The dingy light on the ceiling that was encased in a wire mesh was just bright enough to confirm to me that my shins were cut and bleeding. I sat on the edge of the metal bed shivering then noticed that the door had a few rows of small holes at the centre top of this solid metal door. I walked up to the holes and commenced screaming. "Help. Help me, help".

It must have been at least two hours later before I heard the crashing of boots on the stone steps leading down to this dungeon then up to my cell. Then the silence settled just outside my cell door as if the boots had vanished. After a few seconds the rattling of keys being pushed into my cell door shattered the eerie silence. When the metal cell gate swung open, the two staff members that had frog-marched me down here and threw me into this shit hole, started screaming at me. *"Move It"*. They ran me naked along the dim dungeon passageway and up the dark stairway into my normal dwelling cell and told me to get dressed. Then they ran me up the winding stone staircase and into the mad commandant's office. I was charged with refusing to carry out a direct order and wilful behaviour to a senior member of the staff. I started to speak and explain what had happened when the mad commandant shouted. "You will remain silent". I tried again to continue but he screamed. "You will be silent, you must obey my orders and remain silent". I had no more remission to loose. He had stolen my two months potential parole. I had just under four months left to serve. I was cold, angry and frustrated. I tried for a third time to explain how the bastard Scot had thrown me into a freezing cold shower while the other prisoners were enjoying hot showers. The mad commandant screamed. "Shut up, shut up, you horrible fool. For your impertinence you are sentenced to three days bread and water in solitary confinement. Get this imbecile out of my office".

I checked my bed and cell floor for cockroaches and other
creepy crawly beetles once my eyes were accustomed to the dim light.

As the two prison staff officers were rushing me back down to my normal cell that I shared with the other prisoners I was trying to imagine what the mad commandant was shouting about with this bread, water and confinement. Once back in my normal cell one of the prison officers tipped everything that was neatly laid out on my bed into one of my bed blankets whilst the other one grabbed the remainder my bedding as they both screamed at me to grab my mattress. Dragging my mattress behind me I was rushed back down into the dungeon with the two screws behind me with my bedding and kit. They threw all my bedding and kit into the empty cell I had been in previously then pushed me and my mattress in before locking the solid metal door. One of them shouted through the tiny holes near the top of the metal door that I was to make up my bed and lay all my kit out for inspection because they would be back in an hour. I had no idea what I was suppose to do, I could hardly see anything because it was so dark and my movement was so restricted. I placed my mattress on the bed and sat down, then after a few minutes my eyes appeared to be adjusting to the dimness so I started lifting things up off the stone floor and placing them on the bed. Eventually I was beginning see things a wee bit better not because it was getting any brighter, it was probably because my eyes were beginning to adjust to the shadows. I decided to make up my bed as it had been made up in the large cell that I shared with the other four prisoners. I noticed that the iron bed frame was rusty and the foul smell was emanating from the black metal container in the corner that turned out to be a dry-toilet. It looked like this cell, or indeed this entire dungeon area had not been inhabited for a considerable time. It also looked like I had just been introduced to a new hell, I felt as if I was in the worst place in the world and there was nobody to help me. I was now very concerned and perhaps a wee bit afraid. I remember thinking about praying for guidance and help and then I thought. I think it was *Joan of Arc* who said, '*We suffer at the hands of men, not God*'. Therefore in this particular instance, God had nothing to do with it, and I had no intention of pleading for help from the lunatics that administer this prison, so I would just have to get on with it. Another two prison staff members eventually returned and after unlocking the metal cell door tipped my bed up onto its side again, accused me of being shabby and screamed at me to make it up again for a further inspection. After locking the metal cell door they remained there at the other side of the locked door in silence. I immediately assumed that they were spying on me through the peep-holes located at eye level in the door. I picked up my heavy canvas small-pack and threw it at the peep-holes on the door. The second that the small-pack hit the door and fell to the stone floor one of the prison staff kicked the metal door violently then I heard the clatter off their heavy boots leaving the dungeon. I decided that they were not as smart as they obviously believe they are if they hadn't realized that I know every move they make outside my cell. The cruelty and insanity in this prison is so intense one would have to have wings to avoid it. I would have to find a way to convince myself that one day all this will end or I will survive this place.

I had no idea what time it was when I heard more heavy boots returning to my cell, however whoever they were they did not unlock the cell or speak. Then I heard a scratching sort of noise and discovered that there was a hinged slot at the bottom of the metal door at floor level. Someone pushed into my cell a paper plate with three thick slices of dry bread and a plastic mug filled with cold water. Then as loudly as they had arrived they very briskly departed. I was now beginning to understand what this eccentric punishment was all about. I was not that hungry but did eventually eat my dry bread and drink my cold water. After another hour or so another couple of prison staff returned and shouted at me to return the plate and mug, then the hinged slot was opened, so I pushed the mug and plate through the opening. After they had gone I counted the small holes in the steel door at eye level. There was one line with seven holes, then underneath that line there was another line with six holes and underneath that line there was another line with seven holes, making a total of twenty small round holes approximately a half an inch in diameter.

Even in this very dim light that came from the small bulb that was caged in the ceiling, I froze slightly when I caught sight of a few cockroaches when I accidentally hit the portable toilet in the corner adjacent to the door. The cockroach's scampered across the cold stone floor and ran underneath my bed because there was nowhere else they could go to hide. It was so tranquil in this dungeon that it was eerie and I was thinking that it must be getting late into the evening when the clattering of the heavy boots again broke the eerie silence and brought me back to reality. The boots stopped outside my cell door and there was the silence again and I could feel someone eavesdropping and spying on me again through the twenty peep-holes. Then someone shouted. "Its lights out time, remove your kit from your bed and make it up, move it". I immediately started putting all my kit on the floor and proceeded to dismantle my square box of blankets and bed sheets and proceeded to make my bed. After a few minutes, the prison staff on the outside were walking away and the noisy army boots echoed away into the distance. I was once more left alone in my dungeon cell with only the cockroaches and my thoughts. I was grateful that the dim light on the ceiling had been left on, because I shuddered at the thought of being left alone in complete blackness.

I was finding it very difficult to sleep because I was still thinking about this unusual form of punishment. I was trying to think what it was that I had done to be treated like this? and how these people can get away with treating me like this. Eventually I must have fallen asleep until sometime during the night something was irritating my nose and it felt itchy. I put my fingers up to scratch it and felt something on my finger tips, so I sat up in bed with this thing held between my forefinger and my thumb. In the dimness' and not seeing clearly or able to focus, I stood up on my bed and held my hand up to the dim light on the ceiling. It was cockroach that was squirming in-between my fingers and thumb and in panic I threw the damn thing into the air then jumped off the bed onto the cold stone floor in an effort to find and destroyed it. I felt sick, the thought of this long brown slimy thing trying to crawl up my nose. I removed the bed sheet that I was using to cover me to see if there were any more of them, but it was impossible in this dim light to identify anything so I spent the remainder of the night lying on top of my bed wide awake. Eventually I heard the noisy army boots clattering down the steep stone steps leading down into the dungeon. Then the jangling of keys being inserted into my cell door and when it was opened two prison staff members were standing shoulder to shoulder. One shouted. "Slop out prisoner, move it". I was already standing at the side of my bed and told them both that I had not used the loo. He screamed. "I said slop out. When I say slop out you will slop out so move it". I grabbed the handle of my metal portable loo and they marched me to another metal door. One of the staff members pushed it open. It was one of those squat toilets on the floor and there was a brass water tap on the wall. I ran some water into my loo and poured it down the squat toilet drain. As I was about to leave, one off the staff members screamed at me to leave some water in the bottom of my portable loo, then suggested. "You may need a drink". Then they both laughed. After returning to my cell with the portable toilet, they instructed me to grab my toilet goods then marched me back to the same squat toilet room and told me to get washed. As they both watched over me I had a brisk wash from the cold water from the brass tap on the wall. After a quick wash, I was locked up again but not before being instructed to make up my bed and kit for inspection. As I was preparing my bed, the noise of their heavy boots confirmed that they were now leaving the dungeon. Two prison staff members eventually returned to inspect my bed layout and without actually inspecting my bed they immediately tipped my bed onto its side spilling all my kit and the folded sheets and blankets on to the floor and told me to re-make it for further inspection. They returned two hours later and tipped it all onto the floor again. This went on all day and every day during my three days of solitary confinement in the dungeon cell. I was fed three thick slices of dry bread and a mug of water once a day around lunch time. During this three days in the dungeon I was never allowed to see daylight. On the morning of the fourth day I was frog marched on three separate occasions up and down the dungeon steep stone steps returning all my belongings including my bed mattress back into the larger communal cell. I was given my first hot shower, then double marched up into the kitchen. In spite of the fact that it was still morning I was served a three course meal that I could not eat and two staff members stood over me and took turns each at screaming and shouting at me to eat it!

Getting back to normal was easy for me because now I had now been in San Gesto as a prisoner for three months and of course I had already done a month whilst waiting for my court-martial so I was pretty well clued-up to most things that happened in here and could take almost anything that these offensive staff members and the mad commandant could do to me. There were always a string of new faces among the prisoners because there was a continuous change of inmates. Most prisoners that were incarcerated never ever spent anymore than fourteen days in San Gesto, in fact the norm was seven days and the majority of them were from the Fusilier Regiment and there were always more prison staff than prisoners to give us a hard time. Unlike Articulate Richard, I was not a model prisoner and therefore was never ever offered a white band. The cleaning up of the sea-weed on the officers private beach continued, but not as often as it was when Richard and I were doing it. Because there were no white band model prisoners or anyone waiting for a court-martial, they would occasionally take a few of the inmates and it was pathetic listening to them in the evening complaining about it. Whereas both Richard and I looked forward to the privilege and freedom of it.

A few weeks after my spell in the dungeon cell I was scrubbing the floor and cleaning the staff members rest room and spotted a large cigarette-end lying in one of the ash trays. The staff member that was supervising me had left the room temporarily therefore I had not much time to make a decision so I grabbed it and tucked it into my sock. Within seconds of hiding the cigarette - end in my sock two wardens entered the staff room and immediately commenced screaming at me. "Come on move it". When I finished scrubbing the floor they instructed me to leave my bucket, scrubbing brush and floor cloth and shouted. "Okay prisoner, double march. Left right, left right, move it". They marched me directly into the search room. I could not stop myself whispering to them. "You b******* have set me up?". They were both grinning like Cheshire cats as they stripped me naked and eventually found the cigarette end that they had deliberately put into the ash-tray. I was marched in front of the mad commandant who found me guilty of unlawful possession, gross insubordination to two senior members of his staff and sentenced me to three days solitary confinement with bread and water.

This time it was easier because I knew the drill and was much wiser. I checked my bed and cell floor for roaches and other creepy crawly beetle's once my eyes were accustomed to the dim light . When they tipped my bed, I just threw every thing back onto it instead of trying to make it better. I was becoming hardened, silently angry inwardly and refusing to conform. During this spell I decided that I had to think positively and not get too concerned about anything. I had to be optimistic because it was just another three days in a different cell. I decided to think about the benefits of being locked-up down here in the dungeon. How serene and cool it was and that I was not being screamed and shouted at every minute of the day and having to run around everywhere like some half-wit. I decided that I was going to relax and enjoy this break away from the anarchy that was taking place above me. Every time the staff members screamed at me through the twenty tiny holes in the metal door I pretended not to hear them. This left them with only two choices, ignore me and go away or open the cell door and repeat themselves. Unlocking the cell door and repeating themselves involved additional effort on their behalf and proved nothing except that perhaps that I was going deaf. Eventually, they decided to ignore me. I ended my additional three days in the dungeon cell with the bread and water high spirited, even smiling on the morning of the fourth day when they opened my cell to release me. I knew that I was upsetting some of the staff members especially the fellow Scot who was somewhat despondent and appeared to be avoiding me, where as previously he had made a point of singling me out for special treatment. I was playing these prison officers at their own game and in spite of the great advantages they had over me as an individual, I felt that I was injuring them some what. During judo lessons, the fellow Scot, staff member Gilmore no longer continually taunted me because when he did, I no longer lounged at him. When he made me face him on the matt with the blunt artificial knife in my hand, I never went anywhere near him and just wandered around aimlessly in circles. When he did eventually have to attack me, he could hardly grab a hold off me because as I would immediately make myself lithe and supple that it made it very difficult for him to lift me and slam me onto the thin mat. I was learning how best to survive in this dreadful place and how best to react with its sadistic staff members, in fact what often concerned me most was my own desire to actually confront them.

One day while we were being badly chased around our parade ground in full pack and rifles with the blazing sun beating down relentlessly on us, I just suddenly stopped. The other three prisoners that were the only other inmates at this particular period all smashed into me and each other. I grabbed my rifle in both hands and hurdled it high up into the air. I have no idea why, perhaps I was going mad but whatever it was it made me feel so good, especially when I watched the expression on the faces of the two prison staff members who were drilling us as the rifle twisted in the air and came hurling back downwards and crashed onto the stone parade ground as the other three prisoners ran for cover. After the rifle had crashed back onto the ground I was rushed off the parade ground and locked in a single cell. Eventually after an hour or so I was taken in front of the crazy commandant. I can't remember exactly what I was charged with because quit frankly, I wasn't interested and didn't pay too much attention. I was sentenced by the deranged commandant to nine days solitary confinement with dry bread and water. The only difference was that I was to be examined by a doctor every third day. I will never ever forget the confused and disorientated look on the mad commandant's face as he sentenced me. That alone was worth three days bread and water.

The staff members were finding it difficult, if not impossible to intimidate me, especially in my solitary confinement cell in the dungeons. I could feel it. I was now at the stage in my incarceration where I was rolling down the hill. I was over the top and only had another one month to do then I was free. I had only recently found out after a military cleric had visited me and inform me that I had to write a letter to my parents as they were extremely concerned about my well-being. In fact he insisted that I write a letter immediately and refused to leave until I did. He left with my letter in its envelope and promised that it would

91

be posted that very day. His story unfolded the fact that immediately after my court-martial and sentence, my army pay was automatically stopped, therefore the small amount of money that was being paid to my mum was also stopped. With that and the fact that I had stopped sending the odd postcard, my mum in particular had became extremely concerned and had contacted some military organization in Edinburgh. I thought that it was a pretty dirty mean trick to play on decent working class people struggling to bring up their family. I think that was the last thing I needed to know about the military bureaucracy. I had already more or less decided not to allow these San Gesto people to intimidate me anymore. I decided that I was going to do everything I can to retaliate. There was not a great deal I could do to harm them but I sure as hell could frustrate and disillusion them.

On my second day in the dungeon cell, staff Holburn and another staff member opened up and entered my cell one afternoon without saying a single word. Staff Holburn sat on my bed while the other staff member appeared to just stand guard at the open cell metal door. Holburn asked me. "What are you doing?" I had a certain amount of respect for staff Holburn because I got to know him as an individual during the times he escorted Richard and myself to the officers beach to clean up the seaweed. He was also responsible for getting me my white-band and extra cigarettes during the time I was awaiting my court martial. I was a wee bit hesitant when he asked the question because I wasn't too sure what he actually meant so I asked him. "I'm sorry staff, I don't understand what you mean". He was now hesitant. He removed his cap and wiped his brow with the back of his right hand and said. "What did you do before you came into the Army?" I explained that I was training to be a heating engineer. He immediately suggested that I don't belong in the Army and certainly should not be in San Gesto. He went on to explain to me that in his opinion I am the first inmate ever to be sentenced to nine days in a dungeon cell on bread and water. He further explained that I would be examined every third day by a doctor. I explained that I was aware of that. He nodded his head as if in agreement, stood upright and replaced his cap, he looked around my cell and nodded his head once more then indicated to the other staff member that they were finished here! As the other staff member was locking the door staff Holburn stopped him and wandered back into the cell and sort of whispered. "Be very careful what you are doing, if you push it too far, you could face another court-martial". Then he left me alone with my thoughts.

Before dawn and like every other morning, I heard the heavy footsteps of the staff members descending the steep stone steps down into the dungeon area. Then the silence as they spied on me through the twenty peep holes, then the jangling of the keys as they unlocked my cell door, then one of them would shout. "Stand-by to slop out. Move it". I was always away-in-front of these people because I had already moved it and was already standing at the metal cell door fully dressed and watching them watching me through the twenty tiny peep-holes. I was now fully aware off nearly everything these prison warders were intending to do before they even did it, therefore I was always one-step ahead of them. On this particular morning I was already aware that it was my fourth day, therefore I was due the examination by a doctor. After slopping out my portable toilet, having a quick wash, eating my three thick slices of dry bread and drinking my mug of water, I prepared my bed with all my kit laid out on it for the morning inspection. I no longer paid any attention to detail because I knew that the staff would lift up my bed onto its side and tip everything onto the floor. Sure enough, they arrived tipped my bed and as they were leaving I shouted. "Staff, at what time to-day should I expect the doctor?". They both looked at each, ignored me and locked the cell door. When two different staff members returned a few hours later they were escorting a civilian male, he was the doctor! He was a middle aged very slim person and most certainly did not look Italian, more Asian looking. It was difficult for me to tell because he never uttered a single word. As he was removing a stethoscope from his small bag one of the staff members shouted. "Remove your shirt prisoner". The doctor put the instrument to my chest, listened for a few minutes, pushed my right shoulder indicating that I should rotate. I felt his stethoscope on my back, then after a few seconds one of the staff members shouted. "As you are prisoner, get dressed". I didn't even see or hear the doctor leave the cell. As the two staff members were leaving the cell one of them stepped back, tipped my bed up onto its side and shouted. "You have failed this second inspection prisoner. Move it. We will be back, now move it you lazy slob". I knew they would be back, I also knew that they would tip my bed onto it's side, it was a stupid and pointless exercise. However all I did was put the bed upright stretch myself out on it until I heard the clatter of their army boots, I would lift everything off the floor and spread in on the bed. They would unlock the cell door and tip the bed onto its side again. I do believe that I was not wasting as much energy as they were and I have to say that I was getting to the stage where I was not only surviving in this dungeon cell on the bread and water, I was beginning to get concerned about being taken back up into the mad house upstairs. The same little doctor visited me another twice and not once did he converse with me.

On the morning of the tenth day I was taken up and out of the dungeon. After moving all my kit and bedding back up into another six person communal cell, I was allowed to have a hot shower and a shave. I noticed that I had not been taken back to my normal cell where I had my flint and some dried tea leaves hidden. This cell was half empty, only two other beds were being used, I just couldn't understand it but my train of thoughts were suddenly disturbed when two staff members returned and double marched me up to the kitchen dining room. I was once more served a full three course meal. After spending nine days eating dry bread and water I just felt nauseated looking at it being served. I was rushed over to a table in the dining area where the two staff members took turns each barking at me to. "Eat, eat". The barking intimidation did not last very long and was eventually abruptly stopped when I was violently sick. Fortunately for me I did not have a lot of cleaning up to do as I had not eaten a lot. I was returned to the cell and instructed to prepare my bed complete with all my kit on show for inspection. Eventually I was rushed up onto the parade ground dressed in full kit to join the eight other inmates and was soon sweating under the sweltering Italian sun as I shouted out the drill-timing, *one, two three, one* and wishing I was back in my dungeon. At the end of my first day up and out of the dungeon, when all nine of us inmates were having our thirty minutes rest and relaxation in our recreation room I noticed that all of the other inmates were all new faces, all new prisoners in San Gesto and every one of them eyed me sideways and with great suspicion, mistrust and doubt!!

This was the most prisoners I had ever seen in San Gesto, eight other prisoners was the largest intake of inmates I had witnessed. Two communal cells were now being used and quite frankly I was concerned about me loosing my normal cell, the cell that I had nearly spent six months in. The cell where my flint and dried tea-leaves were hidden. Whenever we had new inmates I always tried to assure them that they were going to be okay in spite of the uncertainty and often cruel acts that were unfolding before them. However I never ever got too close to any of them like I did with Richard. As usual and as soon as the opportunity presented itself I had a few words with the two prisoners that I was presently sharing the cell with. One of them was a Fusilier who was quite an amusing person whom I knew instantly would survive all that the San Gesto staff members could throw at him, he was from Yorkshire. The other young guy was from the Catering Corp and he was still in a state of shock in spite of the fact that he was on his third day in San Gesto. He looked and behaved like an only-child type of person with a very middle-class background. They had both been sentenced to seven days. I tried to talk to the young guy that appeared to be traumatised. I tried to reassure him that he was going to be okay and that in another few days he would be outside again and far away from this place. He did not look as if he was listening or was too preoccupied thinking about something else. However a few days later they were both gone and in another day or so another part timer was gone and I was back in my old cell and reunited with my flint and dried out tea-leaves. I was surprised to find out that a few of the new prisoners had been sentenced to fourteen days which was unusual, the norm was normally seven days. Most of the prisoners in my old cell were from the Fusiliers Infantry Regiment.

On the Friday morning staff Holburn collected four of the prisoners to take them to the officers private beach to collect and clean up the sea-weed. I sure envied these four prisoners as I watched them being driven out of the San Gesto gates. The last time I had a glimpse of the outside world was the day of my court-martial and that was five months ago. In spite of the fact that there were only myself and another young prisoner left in the prison they still had us up in the parade square in full kit with rifles running around like two maniacs. To make matters worse this new young inmate was useless and making all sort of blundering errors by turning left when it should have been right. On the about turn order he was too slow therefore we were bumping into each other. For me it was a night-mare because I was an expert and it was driving the two staff members that were drilling us insane. Eventually we had to stop for lunch and I was surprised that after we had collected our food on our tray's we were not allowed to use the dining area and instead we were both marched back down to the cells. I was further surprised when the staff members locked the two of us up in our cell. Apparently no two inmates should never ever be locked up in pairs. It must be one, three or more prisoners in any one cell, but never ever two. My friend Richard had put me wise to most of the knowledge that I now had about San Gesto. This young lad had only just arrived the day that I had been taken out of the dungeon. He was another Fusilier and had been sentenced to seven days. God only knows why and for what, in fact I thought he should have been in hospital and not in a prison. We were on our own in our cell and I tried to ask him what had happened to him up in the parade ground. He would not speak. He started cleaning his kit and I suggested that he should eat his food before it gets cold and further suggested that it was our lunch break and he must relax. He started to try and tear his towel and then his bed sheets, I knew that something was terribly wrong. I stopped him and tried to calm him down because I had no idea what else I should do and I didn't want to shout to try and get the attention of some staff members, who knows what the hell they would do to him. He had calmed down and we were both sitting on the floor like we all do during lock-up breaks but this guy just held his head in both his hands. I suggested a couple of times that he should eat his lunch but he never made any response. When the staff members eventually arrived and shouted. "Stand by your cell gate. Move it, move it". He didn't move and that's when I knew that he had lost it, all I could do was run to the cell gate to present myself being present. One of the staff members screamed again. "Stand by your cell gate". Obviously a final order to the absent young inmate who was still sitting on the floor with his head in his hands. They unlocked the cell gate and one of the staff members rushed past me. I heard the screaming and abuse being shouted at the young inmate that had failed to stand-by his cell gate. The two staff members eventually dragged the young inmate up onto his feet and dragged him away.

I must have been locked up on my own for about thirty minutes when the same two staff members returned. They questioned me about the other inmate and asked me what had happened. I wanted to suggest to them that they had driven the boy insane, but instead, I told them that I had no idea what had happened. They accused me of dumb insolence because of the way I behaved and looked at them. They double marched me up the spiralling stone stairway and back onto the small parade ground and it was still a sweltering boiling hot day and the sun was still scorching hot. Another two staff members arrived dragging what looked like two army kit bags with ropes attached to both ends of them. They stopped adjacent to one of the prisons external ancient of tall escarpment castle wall's. I was left standing to attention in the middle of this square under the sweltering hot sun watching this weird scenario. The staff emptied one of the kit bags spilling dozens of pairs of metal handcuffs into the grounds. The other kit bag was emptied and its contents appeared to be bundles of newspapers and magazines. They then proceeded to throw handcuffs and newspapers back into one of the empty kit bags and continued doing this until all the handcuffs and newspapers had been repacked back into one of the kit bags. I was standing watching this and wondering what the hell was all this about. Then they tied one end of the rope to a hook that was already fitted into the ancient castle wall. I was marched over to the rope that was tied to the other end of the kit-bag that was full of handcuffs and newspapers and was instructed and ordered to grab hold of the loose end and pull on it until I had lifted the kit bag full of handcuffs and paper off the ground. Then instructed and ordered to lower the bag back onto the ground. I was then ordered to continue doing this repeatedly and continuously. It was fairly easy in the beginning until staff member took turns each standing by my side shouting. "lift, drop, lift, drop, lift, drop, lift, drop" and insisting that I go a little faster each time. After fifteen or so minutes, he would be replaced by another staff member who would continue shouting. Lift, drop, lift, drop". This went on for a considerable time and as the time passed, they made me lift it further away down the rope tied to the now heavy kit bag. This of course was making it more difficult for me to get the bag off the ground. Eventually I was at the end of the rope and at least twelve feet away from the bag. It was becoming extremely difficult for me to lift the kit bag clear off the ground. My back, legs and arms were aching with pain. I was sweating profusely and the top of my head, face ,neck and arms were being burned by the scorching Italian Riviera Sun. I actually felt that my arms were being ripped out off my body so I had to find a way of stopping this. I was about to throw the rope onto the ground and refuse to cooperate but thought about what staff Holburn had said to me about having to face a second court-martial so I reasoned with myself and told the staff member that was shouting out the "Lift, drop" instructions through rasped lips. "I need to urgently go to the toilet". I lowered the rope to the ground. He instantly roared back at me. "Move it you idle loaf". Move it". I was eventually rushed down to the loo. In the loo the doors were only half doors to allow the staff to be able to keep their eyes on you at all times. Some staff members left you to get on with it but others stood at the half door screaming at you. "Move it, move it". This b****** presently stood at the actual loo door watching me pretending to have a bowl movement whilst yelling. "We don't have all day. Move it, move it" I thought I was whispering to myself when I suggest that he was a F****** pervert, until he went berserk and screamed. " Staff attention. Staff attention". Staff Green eventually burst into the loo and after a whispered private conversation between them they pulled both of the loo swing doors open and began to drag me off the toilet seat. I resisted and attempted to push them away from me. The minute that I was fully dressed again and up-standing I was double marched direct to a cell adjacent to the mad commandants office. After a ten fifteen minute delay I was taken in front of the mad commandant. Standing between Staff Green and the other staff member I was charged with physical and verbal assault on senior members of his staff. The raving mad commandant had turned purple as he sentenced me to nine days solitary confinement, with bread and water.

I had the feeling that I had these corrupt staff members a wee bit mystified and that the deranged commandant was embarrassed at me being continually dragged before him. After all he was the big tom cat and we inmates were tiny mice and therefore supposed to be terrified of him. I now realized that there was no rehabilitation programme in this San Gesto military prison. There was no intention to restore any of the prisoners to a former position of rank and grant them their rights and privileges once more. There was no aim or attempt to restore any prisoners good reputation and standing after that prisoner had made an error. This San Gesto military prison was programmed to insert fear and terror and for that to be successful it was managed, controlled and run by merciless individuals. The mad commandant and his relentless staff members did not suffer from their insanity, they enjoyed every minute of it.

When the staff members rattled their bunch of keys against the cell gate and this happened every morning, after lunch and after the evening meal they shouted. "Stand by the cell door. Move it, move it. Stand by the cell door". The person that was last in the line-up in front of the cell door was charged with being lazy and idle. They did not go in front of the mad commandant for this offence because it was obvious that someone, had to be last. This was just another special

97

privilege to allow the staff to vent their sadistic mental cruelty on individual prisoners. To me it was sad, senseless and pointless. This silly rule only created a feeling of unnecessary anxiety, concern and riotous unrest among the inmates. Just another reason to create an atmosphere of distress and panic. The idle lazy last person had to carry out extra duties, like scrubbing floors or washing the toilets when the other prisoners where allowed a rest period between meals and in the evening when in the recreation room. When I was not in solitary confinement, I made a point of being last as often as I thought I could get away with it without making it obvious. I would advise every new inmate to ignore the order to rush to the cell gate in the morning because I would deliberately wait until everyone was on their way to the cell door then I would run in last. The staff were furious and knew that by me doing this, it deprived them off their sick and sadistic game of having all the prisoners scampering and often fighting not to be last.

I finished my nine days of solitary confinement and eventually my six months of incarceration in San Gesto was over and the day finally arrived for my release. I was taken in front of the mad commandant who had stolen my two months remission, he lectured me and informed me that he had no doubt that he would never see me again. Then he concluded by screaming. "Nobody ever returns to San Gesto. Get him out off here".

Indifferent: 9

On that wonderful morning when I was released from San Gesto military prison, I was handed over to my platoon sergeant and two off our regimental policemen. The journey back to my own company was one that could only described as being indifferent. For the first time, in a long time I was travelling in a vehicle without being in handcuffs and enjoying the picturesque scenery. The sergeant sat in the front of the land rover beside the driver who was a stranger to me. The two regimental policeman that were sitting in the rear with me were also strangers and appeared to be afraid to look at me, let alone talk to me. We arrived back in 65 Coy R.A.S.C. barracks just before ten-o-clock that delightful morning. I was put on company orders even before I was allowed to get unpacked. Around 1030 H, I was standing to attention between my platoon officer and our Coy sergeant major outside my Co.'s office. I honestly thought I was going in front of my C.O. to be informed. *'Well you have done your time soldier, welcome back to 65 Coy'.* My Commanding Officer read the riot act to me. "You will be under very strict observation for the remainder of your time in this company. One hair out of place, one step out of tune and you will be back in San Gesto. You will not be allowed any passes for at least a month therefore you will be confined to the barracks for a month. You will not be allowed to wear civilian cloths for at least two months. Dismissed".

I was shocked and trembling with anger and to make matters worse, my platoon officer gave me the day off duty to unpack and settle in, unwittingly rendering me the whole day to think about what I thought was a grave injustice. At lunch time I met up with the few soldiers that were still around that I knew including Falconer and Hansen. I was made most welcome and felt good sitting among them, but still extremely angry and very offended. When I explained to them what had happened they were all surprised and concerned. I had been so happy and felt so fit and healthy that I just wanted to get back to normal duty and go down town for a few beers with Hansen and Falconer. That was until my commanding officer decided to treat me like a criminal

That afternoon I had arranged some pay and had collected some Lira and had also collected all my personal possessions from the store room. Just before dinner that evening as I was getting dressed in my raven wing suit, blue shirt, fawn tie, dark blue socks and dark brown ox blood coloured shoes, Falconer and Hansen wandered into my billet. They both stopped dead at the open door when they realized what I was doing and immediately asked. "What the hell are you doing?". I did not respond as they asked again "What the hell are you doing Cass?". "I'm going down town for a few beers". Was my instant response. "You cant for Christ-sake.

You have no pass, you're confined to barracks and you have a bloody civy-suit on, are you F****** crazy?". The other five young soldiers in the room were all strangers to me and were sitting on their beds listening to every word and watching every move I made. "Falconer, you don't understand". Was all I could think of to say. I opened the large hinged windows and looked down into the street below. I was on the fourth floor and had already checked out the rain water pipe that was adjacent to the window that ran from the roof down to the pavement on the street below. Falconer grabbed my arm and shouted. "For Christ sake Cass this is crazy. These pipes could break and even if they don't, you just can't get away with this. Take your suit off and let's go for dinner then we will have a few beers in our NAAFI downstairs and at least lets talk about this". I responded angrily. "Falconer let go of my arms, no matter what you think I am going down town for a few beers, so let go, please". Hansen walked forward and suggested to Falconer that he let go off my arms and he did. As a semi-qualified heating engineer / plumber, I knew better than most how easily these brackets that hold these rain-water-pipes in place can be torn out of the wall.. I knew that any one of these pipes could come loose at any time causing both of us to go tumbling and crashing down onto the street over twenty five feet below. I stood up onto the window ledge and edged myself out and around on to the rain-water pipe. I slithered very slowly and very carefully down the pipe without looking up or down. When I eventually touched the ground I thought I saw one of the guards at the main entrance gate watching me. I did not hang around long enough to find out as I was off down the road heading towards the crowded town centre.

After a ham Panini washed down with a couple of glasses of nice cold bianco wine, I felt slightly inebriated so decided to move on. I wandered around aimlessly and just soaked up the feeling of freedom. The noisy traffic with their headlights now blazing roared around me as I touched shoulders with other pedestrians that unlike me, were in a hurry to get home. I felt great and continued to wander around without any particular destination in mind. I have to say that I do believe that I was actually talking to myself about my predicament and had to admit that the future was bleak, so I entered the next caffettiera that I came across for another ham Panini washed down with another few vino bianco. I was dozing of to sleep so gathered myself together and moved on. The traffic and most of the pedestrians had gone except for a few scooters that roared noisily past me. Without any warning, it started raining and I suddenly remembered how ferocious and violent the rain can be in sunny Trieste. Within seconds the huge raindrops were bouncing of the ground and I was soaked. There was nothing I could do except take shelter in a closed shop doorway that looked inviting. I noticed some other unfortunate pedestrians running towards what turned out to be a very brightly lit ristorante. I waited until the heavy rain diminished in its intensity then made a dash for the sanctuary of the ristorante . Within fifteen minutes of me entering the bar it had become a very welcoming vibrating refuge shelter for us poor souls of the night. I remember wishing that I could speak Italian because a couple of the other customers, male and female, had tried to converse with me but soon lost interest, so I sat alone drinking a few more large glasses of rosso vino. It must have been after midnight when two military policemen wandered into the ristorante. I was so naive I thought, *these b******* are going to have a drink whilst on duty so perhaps I could report them!* They wandered around as if they owned the place then stopped at my table and asked me. "Can we check your pass soldier?"

I knew that I was slightly inebriated and I knew that I did not have a uniform on, so my first train of thought was, *how the hell do you b******* know that I am a soldier,* so I did not immediately respond to their intrusion. Perhaps that was because I was not in possession off a pass. I was suddenly rudely shaken back to reality when one of the military policemen prodded me with his long timber baton and asked. "Where is your pass soldier?" Of course, I had no pass to show them and I had no space around me to attempt to do a runner, so I did ask them. "What makes you think that I'm a soldier?" I have to admit, I was pleasantly surprised at their obvious surprised awareness at my questionable response. They looked at each other as if for reassurance, then the one with his baton still in its sheath on his broad pure white belt asked me. "Your not a member of the military force in Trieste?" I waited for a few seconds to think, then replied. "Excuse me, I asked you the question first". The guy with the baton immediately lifted it very slowly and placed the thick end of it into the open palm of his left hand. The one that asked me the question replied. "Sir, we have to see some identification. A driving licence or passport. Or we call the polizia". I liked that, I liked being addressed as Sir, especially by the military. I replied. "Why would you want to call the police and why don't you go and ask these other gentlemen for their pass or passports?" I could I see and feel that they were getting embarrassed and annoyed. Then the one that was doing all the interrogation said. "These people are not foreigners, they are not English". I just could not resist, so I put my hand up to stop him and said. "There you go now. I'm not English either so I'm also a foreigner, therefore also not required to identify myself". By this time one could have heard a pin drop in what was once a very relaxed and gossipy atmosphere. Everyone in the ristorante had focused their attention on the two military policemen and myself. I could feel that the one that was wielding the baton was about to express serious agitated emotion so I put both my hands in the air as in surrender and said. "let's go". Both military policemen appeared to say simultaneously. "Go where?" I replied. "65 Company Royal Army Service Corp".

I have to say that I was pleasantly surprised in the decent manner in which the two military policemen escorted me out of the ristorante and into their Land Rover. We drove through the deserted city of Trieste with the baton wielding military policemen sitting beside me in the cage in the rear of the vehicle until we eventually arrived at what I assumed was their headquarters. I was interrogated further for a while and once more was impressed by the casual nature of the cross-examination. The conclusion was that I was AOL [Absent without leave] therefore it was a matter for my commanding officer to deal with. I was once more back in the cage in the rear of a Land Rover with my baton wielding military policeman sitting beside me and driven back to 65 Coy R.A.S.C. I was handed over to the duty guard officer in my own barracks and after some paper work, a few telephone calls I was locked up in a cell in one of our cell blocks and slept like a baby. In the morning, my furious Commanding Officer charged me and found me guilty of being absent without leave and wearing civilian cloths without due permission and sentenced me to fourteen days prison to be served in San Gesto military prison. To me personally, it was all worth while just to see the look of bewilderment on his face when I was marched in front of him. Perhaps in future when some soldier who has wronged and has served his punishment, he may consider showing some understanding and compassion, instead of more hostility.

When I was escorted back to San Gesto in handcuffs by the military police later that morning, I rejoiced at the look of shock on the faces of the prison staff wardens when I was pulled out of the rear of the Land Rover by the military police into the San Gesto security enclosed compound. After all the bureaucratic official paper work, cropping of my head of hair and collecting my bedding, I was ran in front off the mad commandant. Through taught lips and attempting to avoid direct eye contact with me he promised me that I will live to regret ever coming back to San Gesto. He also promised me that If I refuse to conform, I will spend my fourteen days in solitary confinement and if given the opportunity he will have me before a court martial for refusing to *Soldier!* Apparently, I had previously broken the record for solitary confinement with bread and water in San Gesto, especially when I had been sentenced to nine days. Now apparently, no prisoner had ever returned to San Gesto after having been incarcerated inside this place. Not only was I back, I had returned within twenty four hours of being released. The mad commandant partially kept his promise, I did spend nine days in solitary confinement on bread and water and the remaining five days dodging facing a court martial for refusing to *Soldier.*

In spite of all this misfortune, after being released and returned to 65 Coy I was to find out that a National Service soldier's army service time is automatically suspended the minute that soldier is imprisoned. When I returned to my company my Commanding Officer informed me that the time I had spent in San Gesto does not count as part of my National Service. I was an Eighteen Month National Service soldier. Now, I would have to serve two years and a few weeks, an additional service of over six months. I was absolutely shocked. No one had ever had the decency to explain that to me. I thought that I only had a few more weeks to do in this mans army prior of going back into San Gesto for the second time. On the contrary, I still had just over six more months to do until I was free. For the first time I suddenly realized that they had all defeated and had beaten me after all. All I could do now was get on with it and accept the stupidity of my ways and ensure that I do not return to San Gesto, If I do, I could spend the rest of my life in the San Gesto prison dungeons

I got myself settled into 65 Coy's routines and started to adjust and conform. I have to say that I missed Hansen and Falconer because they had been demobbed and were now at home after completing their eighteen months National Service. I should have gone with them. We did promised to keep in touch. I had been confined to barracks for a month and was driving three tonne Bedford truck's around Trieste. My worst assignments were during weekends when I had to drive our own R.A.S.C. drivers that were not on duty to a beautiful beach at place named Udine for rest and relaxation. Because I was on duty, I was not allowed to rest, relax, swim or even remove my jacket in this scorching heat. Then there were these damn mock wars when I had to drive these huge troop-carrier vehicles.

That's when I realized that my 65 Coy Sergeant Major had just volunteered me to be the first member of the new Coy Regimental Police Force.

In one of these planned mock battles the Fusiliers were fighting the Americans. We spent weeks attending meetings and getting involved in map-reading and many other logistics. I was surprised when I realized that I was going to have quite an important role to play in this exercise. Then of course I was the most experienced driver in the entire R.A.S.C. 65 Coy. This scheme was to last for at least two weeks, two bloody weeks sleeping in trucks and eating rubbish food from our metal mess cans, the only consolation was that it was usually dark when one ate, therefore you could not see what you were eating. We would have no access to water for washing and probably very little to drink. It is likely that I had more water to drink when I was in solitary confinement in San Gesto than I was going to have access to during the next fourteen days. I had done this before many times and I was not very happy about it but unfortunately it was a huge exercise and our entire company was involved.

On day of the start of the combat, along with my co-driver, we checked out

103

and filled-up our huge fuel tanker, double checked all our tyre pressures, engine, lights, camouflaging and emergency rationing. We checked all our maps, night torches and personal kit . We as a company would not be directly involved in any combat as such, we only supplied the transport for moving the Fusilier foot soldiers, supply water and fuel for all the vehicles and I was in charge of the fuel tanker. We left our barracks parking lot in a huge convoy, collected the hundreds of Fusilier foot soldiers at their headquarters barracks and headed directly into the Italian hills. After driving for a few hours and after various vehicles had been sent off in different direction with their Fusiliers foot soldiers, it was our turn. We were given our map references and instructions to report to the officer in charge of a temporary depot . We were soon off on our own and within an hour we left the hard tar road and were now driving along a narrow laterite B road. The terrain was bushy and flat with many small tracks breaking off the main road to both the left and the right hand side of us. I stopped to check the map, we were okay and going in the correct direction, I estimated that we had another ten or twelve miles to go until we come to a cross-road then we do a left in order to reach the depot camp. That's when I noticed that the Americans had a camp about twenty miles or so down the road to the right. I handed the map to the co-driver and asked him to check that the coordinates and map references were correct for our destination and final location. I leapt out of the tanker to stretch my legs and kick all the tyres to ensure our vehicle was still in good condition. Before I had completed my inspection he had joined me and confirmed that all the map references were okay for our final destination. I knew that he could never have checked these coordinates in such a short time, I also knew that he was not interested. When we reached the cross-road, I stopped and suggested to my co-driver. "We should do a right turn here, is that correct?" Then I handed him the map. Then after a few minutes, he replied. "Yes, yes that's correct Cass, turn right". I knew that it was a left turn, in order to reach our base camp. I knew that this idiot of a co-driver had not checked the map or any of the coordinates. However, I made my decision and that was that I didn't want anymore to do with these mock-wars and turned right. I had also considered the complications of being taken a prisoner by the Americans and possible consequences. This would be classed as an incorrect interpretation of map references and co-ordinations. After driving for ten minutes I stopped and told my co-driver. "Okay, It's time you gave me a break, Its about another forty-five minutes driving until you reach our depot camp". Within half an hour we were ambushed and surrounded by American troops and taken prisoner's.

The Yanks appeared to be delighted at capturing and confiscating such a booty as a tanker full of precious fuel on the first day of combat. I personally did not bat an eye-lid except glance sideways at my incompetent and now confused co-driver. We were triumphantly escorted the next few miles to their camp. Once my co-driver had parked our fuel tanker, we were both ordered to leave the vehicle, collect our personal kit and were escorted to an office. We were interviewed and I mean interviewed as opposed to being interrogated. These Yanks were very civilised and that made me feel very comfortable immediately. After we had given the American officer our personal army details such as name, rank and army number, we were escorted by a corporal to a huge tent. Inside this huge tent there were a couple of dozen single beds all very neatly distributed around the four sides of the tent and folded on each bed were brand new mattresses. In the centre of this tent there was at least a dozen or so foldable tables and chairs just waiting to be unfolded. The corporal suggested that we throw our kit on a selected bed and follow him. He escorted us to a portable cabin where we collected bed sheets and a blanket. I was shocked beyond belief. We Brit's would be sleeping for the next two weeks in our clothes on a ground sheet and in the open. We were also given a small booklet indicating where the cookhouse and cinema were. After being escorted back to our tent with our bed sheets the corporal informed us that the cookhouse was open 24 hours a day and if we check out the cinema we would get a timetable for the movies, then he left us to do what ever it was we wanted to do. These Yanks had it made, this was without a doubt a five star prisoner-of-combat camp. After we made our beds-up we decided to check-out the cookhouse The cookhouse was similar to a restaurant with chef's with big white hats. Self service with choices off eggs and steaks done to our choice and served with fries. I could not believe it. Machines with ice cold drinks of your choice, including iced tea. It was unbelievable, I had never witnessed anything so spectacular in all my life. In our own barracks back in 65 coy the mashed potato with huge lumps were thrown onto your plate. The meat was riddled with gristle and the diced carrots, wet cabbage and grey gravy made you fart all evening. The only drinks we had was tea aced with bromide which will probably make us all impotent for the next few years. I was so content that after we had eaten, I wasn't interested in movies, I just wanted to get back to the tent whilst secretly whishing that this mock war would last for six months. My co-driver appeared to lack any skills whatsoever and just followed me wherever I went. I have to say that I was privately hoping and praying that he was not following me back into San Gesto.

In this camp, we were the first and only two prisoner for the first five days then a few infantry Fusiliers joined us and eventually there were twenty seven of us. My co-driver and myself were the only prisoners from 65 Coy R.A.S.C. After our evening meal we watched a different movie every evening and then went for a late supper before retiring for the night, it was just wonderful. When the mock war scheme eventually ended after sixteen days all of us prisoners were released. The Yanks took all of the infantry troops back to wherever they had to go but not before what I thought was one of the most embarrassing moments in my life. Whilst the twenty seven of us were hanging around on that final day just waiting to see what was happening, we were all told to line up as if on duty. An American officer announced that five sets of bed sheets were lost. He very diplomatically suggest that some of us may have misunderstood the rules of engagement, and suggested that each and every one off us complete with all our kit return to our billet tent alone. He further announced that a basket had been placed in the centre of the tent. After a delay that person will leave the tent and return to this parade. He said that he was confident that the misunderstanding will be amended. Every single one off us had to go back into the tent with all our kit and of course the thieving infantry men would hopefully put the bed sheets that they had taken back into the basket. It worked, after the twenty seven of us Brits had been back into the tents, the lost bed sheets were found. I was so ashamed and regretful that this had to happen especially after the way these Americans had treated us and I just couldn't help feeling hurt about what they must be thinking about us Brits. One large American type troop carrier-vehicle left the camp with all the infantry troops on board including the thieves. I jumped into my vehicle with my co-driver at my side and I have to say that I felt unwell at the thought of going back to my own company because I was certainly not looking forward to the interrogation that I was going to be subjected to.

When I eventually got back to my barracks parking lot with my full fuel tank, it was utter chaos with all sorts of vehicles arriving covered in mud and battle scars. Some of them still had camouflage netting hanging loose. Drivers in general were running around like ants. I spotted a few of the drivers that I knew and they all looked like shit and looked as if they had been dragged through paddy fields. I spotted a corporal with a clip board and sent my co-driver over to him find out where he wanted this fuel tanker parked. When he returned he said if I still had fuel in it I was to park it in the in fuel storage area then check ourselves in with our respective platoons. I dismissed the co-driver because the fuel storage depot was a separate area unit from the normal parking lot and I would probably have to wait for a lift back. After parking and signing the vehicle in, I got a lift almost immediately back to the main parking lot adjacent to the barracks. I checked in with my own platoon and suddenly wished that I was somewhere else or at least could find some way to look dishevelled. Everyone else looked bedraggled and in need of a wash and shave and even their uniforms were filthy. Up until now, no one appeared to know that I had been a prisoner off this mock war which surprised me somewhat, but made me feel a wee bit more comfortable. That was until my platoon sergeant suddenly appeared and asked me. "What the hell happened to you?" I knew that eventually I would have to face the consequences, so I said. "Serg, I have no idea, It's not as if I got lost. I must have got my coordinates mixed up and before I was aware of it I was surrounded my Americans. They appeared to come from nowhere, as if they had parachuted on top of me". "You had better come with me, our platoon officer wants to see you" He was not in his office. But after a few minutes we found him talking to another officer. He looked even more bedraggled than most. He was filthy and looked as if he had taken this war too seriously and had not had time to wash for days. I had to repeat to him how I had been over powered by American infantry. He shouted. "You're a bloody fool Cassidy. A bloody fool. I will deal with you in the morning". As he was about to depart he told the sergeant that he wanted my co-driver to be present at our meeting in the morning. In the morning our platoon parade was dismissed, the sergeant myself and my co-driver were on parade again, to go in front of our platoon officer. I was first to be interrogated by my platoon officer in the presence of my platoon sergeant. Off course I repeated my story and reiterated that I had been shocked, taken by complete surprise and extremely saddened when I was ambushed and taken prisoner by the Americans. However when our officer interviewed my co-driver, I think he was shaken when he was suddenly aware that it was my co-driver who was driving the fuel tanker when we were ambushed and captured by the Americans! The enquiry was suspended until such time as further enquiries can be made. It was around this time, September 1954 that the Anglo / American troops were being pulled out of Italy. It was probably because of this that I never heard another word about the incident when my co-driver and myself were the only two R.A.S.C. drivers were taken prisoners by the Americans during that mock-war.

It was the scheme of all scheme's when we, the R.A.S.C. 65 Coy pulled out of Trieste Italy Zone A. We drove in convoy from Trieste in Italy to Monchengladbach in Germany. Although the distance was only just over seven hundred miles, it took us five days. We left Italy and entered Switzerland then into Austria and set up camp. On the second day we entered Germany and on the outskirts of a place named Munchen, we set up camp. On the third day we by passed Nuremberg and set-up camp. On the fourth day we by-passed Frankfurt, stopped and set up-camp. Then on the fifth and final day we drove into a camp in Monchengladbach, Germany. In the morning our entire company was on parade. The company sergeant-major instructed me to take two steps forward, then stand easy. In spite of the fact that I was shocked at being singled out in this manner. I very smartly took two sharp steps forward, smashed my highly polished boots very noisily onto the concrete parade ground to stand to attention, then stood easy. The sergeant-major then explained to the parade that he was looking for volunteers to be considered for our Regimental Police Force, any one interested should take two-steps forward and stand easy. That's when I realized that my sergeant-major had volunteered me to be the first member of our new Regimental Police Force. Apparently over twenty drivers volunteered and out of that twenty only seven were required as the company Regimental Police Force was mad up of eight policemen. After the other seven had been chosen by the sergeant-major, we were all interviewed, interrogated, drilled and taught our duties and rules of engagement and for me it was no problem. I was truly shocked and somewhat amazed at the control and influence we police had over our fellow soldiers and the responsibility was just as awesome. I very soon realized that I was going to enjoy the remainder of my time in this mans army. Not because of the impressive control over others. I just loved the military police turn-out that we had to maintain to be the best dressed soldiers in the company. We wore pure white belts, white gaiters, a black bandolier and a black arm band with two highly polished brass R.P. [Regimental Police] letters on the arm bands.

Another Scot from Glasgow had volunteered and had been selected, although I had never met him previously until now and we soon became inseparable. We spent most off our first few weeks on duty controlling the main entrance gate to the camp. Nothing entered and or left the camp without us checking their credentials. We were responsible to ensure that no soldier in our company was inappropriately dressed, or behaving in any manner unbecoming to our company. Our company, 65 Coy, R.A.S.C. was eventually sent back to Salisbury England. I had now been in the army for over twenty two months and still had another two months to do. Because of my time in detention, instead doing the eighteen months National Service I was having to serve just over twenty four months. The damage to me personally was minimum. I did eventually realize that if I had allowed the prison warders in San Gesto prison to break me, I could have received two months remission and would have been out of the army two months earlier. But, I doubt if I would have been the same person that I am, and what the hell is two months between the devil and the deep blue sea. I do know that I suffered in San Gesto, but have the benefit of believing that I defeated the mad commandant and his sadistic prison staff by not allowing them to have total control of me.

My last two months in Salisbury England as a Regimental Policeman was exceedingly pleasing for me . I had chosen and preferred to being tidy and smart and being one of the smartest dressed soldiers in our company, because it made me feel good and I did for me, not the army. In fact, I was now the smartest of the eight Regimental Policeman therefore must have been the smartest guy in the entire company, perhaps even smarter than the sergeant-major. We had to do twenty four hour shifts as Regimental Policeman. Twenty four hours on duty and twenty four hours off duty. During the twenty four hours off, one was expected and did spend hours cleaning and ironing your entire uniform, scrubbing your kit and re-laying additional white blanco on your belt and gaiters and off course spit and polishing your boots. The other Scot, Jamie and myself ended up as permanent partners doing our twenty four hour's police duties together. Most of the soldiers in our company were young English lads. There were a few Scots and Welsh guys but ninety per cent of them were young English lads. Therefore every weekend a few dozen of our company squaddies were issued passes for a thirty six or forty eight hour leave. The forty eight hour passes left the camp on the Friday evening after duty. The thirty six hour passes could only leave after midday Saturday. If Jamie and I were on duty at weekends when everyone with a weekend pass were due back before midnight, we never ever put anyone that was late on a charge. We always suggested to them that if they left the parcel that they had in their possession in the guard room, we would not charge them and would allow them to run silently and secretively to their beds in their billets. It never failed. The parcels in their possessions were always goodies that their parents had made up for them to share with their friends who had not been on leave and normally contain home made cookies. Of course, it was a very good deal for the individual because if he was charged he would be in trouble and also have to forfeit other weekend passes. We, on the other hand had earned a few cookies, because if the duty officer had discovered our leniency, we would have been in very serious trouble indeed. I do believe that Jamie and I only ever charged anyone who arrived back late from weekend pass when we had no other choice and that would be when the duty officer was present. We may have eaten a few home made cakes and scones but there were others that were late that had no goodie parcels that we also allowed to escape away swiftly to their beds. From the guard-room we had a panoramic view of the main gate entrance into the barracks. We could watch the headlights of the approaching vehicle as it raced towards the barracks. The vehicle would screech to halt at the gates as if in an attempt to impress the people in the guard room that they had tried not to be late. One of the car doors would swing open and the pathetic young soldier would leap out and run to the now locked pedestrian gate. Jamie and I would take turns each in going out and opening the gate. Often one of the parents would also climb out of the vehicle in an attempt to offer an explanation. Of course we had no jurisdiction under our rules and regulations to even listen, so all we could was raise a hand to indicate to them to stop, and then wave them away. Most of these soldiers we are talking about are raw-recruits, young eighteen year old National Service soldiers. Just like I was two years ago and my heart went out to them and that was the reason I was absolutely reluctant to charge any of them, unless I had no other choice.

I had always thought that it was extremely unfair that we Scots stationed in England were never considered for leave passes. I could understand why, because it would take us that long to travel home to Scotland. However, should have qualified for a monthly five days leave. On the other hand perhaps we deserved all we got. If we had joined one of our own Scot's regiments like the Argyll and Southern Highlanders or the Cameronians we would have qualified for leave passes if we were stationed in Scotland. Actually, it was my original intention to do my National Service in the Cameronians, but my brother Hugh warned me against it. He suggested all infantry regiments spend most of their time in fields on schemes and mock-wars and that it was tough. Whereas in the R.A.S.C. all we do is drive them to the fields, then at worse we just sleep in our trucks until it's time to take them back to their barracks. It sounded like good advice to me and that's the reason I selected the R.A.S.C. Hugh's mate, Tully Leonard had decided to do his National Service with the Cameronians who were an infantry regiment and he actually ended up fighting in the Korea War. Perhaps I would have preferred that, however we will never know.

Indifferent: 10

On December 1954, I was finally demobbed after spending just over two difficult years in the Army, so now I was free. I was not resentful about my detention, but extremely resentful about having been treated so badly. I had committed a serious offence, faced a court martial, was found guilty and had accepted my punishment in spite of the fact that my court martial was meaningless and my defence lawyer farcical. Whilst being incarcerated, I was subjected to unnecessary mental and physical brutality and I intended at that time when I was demobbed in 1954 to write a book about that dreadful experience. I did start writing *Indifferent* when I got married in 1957 because I still had a copy of the manuscript of my court martial and remembered vividly the good, bad and indifferent incidents that had unfolded during my spell whilst in Trieste, however I lost interest, perhaps that was because I had better things to do. The military powers to be had classified me as being *Indifferent,* which had been logged in my discharge book after I had been demobbed. Perhaps I was indifferent when I was in the army, however there are times when one has to be strong and resilient, otherwise you may be overwhelmed . I don't necessarily mean strong physically, I mean mentally, after all I have never been a physically strong individual.

I had managed to catch the overnight train from Kings-Cross railway station in London to the Waverly railway station in Edinburgh. I have to say that it was a pleasant journey compared to the one that I had taken over two years ago when I travelled down to London as a rookie soldier. I was now older and much wiser. Walking down Arthur Street that very cold quiet winter morning I turned right into Middle Arthur Place and suddenly realized that I was apprehensive. I had not contacted my parents for such a long time. In fact, the last time I contacted them was when I sent a post card after I was released from San-Gesto after my second spell in that hell-hole. Telephones in the 1950s were for rich people and none of us Cassidy's were very good at putting pen to paper. Nobody, except myself was aware of the fact that I was actually walking towards our house in 7 Middle Arthur Place. It must have been just before eight o clock on a Thursday morning. Mr Bertram, a neighbour from No 5 walked passed me, I stopped and turned to look after him and wondered why he had not recognised me. I thought, well he's probably late for work and in a hurry, that's why he did not speak to me. As I passed No 5 the entrance to his tenement building, I realised that the next house, the main door No 7, was our house. I stopped and was standing at our door when Rosie and Ann Leonard came bounding out of the tenement building which was opposite us. Our families had been neighbours and friends all our lives, they shouted at me. "Oh hi Cass, when did you get home?" I smiled and felt happy that they had recognised me and explained. "Just this very minute, this is me just now". "Oh, your mum will be pleased. We have to rush as we are going to be late for work" They were trotting away when Rosie turned-around and shouted. "Oh Cass, Tully is back from Korea and working with our dad in Leith Docks. See you later".

The Leonard's has been neighbours and friends of our families for ever. Rosie Leonard was about a year older than me so she would be about twenty one. Ann was younger, about sixteen, maybe seventeen. We were never out of each other's house's. Tully, one of their elder brothers was same age as Hugh, twenty two and were best mate's. Before they both went into the army, Hugh and Tully both worked as stokers on the steam trains. The Leonard's parents were both Irish but all the six kids, four girls and two boys were born in Scotland. The four girls, Mary, Rosie, Nana, and Ann, were all like sisters to us. They also all lived in a two room flat. Even after they had left school they would still walk about in their underwear in front of Hugh and I if we happened to be in their house. Tully preferred to be called Tam and was an extremely good-looking guy and the double of a handsome film star of the fifties named Jeff Chandler. Tam had that rugged Irish look and his hair, like Jeff Chandler's was jet black with small tight curls with light streaks and also like Jeff Chandler, he was just under six feet all.

I knocked on my door, it was opened instantly by one of my wee sisters, when I went into the army she was a wee twelve year old school girl, this girl standing smiling at me was tall and pretty. She shouted. "Mum, mum, its Davie". Then disappeared back into the house leaving the door wide open. I slowly followed her into the kitchen/dining room which was also my parents bed room. The next person I meet is my other wee sister who was brushing her teeth at the kitchen sink. My mum was helping the baby boy of our family to get dressed, he would be about five years old now. My mum looked over at me and smiled. She looked very tired and exhausted. She walked over, hugged and held me in her arms for a while, then whispered. "Oh son where have you been? You will be the death of me. I have been so worried about you. Why did you not write more often, especially when you were in that penal place. Are you okay?" I whispered. "I'm fine mum". My wee brother looked frightened, and his eyes were like big saucers. I walked over towards him but he reached out for my mum, who said to him. "You've no to be frightened. This is your other big brother Davie, he's going to be home for good now". My mum looked at me with a concerned and meaningful expression on her weary face.

My two younger sisters soon left the house to go to their work, I could not believe that they were both now working. My mum explained to me that they both worked as shop assistants in different shops in Clerk Street on the Bridges. My Dad, Cathie and Hugh had already left for work. Hector, my other big brother was still in the R.A.F and my mum was of the opinion that he was now being trained to be a pilot. Our brisk conversation was interrupted when my mum had to rush away to take my wee brother to Drummond Street School. On her return she said that she had forgot to tell me that Hugh was engaged to a girl called Ann Murray. When I enquired if he had gone back to work in the railway she said that he was now driving a big delivery van for the Co-op. She went silent for a wee while then suggested that she was worried about Hugh. Then silent again. When I enquired what she was concerned about, she said. "Oh, well some weekends he doesn't come home". I thought, oh my god, Hugh's nearly twenty three years old and my mum is worried about him because he doesn't come home some nights. Mum would never think that the reason could be because he has to share his bed with his wee brother and the bedroom with his three sisters. She would never think that perhaps he is sharing his bed with his fiancée in their own private bedroom. Good luck to him was what I thought and as far as I was concerned, I hope he spends more nights with his girl friend and less time sharing my bed that I will have to share with my wee brother. I put the big black kettle closer to the small coal fire that was glowing and it started boiling instantly so I withdrew it away from the fire because it was now boiling and ready for making some tea. My mum had brought morning rolls from Jackson's the bakers back with her when she had returned from taking my wee brother to school. My mother was doing most of the talking whilst we sat drinking tea and enjoying Jackson's rolls. She complimented me and told me that I was looking good and then spoiled it by suggesting that I looked a lot older. We laughed and I felt at times that we both wanted to cry, but we didn't want to spoil the moment, so we didn't cry.

Eventually I wandered through to our only bedroom and sat on the edge of the double bed that from now on I would be sharing with Hugh and my wee brother. I only had a small battered dark brown luggage suit case which I had dropped on the three seater settee that when folded down was the bed which my elder sister Cathie shared with our two younger sisters. I was beginning to wonder how I was going to fit in here because I felt like a stranger. From my luggage case I removed the copy of the full manuscript of my Court Martial. I started to thumb through it and promised myself that one day I will write a book about my experience in the army and San-Gesto. Then I picked up my army discharge book and stopped at the page with *Indifferent printed* in bold letters under discharge characterization. I heard my mum open the kitchen door so she was obviously on her way into the bedroom so I threw both discharge book and manuscript back into my luggage case and closed it.

My Mum collected my wee brother from school around twelve noon. My Dad was the first to arrive home around four thirty, then shortly after that my two younger sisters then Cathie, the eldest. I thought I spotted a wee wet tear drop in her eyes as Cathie hugged me then told me off for not writing more often. Hugh, who was last just laughed when he saw me. My Dad, as usual was the quiet man and eventually complimented me when he told me that I looked well and insulted me when he suggested that the army must have been good to me. We all sat down to mince and tatties for dinner around six thirty and most of them, except my Dad and Hugh wanted to know all about me in Trieste. I felt awkward and uneasy attempting to talk about Trieste and was relieved when Hugh suggested that we give Tully Leonard a shout and go for a couple of pints of beer to celebrate my home coming. Our first stop was at Airds bar at the top of Arthur Street, but after one pint of Younger's beer, Hugh and Tully decided that they wanted to go to the Woolpack bar , as it sold McEwen's beer. The conversation was mostly between Hugh and Tully about girl friends and work and I was more or less left out off it and that was fine. As we were eventually saying goodnight, Tully asked Hugh what time they would meet tomorrow which was the Friday night for the usual few beers, then Fairlie's dance hall on Leith Walk. Hugh confirmed that he would not be going for a few beers or Fairlie's dance hall as he was meeting his fiancée, Ann Murray. Tully laughed and teased Hugh a bit then asked me what my plans were. Off course I had no plans so It was agreed that we would meet around six thirty tomorrow night. That was to be the beginning of my long friendship with Tully alias Tam Leonard, *Jeff Chandler the movie stars double.*

Tam was working as a labourer with his dad who was the ganger on part of the Leith Docks Project and soon got me fixed up with a job as a labourer. The pay was very good which is exactly what I was after. Tam and I worked together in the same gang. Paddy, his dad was in charge off a few gangs and we always got the chance of any overtime work that was going including weekend work. Xmas and the New year came and went. We Cassidy's had a couple of chickens on Xmas day. Hugh spent most of the holidays staying with a pal, ?? [Ann Murray]. Tully my dad and I went to the Tron Church at the top of the Royal Mile on the High Street to bring in the New Year as the bell struck midnight. This was a bit of a ritual at the time and a few thousand other people of all ages gathered around the Tron Church drinking and singing and generally celebrating the old year out and the new year in. On our way back home to Middle Arthur Place around one-o-clock on new years morning my old man was walking in front of us playing his accordion. Just as we were about to turn of Arthur Street into Middle Arthur Place, three men that were about to pass us going in the opposite direction suddenly smashed Tully and I against the wall and demanded that we hand over any cash or bottles of alcohol we had. As Two of them were squashing us against the wall by our necks the third man was frisking into our pockets. The two that were holding us were shouting. "Get their bottles as well". My old man must have heard the commotion, and from a sideways glance, I watched him very sharply putting his accordion on the ground then silently skipped and trotted towards us. He very swiftly turned the guy around that was going through our pockets and with a short left hand jab to his jaw, sent him sprawling to the ground. The guy who had me by the throat released me and was instantly hit under chin the minute he turned around to face my old man. He also went down in a heap and fell down like a log onto the road. It was all happening so fast and now the guy that was holding Tam started lashing out at my old man who appeared to be backing off some whilst curled up like a ball. Then my old man let rip into his body then his head and face with rapid left's and rights until he was also smashed to the ground. Not one off these three men got up off the ground. They were not even making any noises as my old man shepherded us away towards our street and house. After he had collected his precious accordion I glanced back at the three figures who were still sprawled out over the ground.

One of my younger sisters changed her job and started work in a Lodge at the top of The Mound of Princess Street. It was a residential lodge for student bankers for the Commercial Bank of Scotland. Because of the hours she worked she was residential therefore it was one less person sleeping in our bedroom. Hugh eventually got married to Ann Murray and we had the reception in our bedroom at Seven Middle Arthur Place. It was indeed an unbelievable achievement. Our bedroom was converted and transformed into a respectable looking lounge for a wedding reception. We very quickly stripped all the existing wall paper off and re-painted the ceiling with brilliant white emulsion paint, then re-papered the walls. Repainted the door, skirting boards and fire-place with fresh white oil-paint and relocated wardrobe and three seat bed settee. Made hundreds of sandwiches, bought a reasonable wedding cake, a firkin of beer, a few bottles of wine, a couple of bottles of spirits and some soft drinks. We borrowed additional drinking glasses and additional serving plates from the Leonard's and other neighbours. The guests were our family and the brides three brothers and her younger sister as Ann Murray's parents were both deceased. There were also a few of our family friends like the Leonard girls and Tam. In total there must have been about twenty of us in that small bedroom and if my memory is correct, we had a ball. Our old man was playing his accordion and on other occasions the spoons accompanied by Hugh with his mouth- organ. We also had a gramophone player and records of Johnny Ray, Frankie Lane, Alma Cogan, Nat King Cole and many others. It was one hell of a party. We sang and danced for hours. It started on the Saturday afternoon after the church wedding and it went on until early Sunday morning. I was Hugh's best man and Ann's younger sister was the best maid. That night, or should I say that Sunday morning I escorted the bridesmaid home to Granton. After the wedding, the bridesmaid and I dated for a few weeks but it was obvious that we were as like as chalk and cheese, therefore we soon drifted wide apart.

One Friday night Tam Leonard and I were at the Excelsior dance hall and as usual Tam was soon involved with a few girls and undecided which one he intended to take home, so he was kept rather busy flirting between them. I met up with this guy Carlo DeMarco that I used to go to school with and we got talking. Carlo was an Italian, well his father was an Italian his mother a Scot and Carlo was born in Edinburgh. I was telling him that I had just returned from Italy and we were having a bit of a laugh. I suggested that he was looking very affluent and after more laughter he told me that he had his own garage business that serviced and repaired vehicles. Our conversation was suddenly interrupted when these two elegant looking girls joined us. He introduced me to Leila his fiancée and the other girl Marie, who was his fiancée's friend. His fiancée eventually insisted that Carlo dance with her, so they did, leaving Marie and I standing alone together. This Marie was also a very attractive lady therefore I was a wee bit apprehensive about asking her to dance, but in spite of my predicament, I did asked her to dance and was delighted when she replied. "Thank you". As it turned out Marie was not with anyone in particular as the three of them, Carlo, Leila and herself had been at a party and decided to finish the evening off at the Excelsior dance hall. Once more I was pleasantly surprised and felt that we were both relaxed in each others company and she made me feel as if I had known her for a considerable time as apposed to five minutes. Marie lived with her parents in Upper Grey Street which is in the posh Newington area of Edinburgh where I used to work as a butchers messenger boy with Brechin Brothers. That night I walked her home and we agreed to meet next Saturday in the Excelsior Dance Hall. I have no idea why we did this in those days, I mean meet inside the dance hall. I do believe that it had something to do with having a few beers with your male friends before meeting and spending the night with your girl-friend, I honestly have no idea why, but that was the norm.

They often had to defend themselves in the pubs at the weekends
from other drunken hard fighting Irishmen simply because
they had refused them work, or worse still, they had dismissed them.

On that particular Saturday night when I met Marie in the Excelsior dance hall she informed me that she was staying the night with another girl-friend of hers that lives just of South Clerk Street. I remember asking her if she was going to stay with my friend Carlo DeMarco fiancée's house. She laughed and informed me that Carlo and Leila his fiancée live together in Carlo's own

116

house. Eventually I was introduced to Marie's girl-friend Elizabeth and her boy friend and the four of us all walked home together to South Clerk Street. Marie informed during the walk that her girl-friends parents were on a months holiday in their apartment in Cyprus. Marie also suggested that when we get to her girl-friends house she will probably invite me in for a night-cap. When we did arrive arrived at the house in South Clerk Street, Marie's girl-friend did indeed invite me to join them in the house for a night cap. I was overwhelmed at the obvious opulence, it was a huge house on the top landing of a tenement building off Clerk Street Newington. The view from the huge bay windows in the lounge overlooking Edinburgh was amazing and the fact that it was now after midnight, the dancing lights made the city so enticing. The four off us sat in this huge beautifully furnished lounge drinking whatever was our fancy. Our guest Elizabeth had opened-up this two door cupboard that exposed bottles of every make of liquor one could imagine, including wines. The bottom section was a large fridge full of bottled beer, white wine and all sorts of soft drinks, it was unlike anything that I had ever witnessed. In fact I had no idea that people living in houses could afford to maintain a stock of alcohol similar to that of a license bar. That was until Elizabeth explained that her father was the head brewer for McEwen's Brewery.

During the conversation I discovered that Elizabeth and her boy-friend were both attending Edinburgh University. When I was asked what line of business I was in, I lied and told them that I was finalizing my five year apprenticeship as a Heating Engineer. I was relieved that they did not find that interesting enough to pursue it any further although I was feeling a wee bit uncomfortable with Elizabeth's boy friends attitude but at the same time I was relaxed and enjoying myself and having a good time. little did I know that it was about to become much more exciting. Eventually Elizabeth, without any hesitation wished Marie and myself goodnight, then taking her boyfriends hand, vanished. Marie and I sat for a while necking and messing around until she excused herself and returned to the lounge in a night-dress. She did not sit down beside me, instead she held both her hands out towards me. I was shocked, then very slowly eased myself out of my arm chair and walked very slowly towards her. Marie took hold of one my hands and ever so gently guided me through a long hall and into a bedroom. I had not been with any girls since I had come home from the army and after consuming all that bromide whilst in the army and especially whilst in San - Gesto, I was suddenly very concerned, then scared. I was still very much a rookie when it came to having sex with girls and was certainly not prepared for this. During the night, Marie very diplomatically and delicately suggested to me that I was a sexual student with great potential. In the morning Marie informed me that I aroused her immensely and that I was now an undergraduate and heading for a first degree in making love. Marie and I were guests in that house every Friday and Saturday night for the next three weeks. Elizabeth's boy friend was an arrogant and condescending snob, therefore I avoided having any conversation whatsoever with him. Elizabeth on the other hand was a lovely friendly girl and I got on great with her and I knew that she was fond of me, perhaps that was because Marie had informed her that I was a potential first degree undergraduate in the art of love making.

Tam and I had changed jobs, because whilst working with his dad we always got singled out by his dad to do the most difficult and often filthy jobs. Every time a delivery off cement arrived, he always instructed us to unload the thousand's of heavy cement bags. It would take hours and by the time we were finished there was cement dust in our hair, ear's, eye's and we even found cement dust on our foreskins when we went to the loo and that was the last straw. The next time he gave us the job it was late on a Friday afternoon and we had already been paid. We unloaded the truck and its trailer, then went direct to the site office and told the time keeper that we were leaving and were no longer returning to work for them. We left the huge Leith Docks construction site and went directly to the Infirmary Street Baths. We both had a hot bath on the top floor in order to free ourselves of all the cement dust, then finished off with a swim in the swimming pool. However on getting dressed, we discovered that we should have bathed with all of our to our clothes still on because they were all impregnated with the damn invisible cement dust. We had not informed Tam's Dad that we had left our employment and would no longer be working for him and that was going to prove to have been a grave mistake. That Friday night we were in the pub at the top of St Mary street when Paddy Leonard, Tam's dad, technically our ex-boss wandered inside and of course when he caught sight of us he wandered over and joined us and bought us a drink. After he had drank his dark rum and had a few sips of his Guinness he started talking about work. Eventually he informed us that he wanted both of us to turn out for work on Saturday morning because he had a wee job that needed to be done and that we would probably get the Sunday shift out of it as well. Tam and I just looked at each other then I pointed my finger at Tam, indicating that as it was his dad, therefore he should tell him. I actually thought that Paddy Leonard was about to hit his own son when Tam told him that we had resigned and no longer worked for Wimpy, or him. He went berserk and accused us of being traitors because we had not discussed it with him. Then he went on about him being two labourers short tomorrow morning. It's just as well it was early on in the evening, because I do believe if he had been drunk he would have knocked the both us to the floor without any hesitation. Paddy Leonard, like most Irishmen, was a hard man and the fact is, the Irish gangers had to be tough. They often had to defend themselves in the

118

pubs at the weekends from other drunken hard fighting Irishmen simply because they had refused them work or worse still, had dismissed them.

Tam and I were back to work within days, working for Tarmac Adam, a company that had the contract for ripping up all the tram lines around Edinburgh. We both laboured hard digging-out and removing the huge granite cobble-stones between the tram-lines and then manually loading these heavy granite cobble-stones onto lorries. After the heavy steel tram-lines themselves had been removed we had to physically lift and load them onto huge low-loader lorries. Every night we went home with bloodstained hands, aching backs and ears that were numb caused by the continuous thumping noise from the compressed-air operated jack-hammers. There were no gloves or ear plugs in those days. We laboured on the removal of these tram lines from Waterloo Road, along Princess Street, Shandwick Place and all the way to the Haymarket Railway Station whilst working adjacent to the thundering rattle of the huge Jack-Hammers. It was hard and bloody work, at times one would spend hours at a time bent-over making it almost impossible to stand upright again without holding onto something or some other person. After the first day we had both regretted leaving the job we had with Paddy Leonard, but unfortunately we could not go back to ask him for our jobs back, not after what we had done. The one consolation was that on this removal of the tram-line project we were getting very well paid and that's what it was all about.

Indifferent: 11

Marie and I were meeting each other every weekend inside the Excelsior dance hall after Tam and I had spent a few hours having a couple of pints of beer and playing a few games of darts. On a Wednesday night we would meet and spend the night sitting in the rear seats of some picture-house attempting to eat each other and after it was over we didn't even know what the movie was! She was a lovely girl and I liked her a lot and we appeared to be good for each other. She was a clever posh girl with no snobbish desires. There was only one thing that concerned me a lot and that was that Marie repeatedly invited me to come to her house to meet her parents. I was not prepared to even consider such an occasion. Marie was an only child and it was obvious that her parents who lived in Upper Grey Street in the posh Newington area of Edinburgh were extremely affluent. Her father was a solicitor who had offices at the west-end of Princess Street and Marie herself had attended a private school and was still sitting some exams and presently employed as a private secretary in another lawyers office in the west-end of Princess street. I personally did not have the confidence or the desire to meet her parents and I had certainly had no intention of ever taking her anywhere near Arthur Street. As usual, she was told and believed that I lived in the Pleasance. The lord only knows what Marie would have said or indeed do, if she ever found out that I was a labourer and not a promising Heating Engineer. Its not that I was ashamed of being a labourer after all it was honest and hard work but I had lied about being a qualified heating engineer and I was not ashamed of my parents but I was ashamed of living in the poor area of Arthur Street. However it was all in vain and the crunch came when one Wednesday evening after we had been to the movies she insisted that I must meet her parents now because she had informed them that she wanted us to get married. I was shocked and speechless. I was never ever aware that I had ever given Marie the impression that I would get married to her. I was twenty one years old and had nothing, getting married to Marie or any other girl was out of the question and certainly not an option. I tried to be as diplomatic as possible when I explained all this to her but after that incident things were not the same and eventually we decided to go our own way's and I have to say, I did miss her for a while and often wondered why she had to go and spoil everything.

Tam Leonard and I were now working for Scottish Gas digging the huge trenches for new gas mains pipes that were being laid throughout Edinburgh. It was about this time that I had come up with the idea that instead of hanging around the pubs at the weekends drinking pints of beer and playing darts. We should be hanging around the lounges of the smart hotels in Princess Street.

Instead of drinking large vulgar big pints of beer, we should be drinking delicate small glasses of beer and mixing with the silver haired lonely mature ladies. My plan was that by mixing with the privileged minority of middle-aged or elderly prosperous widows in these posh lounges in the posh hotels in Princess Street, perhaps we could benefit from such an activity. Perhaps we could attract the attention of some lonesome mature and wealthy widows that we could charm and satisfy. Perhaps we could make ourselves indispensable to these middle-aged lonely rich widows and marry them. Perhaps one could live a life of reasonable luxury until the dear elderly wife departs this life and leaves us her entire prosperous estate and then, the world is your oyster to enjoy. I managed to convince Tam that it was worth pursuing. One Friday night, both dressed immaculately and in our best behaviour we ventured into our first encounter pursuing elderly prosperous widows that frequented posh hotels in and around the Princess Street area of Edinburgh. The Waverly hotel was our first choice and although we met some interesting elderly ladies we were both reluctant to make a move so we ended up in Fairley's dance hall. On the Saturday night we spent a few hours in the Scotsman Hotel but once more ended up in the Excelsior dance hall. The following weekend we spent hours in both the posh lounges of the George and Carlton hotel and this pursuit of striving to encounter, entertain and satisfy some mature wealthy widows and eventually become the recipient of their fortunes, was proving to be tiresome. We were both becoming very impatient and had expected to meet a beautiful middle-aged affluent widow on our first Friday night at the Waverly hotel, so It was not happening as planned. We did meet some very interesting elderly ladies but they were as sharp as razors and most probably would have taken everything that we had, then abandoned us. Eventually after a few weeks of prancing around posh hotel lounges like a couple of fairies sipping a tiny glass of beer and winking at elderly ladies with pink coloured hair who were drinking expensive pink gins and cocktails, we were back in the pubs drinking pints of beer, playing darts and going to a dance hall looking for a nice girl to have some fun with. We were still affected by poverty but enjoying our state of being poor and ourselves again. I have to say that the whole idea was mine and maybe my intentions were dishonourable because I was taking advantage of Tam Leonard's film star looks, perhaps that's why it just didn't work, but at least it was worth a try. Who knows.

One of my younger sisters, the one that was working and living in the Lodge at the top of the Mound off Princess Street arrived home one evening on one of her usual visits to see our parents. She had another couple of girl friends with her. One of the girls was a very attractive girl with long jet black hair and wearing a nurses uniform. I never normally paid much attention to my sisters girl-friends because I had three sisters and there were always girls in and out of our house.

121

As it turned out this particular girl was Irish and only lived a few streets away from us in Lower View Craigrow. The nurse and my sister were to become very good friends and the nurse became a regular visitor to our house. I had just got home from work one Saturday afternoon when my younger sister arrived with her friend the Irish nurse who's name was Kathleen and they were both riding bicycles. My young sister told our dad that Kathleen's bicycle was making a strange noise and asked our dad if he would have a look at it. Of course our dad was an expert on bicycle's and after he had went outside to inspect her bicycle he returned in a rage and asked them both if they had just come down Arthur Street on these bicycles. When they both confirmed that they had he read the riot act to them and suggested that the bicycles were not fit for purpose and should not be on the road, let alone be ridden down the dangerous extremely steep graded slope of Arthur Street. He confirmed that the brake pads on both bicycles were worn and inadequate. He spent the next two hours replacing the brake pads and cables on both the bicycles and essentially overhauling them. Then on completion suggested that I assist him in testing out both the bicycles new brake systems on the Arthur Street slopes.

Tam Leonard and I were working like two beavers building dams, we never ever turned down any offer of working weekends or overtime in the evening. We were labouring like a couple of slaves but still unable to open a saving account. It's not as if we were big spenders or heavy drinkers or gamblers. The only time we went out and spent our money was a Friday and Saturday night. We would have a few beers, a game of darts then off to the dance hall and that was all.. On the odd occasion if you managed to pick up a nice friendly good looking girl during the weekend at the dance hall and you fancied your chances, you take her to the movies on the Wednesday night. During the rest of the week we were normally to tired after digging trenches all day to do anything else except sleep and as I said previously, we still had no loose change.

We decided to go to London and make our fortunes. We packed in our jobs with the Gas Board and said our farewells to our families, friends and enemy's. The overnight bus from Edinburgh to London was the cheapest way to get there so that's what we did. We each bought ourselves a cheap brown coloured cardboard suitcase and filled them to the brim with our clothes then jumped on the all-night bus to London at St Andrews bus station Edinburgh. We arrived in the centre of London in mid August the next morning just after eight-o-clock and it looked as if it was going to be a beautiful day. We had no plans and had no idea what the hell we should be doing. Tam like myself was not a stranger to travelling, after all he had been in Korea with the army and I had been in Italy and Germany. But this was completely different, in the army everybody tells you what to do, how to do it and when to do it. The first thing we did was check our bulky suitcase's into the left-luggage department at the bus station. Then we checked a few B&Bs and soon realized that Scotsmen and Irishmen were not made welcome in many of them and that the ones that did, were far too expensive. We asked a few people where the Labour Exchange was, but nobody seemed to know what the hell we were talking about. Before we were aware of it, our first day in London looking for our fortune was over, it was getting dark we had achieved nothing and we had nowhere to sleep. After a pint of beer and a meat pie with chips, we stumbled across an all-night cinema. We purchased two of the cheapest tickets and found ourselves sitting in the front row. The screen was so high-up in front of us that one would have had to lay flat on the floor to view the picture on the screen. By the time we had watched the movies for the second time we both had very sore necks. It must have been getting very late when we managed to creep quietly and secretly up to the back row where we found twin seats that must have been for courting couples. Very swiftly we claimed a couple of them and managed to get some sleep before an attendant asked to check our tickets and escorted us out of the cinema. We had managed to stay in the all-night cinema for over five hours so we were back on the streets of London just as the daily newspapers were being thrown in their bundles at closed doors of the newsagent shops around Five-O-clock in the morning.

Once more we were carrying our luggage in our left hand, in our right hand, on our shoulders and heads whilst we staggered along the road to Wolverhampton.

We acquired a few newspapers, eventually found a cafe that was just opening and purchased bacon rolls and mugs of tea for our breakfast. We scanned the newspapers that we had come across hoping to find some adverts for vacancies but the only jobs advertised were for waiters, chefs and hotel porters and this type of work was not on our resume We eventually found Kings Cross railway station and managed to get a wash in the gents toilet. That night it was back to the all-night cinema and we would remain there until we were escorted out of the premises again. After wandering around the streets of London all day looking for contractors who were digging up the streets, digging trenches and enquiring for work, it was a pie with chips washed down with a pint of beer than back to the all-night cinema. During the night and after we had promoted ourselves again to the rear seats, I was molested by a guy who sat down beside me, well what I should say is a guy tried to molest me by groping me, anyway that night we didn't wait to be thrown out I got a hold of Tam and we both swiftly headed for the exit door and never returned to that all-night cinema. We decided that perhaps by going to the all-night cinema night after night we were sending out the wrong message to these would be homosexuals and paedophiles who were obviously lurking in the dark waiting for us. What I couldn't understand was why the paedophile had groped me!! why hadn't he gone after Tam the one with that looks like a film star! From that night on, not only did we wash ourselves in the gents toilet at Kings Cross railway station every day, we spent the night in the waiting room.

We eventually decided to collect our suitcases and check into a B&B so that we could get a good nights sleep, a shower and shave. That night in our expensive bed & breakfast whilst trying to decide what to do Tam suddenly suggested that perhaps we should get out of London and try Wolverhampton because he had an Aunt living there. We counted our money and decided that we certainly did not have enough to spend on buses or trains to Wolverhampton. However we had to do something so we decided to hitchhike to Wolverhampton and perhaps his Aunts husband would be able to get us some work. Tam's Aunt was his mothers sister who was also Irish and was married to an Irishman, however Tam had never met his Aunt's husband and had no idea what he did for a living, but we both assumed that like Tam's dad, his Aunts husband must be working in the construction building industry and be a ganger in charge of a bunch of labourers. We had no idea how far it was to Wolverhampton or in which direction we should be going and neither did our Landlord. In the morning, carrying our cumbersome suitcases and not even knowing in which direction we should be going, we left our B&B. Eventually we spoke to a couple of traffic cops who suggested that we take a local council bus that would get us out of London and drop us off in the general direction of Wolverhampton. They also confirmed the identification number of the bus, where we should go to get that bus and that it was approximately one hundred and fifty miles from London to Wolverhampton. Sure enough the local bus took us to its terminal stop on the outskirts of the big city. The bus conductor and driver had written down on a piece of paper the road reference numbers that we have to keep to in our efforts to get lifts to Wolverhampton. We must have looked like a couple of reckless salesmen carrying suitcases and strolling down a highway that had no pedestrian pavements or even a grass verge to walk on. Nearly every vehicle that ignored our hands out sign for a lift gave us a loud blast on their horns indicating that we should get the hell out off the bloody way! On the first day we must have walked for hours carrying our suitcases in the left hand then the right hand on our heads and even cradled in both our arms before the first vehicle stopped. The driver of the lorry shouted down from his cab. "Where the hell are you people going?" When we told him he said he could only take us a few miles up the road before he branches off. We could hardly climb up onto his empty flatbed lorry and by the time we got ourselves reasonably comfortable, it was time to climb back down again. We got a few more lifts but each time it was only for a dozen or so miles. That night we slept in what appeared to have been at one time a bus shelter but was now derelict. We were off walking at the crack of dawn and it was lunch time before we got our first lift. It was nothing short of a miracle that we were not killed by the huge vehicles that passed us as we staggered along the highway that had no grass verge to walk on. Once the traffic got quiet and it was not light enough for us to be seen by vehicles approaching us from behind, we slept in a field that night still fully clothed. We got a few lifts in lorries first thing in the morning, but it appeared that we were the only two people in the world going to Wolverhampton. Late in the afternoon a small van stopped. I was squatting in the back with both the suitcases and Tam was sitting in the front with the driver. I noticed by the tools and material that it was a plumbers van. Then I noticed a few bars of jointing solder and I knew that this jointing solder had a good value at any scrap merchants and of course we were now seriously financially embarrassed. I picked up a couple of the bars of jointing solder, bent them and was trying to get them into my pocket when the driver must have hit the brakes of the van. I was sent skidding up the van with both the suitcases into the back of the two seats. The young driver jumped out of the van and within seconds had opened up both doors at the rear of the van. He shouted. "Hey mate, what the hell are you doing with my solder?" I realized immediately that he must have seen me in his rear view mirror. Before I could reply he said. "I think you should get out of the van and bring the luggage with you". Tam was still sitting in the front of the van as I was struggling to get out, so I shouted at him to also get out and give me some help. The driver asked me again. "What were you doing with the solder?". I explained that I was an apprentice heating engineer and that I was just testing it by bending it to see it was jointing solder or not. He ignored my explanation and told Tam and I to get the suitcases out of his van and asked me again. "What have you done with my solder?" I looked and found the two bars of solder that I had bent, climbed back into the van, retrieved them and handed them to him. He threw them back into the rear of the van and said. "You were trying to steal them weren't you?" I strenuously denied it. He closed the vans rear doors and drove away leaving Tam and I with both of our suitcases standing at the edge of the road. We commenced our trekking in complete silence as Tam was not very pleased about me getting us thrown off the van. We laboriously walked until we could walk no longer. It was getting dark when we both ceased moving and opened a gate that led us into field. We spotted a small cluster of trees and decided to rest beneath the foliage. As we were getting ourselves settled down we discovered that there was some fruit scattered on the grass under the trees. By the size and shape, we guessed that they were crab apples and the taste confirmed that, so we munched on them until we both fell asleep shattered and our bellies full of crab apples. In the morning, we discovered that the remaining crab apples scattered on the grass around us were crawling with diminutive grubs. Tiny maggots were wriggling in and out of the holes in the apples, we just gazed at each other with opened mouths. We spotted the farm house and decided we would seek some assistance. Before we reached the actual farm house the door opened and a dog ran towards us barking profusely but skidded to halt before it reached us. I think we both silently thanked the lord that it was not a ferocious and violent dog. Someone shouted. "What do you people want, this is private property, now clear off?" The dog started barking again. When we both took our eyes of the dog. There was an elderly man standing in the doorway looking very agitated and angry. I asked him. "We are hitch-hiking to Wolverhampton, are we on the correct road". He replied. "Wolverhampton's about forty miles up that road, now be off with you" The dog started barking again. After a protracted silence I asked. "Could you let us have a drink of water?" His instant reply was. "Now, I will not tell you again, be off with you or I will call the police". Without another word being spoken by either party, Tam and I turned around and wearily wandered away down the track towards the road that would eventually take us too Wolverhampton.

Once more we were carrying our luggage in our left hand, right hand, on our shoulders, and head whilst we staggered along the road to Wolverhampton at the same time as trying to thumb a lift. At times we were being pivoted and buffeted by the draught of cold air swirling around us every time a huge vehicle shot past us. At times I honestly thought that we would be drawn into the side of one of these lorries and crumpled to death. We eventually stopped to have a rest and estimated that we had walked about ten miles therefore we were now about thirty miles outside Wolverhampton.   In spite of our pain and present circumstances, there was a certain amount of blissful satisfaction in that fact. Eventually an elderly couple in a car stopped and it was immediately obvious that they felt very sorry for us and the predicament we were in. In spite of the bulk of both our suitcases compared to the size of their small car they still decided to give us a lift. Tam and myself managed to get one suitcase in their car boot and the other one on our knees as we sat in the rear of the car. An hour later they dropped us off in Wolverhampton outside a local bus station. I do believe that we caught the last bus that evening that would drop us of near Burton Road, Tams Aunty lived in number 77.

We both had higher-purchase accounts with Burtons the Tailor's in Edinburgh, hence the reason it was easy for him to remember the address. It was over ten years since he had last met with his Aunty Sarah in Edinburgh but had never met her husband, Paddy Finnin. Even in the darkness I could feel the apprehension oozing out of Tam as we approached number 77. The brass door name-plate confirmed "S. Finnin" so Tam pushed the door bell. There

126

was no response and I had to persuade Tam to push it again and again. A female voice shouted from above our head. "Who is that?" We both stepped back and away from the door and looked up. A women in a white dressing gown or night shirt was hanging out of an upstairs window. Tam shouted. "It's me Aunty Sarah, Tully". "Tully, Tully who?" Was the women's response. "Tully Leonard. Tully Leonard from Edinburgh". "In the name of God what's wrong? Wait, wait now" Was his Aunty Sarah's instant reply. We heard the window being closed, then after a few minutes a light went on downstairs and the door was opened. The women who opened the door asked. "In the name of God, what has happened, what is wrong?" We both staggered into the house as the women had indicated we should. Tully [Tam] was somewhat incoherent as he tried to explain. "Nothing's wrong Aunt Sahara, nothing, we were just passing" Aunty Sarah stopped him in mid speech by suggesting. "Just passing is it, come sit down, sit down". I kept very quiet and allowed Tully to spin the entire sorry story. In the middle of the sorry story, I assumed it was Aunt Sahara's husband, Tully's uncle, Paddy Finnin joined us. We must have looked like two vagrant's as we had not washed, or shaved for a couple of days. Tully told them a tall story about us being robbed in London as I also listened eagerly. It was difficult to tell if the they believed what he was saying because they just kept looking at each other, then back at us. Eventually Aunty Sahara took us upstairs and into a double bedroom with a double bed and suggested. "You will have to share this room. Now, just wait, just wait now". She disappeared then re-appeared with two large bath towels and further explained. "Now, the bathroom is there". She pointed to another door in the small hallway just outside the bedroom, then further suggested. "You must both have a nice shower before you go to bed. Would you like a sandwich and a cup of tea before we all bed down for the night?" We both looked at each other and once more before we could reply, she said. "I'll go and make some sandwiches, these clothes you are wearing, bring them down, they can go in the washing machine, come now".

After showering, Tully's feet were still foul-smelling as was his socks and shoes. We opened the bedroom window and left the shoes and socks on the sill. I had spotted some powder in the bathroom to we dowsed both his feet with it then he wrapped them in a clean pair of my socks. We dressed ourselves again in fresh clothes and tiptoed back down-stairs with our bundles of dirty clothes. Aunty Sarah confirmed. "Your uncle Sean has gone to bed because he has to work on Saturday mornings. I don't work Saturdays at all. So after some lunch tomorrow, we will decide what to do next" This was the first indication that we had that it was very early Saturday morning, we had been on the road for exactly one week. When we got to bed I pulled Tully's feet over the top of the wooden bed rest at the bottom of the bed so that his feet hang out of the sheets and out off the bed.

Tam had decided that he would have to use his christened name Tully, as opposed to Tam, as long as we lived with his Aunty Sarah. Saturday was the longest day in my life. Tully had told them that we lost all our money in London when we were robbed. On the Saturday afternoon after his uncle Sean had returned from his work in an office in a factory that produced soap, we sat down to our first beautiful meal in weeks. Both his Aunty Sarah and uncle Sean started asking all the obvious questions, how did it happen, where did it happen and did we report it to the police. Our beautiful meal was being ruined, not by the obvious questions, but by Tully's inadequate and witless answers. Whilst our lovely lunch was being ruined, it was very obvious to me that they did not believe him and told us that after Sunday morning mass tomorrow, they were going to purchase for us to single rail tickets to Edinburgh. We arrived back in Edinburgh not only bankrupt but now in debt after spending a few weeks in London where we went to make our fortune. We were in debt and disgraced. On the Tuesday morning we went direct to the Gas Board and after some consideration and deliberation, they agreed to reinstate us. Three weeks later, and after digging a few more miles of deep trenches throughout the streets of Edinburgh for the Scottish Gas Board, we sent a postal order to Tully's Uncle Sean and Aunt Sarah to repay them the cost of our two rail tickets.

Indifferent: 12

No one in my family ever questioned the fact that I had wasted over three years serving my time as an apprentice heating engineer /plumber The irony of it was, that I never ever gave it a second thought myself because I was indifferent. I was earning good money working with the Scottish Gas Board digging their trenches. I now had four different suits of clothing and was about to get measured by Burtons the Tailor's for my fifth. Talking about clothes, I had noticed that the Irish girl, Kathleen McAuley was no longer wearing a nurses uniform. When I asked her why one evening when she was in our house with my wee sister, she mentioned something about it having very little remuneration. She also confirmed that she was now working in a hotel as a waitress and earning twice as much. I also noticed again how slim and very attractive she was and thought how stunning she would look if only she would wear a better quality of clothes.

Hugh my big brother was spending more and more time staying overnight with us, it appeared that he and his wife Anne were always arguing and falling out. Eventually, they separated and ultimately divorced. I was now sharing a bed with him and our wee brother. One Saturday night after the usual three or four pints of beer and a few games of darts, the three of us, Tam Leonard, Hugh and myself ended up in Fairlie's dance hall at the top of Leith Walk. Kathleen McAuley, my sister and a few other girl friends of theirs were also there. It was getting late and near the time for the last waltz. Hugh had already met up with a girl that he was seeing home and had already left the dance-hall. Tam and I met up again after a dance and he was in a furious mood calling some girl all the bitches under the sun. I asked him. "What's the problem, who's the bitch that's upset you?" "That Irish bitch McAuley who goes around with your wee sister. I have just danced with her, asked her home and the stupid little bitch refused me". I have to say that I was surprised, because very few girls ever refuse to go home with the dashing Tam Leonard. I was actually lost for words, so made no response as Tam rushed off as soon as the next dance was announced. I looked over to the group where Kathleen McAuley was standing talking to my sister and a few other girls and sauntered over towards her and she smiled at me when she noticed me. I asked her. "Would you like to dance Kathleen" "Sure, that would be nice". As we were dancing Kathleen smiled into my face and asked me. "You never dance with me, so why to-night?" Before I could reply she continued. "Even your friend Tam Leonard danced with me to-night, what are you two up too?". I looked at her and she was still smiling and looked really adorable. I thought, thank god you refused to let Tam Leonard walk you home. The thought of him sexually romancing her in some staircase made me shiver a little. I replied. "We, are not up to anything, why would you think that?" "Oh, it's just that we have all been coming here for a considerable time now and you guys have never ever asked any of us to dance". "Well, that's true, that's because I never dance with my sister either". "I'm not your sister". Was her instant reply. "I know, but It's like the same to me" Was my reply. We did not talk for a minute or two, then I said. "Tam Leonard has just told me that he asked to walk you home". She smiled and said. "Did he now?" I just couldn't wait to ask. "Why did you say No". Without any hesitation Kathleen McAuley replied. "Because of his reputation and there are not many girls in this dance hall that don't know of his reputation". I said nothing for a few minutes, then replied. "That may be so, but there are not many girls in this dance hall that would not go home with him". She did not reply, just smiled. So I asked her. "If I were to ask to walk you home, would you say No". "Are you asking me if you can walk me home David Cassidy" "Yes, I am". "I would like that, yes, you can".

As we were walking up Leith Walk she stopped me and asked. "Do you want to know what your sister said when I told her you were walking me home?" I immediately asked. "Why did you have to tell her?" She looked at me in surprise, then replied. "She was in the cloakroom with me and asked me if I was going home with anyone. Do you want to know what she said?" I did not answer, so we walked in silence for a few minutes until she eventually told me that my sister was upset and had suggested that she should never have agreed to walk home with me. I have to say that I did feel a wee bit annoyed at my sisters attitude. When we got to the top of Leith Walk I was heading for the North Bridge as one would if going to Lower View Craigrow where she lived. Kathleen stopped me and explained that she was living in the Cockburn Hotel at the bottom of Cockburn Street where she works as a waitress. When we reached the Hotel we eventually stood in the dark doorway of a shop adjacent to the entrance of the Hotel. I have to admit that I was afraid to touch her and the thought of kissing her made me feel awkward because she was like family. Kathleen McAuley broke the silence. "You're very quiet, is it because you have a steady girlfriend?" "Who told you that I had a steady girl-friend?" Was my sharp response. She suddenly went quiet so I lifted my hand and brushed it against her face and she asked me. "Will you get angry again if I ask another question?" I had a feeling that she was smiling so I slipped my hands around her tiny waist and whispered. "I'm not angry and I don't have a girl friend and it was probably my sister who told you that I had a girl-friend". After a few seconds of silence, she said "Yes it was your sister who said you had a girlfriend before you went to London". We were both silent then I explained that I no longer had a girlfriend but did not go into any detail. She asked me why I didn't stay in London and

130

when I suggested that it was a long story she immediately asked me about Italy when I was in the army. I most certainly did not want to talk about Italy or my time in the Army so I decided to change the subject by suggesting. "You ask an awful lot of questions, now let me ask you. "I thought you were going to be a nurse". "Yes, I was a trainee nurse for three years but the pay was so poor that I had to get a proper job". "What work are you actually doing in the Cockburn that qualifies you for residency?" "I'm a waitress and we have to work late into the night some evenings and very early some mornings and the room and food is all part and partial to the job. The pay is good, the tips are great and I have my very own private room. Its good fun and I enjoy it. On my nights off I do whatever I want too, instead of having to study all night in preparation for exams". I thought about that for a second then replied. "But surely being a nurse is a very professional career like being a doctor. That must be better than being a waitress" "Yes I know, I truly wanted to be a nurse, but like your family we are also many and wages are important. Your sister told me that you were training to be an engineer?" "That's completely different because I had to go into the army". "So, why don't you finish your engineering course now that your out of the Army?" "I can't, because the company I was with will not take me back and anyway I'm twenty two years old and could not survive on an apprentice wage". We were silent again and once more I felt awkward so I pulled her gently towards me and we kissed. I no longer felt uneasy embracing and kissing this lovely girl whom I had previously considered as part of our family, like another sister. She whispered. "I should be getting in because I'm on breakfast duty in the morning and it's a very early rise. Thanks for walking me home, it was nice talking to you". I walked with her down to the Hotel Entrance. We both hesitated outside the main entrance until Kathleen pressed a bell for the night porter. Then smiling at me she said. "Well, thanks again David Cassidy, good-night". I felt awkward again and with a little lump in my throat I asked. "What are you doing tomorrow?". "Sunday, well I'm on duty until twelve-o-clock then normally I meet your sister and some of the other girls from the Lodge and we go for a walk in Princess Street Gardens, why?". "No, it's okay, I thought maybe we could meet and do something". "Oh, I would like that, it sounds a lot better than walking around the Mound with your sister" "What will you tell my sister". I asked. "Nothing, if you don't want me too, I just won't go to the Lodge to meet her". She replied "Okay what time will I meet you and where?". I enquired. "One-o-Clock. Here at this very corner". "Okay, see you tomorrow Kathleen but don't tell my sister that you're meeting me". "Okay David, if that's what you want". I waited until the night porter arrived to open the door before I headed home up Cockburn Street. I felt good and wandered slowly up to the top of Cockburn Street home, turned left down the Royal Mile, right down St Mary Street, up the Pleasance,

131

left down Arthur Street and turned right into Middle Arthur Place. In spite of the short walk, it was after one-o-clock on the Sunday morning when I got home. My two sisters, where already in their bed-settee. As I was undressing in the dark, someone asked me "Where's Hugh?" I was somewhat surprised as I thought they were both sleeping and I had been as quiet as a mouse. I whispered. "I don't know". I climbed into the bed beside my wee brother but could not sleep. Then I thought about Tam Leonard and smiled. What the hell should I tell him tomorrow.

Sunday morning and Hugh had not come home and because I was being seriously interrogated by my mother, I wandered across the street to the Leonard's the house. All three girls were prancing about in various stages of dress and undress. Paddy Leonard, their father was shouting at them to make themselves decent then suggested to me that I should go through to the bedroom and get Tam out of bed. Tam was already awake so I sat on the edge of his single bed. He asked me what happened to me last night as he did not see me outside the dance hall. I told him that I had left just before the end. He then asked me if I had got a lumber [Met a girl and walked her home] I confirmed that I did get a lumber. He then asked me if I had scored [had sex with the girl] I confirmed that I had not scored. Then we discussed his achievements. Off course he had got a lumber and yes he had scored. I thought to myself, *Tam you always get a Lumber and you nearly always score, but you didn't score last night with the Irish bitch, Kathleen McAuley! because I walked her home.* I changed the subject when I suggested that Hugh must have lumbered and scored last night because he had not come home. Tam said he knew that Hugh had got a lumber because he had spoke to Hugh before he left Fairlie's. That's when I told Tam. "By the way, I won't see you again today; I'm meeting the bird that I took home last night". "Why do you have a promise?" [A promise means a good possibility of having sex] Before I could respond he enquired further. "Does your promise have her own house?". I wanted to tell him then that I had walked Kathleen McAuley home last night and that's who I was meeting to-day, but instead, I ended up telling him a pack off lies. Then he said. "Okay, I will see you in the morning for work".

I was walking down Cockburn Street just before One-O-Clock and when I reached the bottom Kathleen McAuley was just coming out of the Cockburn Hotel. I was pleasantly stunned. She was dressed in a small dark two piece suit with a short skirt that showed sheen like nylons and black high heeled shoes. She looked stunning. She looked like one of the Hotels posh residents, as opposed to one of its waitress's. Her long shapely graceful legs looked just amazing and with her good looks she was just beautiful. She smiled and waved at me as soon as we made eye contact. We decided to go down the High Street and into the Kings Park. Half way down the High Street she asked me if she could take my arm. "Sure". I think I shouted because I felt wonderful having this long legged beauty hanging on to me. She certainly got some looks from the other guys that we passed. I could feel that she was a little bit uncomfortable with that aspect. She sort of slowed down a wee bit leaned in towards me and sort of whispered. "These high heeled shoes are not really for long walks. I should have put shoes on". I replied without hesitation "I don't agree, they look great, I mean, you look great". She smiled and confessed that that's why she wanted to hold on to my arm. She was afraid that she could slip and fall. [I was to be informed by Kathleen much later that she had borrowed the beautiful appealing two piece suit and high heel shoes from one of the other waitress's.]

When I turned to face him, Tam slammed a fist
into the left hand side of my face.

We spent all day in the park and I managed to find a couple of quiet places were we got some serious necking done and it was certainly improving. By the time the day was over our kissing was getting more savage. Our tongues were eventually twisting together so deep that I thought we were going to choke each other to death. We were sitting on park benches in the most isolated and remote areas in the Kings Park. As soon as anyone ventured anywhere near us, we had to move elsewhere because it was as if we could not keep our hands of each other. As we were kissing I could not keep my mind focused because the short skirt kept crawling further up her long shapely legs that were wrapped in these tanned silky nylons. Kathleen continually kept trying to pull the tiny skirt back down which was proving to be impossible. Eventually Kathleen suggested that it was time to go. I wanted to disagree because I could have spent the entire night here just admiring these long shapely legs, however before parting I did the next best thing. I made another date with this Irish beauty and she agreed to meet me at Fairlie's dance hall on the Friday night.

On the Friday night, Tam and I did our usual tour of the pubs playing darts and drinking a few pints of beer. We always had our last pint in the Black Bull Bar adjacent to Fairlie's dance hall. When the pub closed we would wander across the road into the dance hall. Once inside, Tam was off checking all the talent that was going to be available. I personally was only looking for the Irish beauty, Kathleen McAuley. We eventually found each other and made eye contact. Kathleen was standing with my wee sister and some other girls that also worked in the Lodge. Some guys approached them and they all appeared to disappear onto the dance floor to dance, except Kathleen. This was my cue, so I swiftly headed towards her. We had only danced for a few seconds when Kathleen McAuley informed me that this was the first time she had ever refused someone that had asked her to dance. She then confirmed that she felt dreadful and I could see by the expression on her face that she was genuinely upset about having to refuse the boy that had asked her to dance. I tried to make small of it by suggesting that we did have a date and she did smile. But I realized that this girl was so sincere and sensitive that I suggested to her that she would never have reason to do that again. She smiled and squeezed my left hand very tightly. After a couple of dances, I suggested to Kathleen that we should part company for a wee while and that she could spend some time with my sister and her other friends as I was about to seek out Tam Leonard. We parted and agreed to get together again soon and I suggested the next slow dance. When I caught up with Tam he was furious and demanded to know. "Why the hell are you dancing with that Irish bitch?" I was sincerely shocked at this verbal attack and said. "What's the hell is the matter with you? I can dance with who the hell I want". Before he could reply, Ann Murray, well Ann Cassidy, my brother Hugh's wife appeared beside us. "Hi, how are you doing brother-in-law? Hello Tully" Tam did not like be addressed as Tully and probably because he was already in a foul mood, he ignored her. The next dance was introduced and Tam was off. Ann asked me. "Is your big brother here" "No". Was my instant reply. She touched my arm, then asked me. "Are you going to give me a dance". We danced and it was awful. She reiterated the problems between her and Hugh whilst suggesting that she couldn't wait to be divorced yet snuggling in closer to me.

After the dance I got as far away as possible from my brothers wife and couldn't decide if I should seek out Tam and find out exactly what his problem is or find the Irish beauty and Kathleen McAuley won. Whilst dancing with Kathleen I had decided that I was not going to mention the incident with Tam because I didn't want her to get involved, she was far to sensitive to be involved in this nonsense. We were sitting at a table in the restaurant bar having a laugh and a soft drink when without any warning Tam was standing at our table. Kathleen greeted him, he completely ignored her and said to me. "Id like a word with you". He was now pointing one of his fingers directly at my face. I asked. "What is it about". He lifted his right hand waved his fore finger, then in a very low voice said. "Over here". He walked away, so I eventually followed him. We were walking towards the cloakrooms and the exit doors out into the street when he suddenly stopped. I actually bumped into his back. When he turned around his face was scarlet and he growled at me. "I think you're taking the piss out of me". I was shocked. We were like brothers. I asked him. "What the hell is the matter with you?". His reply was. "Why the hell are you suddenly so interested in that Irish bitch?". "Okay Tam, that's it. I'm out of here, I'm not going to listen to any more shit from you". I turned to walk away when he grabbed my left arm and whispered with a scowl. "I have a good mind to smack you in the mouth". I was speechless and felt the anger boiling up inside me and asked him. "You should what?" "You heard me". I took my time in answering, then suggested. "I would not advise you to try that. You know something Tam, you're f****** sick". He took me by surprise when he swiftly grabbed a lapel of my suit and with a snarl said. "That's it, outside". I pulled myself free from his grip and glanced back towards Kathleen McAuley who was sitting watching us. I turned around again to ask Tam if he was serious but he was already heading for the door. I turned and looked at Kathleen McAuley again, then walked back over to her. Before I could say anything she asked. "Why are you two arguing?" "We have a wee problem that we have to sort out so I have to go. I'll be in touch".

I headed for the door and left the dance hall. Tam was already standing outside on Leith Street and as soon as I approached him he asked me. "Where do you want to do this". "I don't care, somewhere quiet, down their". I pointed down towards the back entrance into Waverly Railway Station. Without another word we both walked quickly down the quiet lonely deserted street. Within a few minutes we were at the bottom of the steps leading up to the railway station. As I turned to face him, Tam slammed a fist into the left hand side of my face and head. I staggered sideways a good six, seven, feet but managed to stay on my feet. When I pulled myself together and looked across at him he was still standing in the same place with his fists at the ready. I thought you bastard, that's your first mistake. I knew that if he had followed that punch up and had went after me throwing a few more punches, he would have been victorious and that would have been the end of it and this encounter would have been all over. He obviously lacked the killer instinct. I ran at him like a mad bull and just before impact bent my head down and smashed into his arms and through onto his chest forcing him to stagger backwards. He tried to knee me, but I was to high up on his chest. I got my arms round his hips as he started throwing punches into my back and neck. I twisted him around in a circle until he tripped and went crashing down onto the hard cobbled ground taking me with him. He was now flat on his back and I very quickly straddled him like a horse. I instantly started pounding my fists into his head, face and ears. I continued to punch both my clenched fists into his head without thought or hesitation. He did not or could not retaliate so I stopped beating into him and leaped up onto my feet. Tam remained flat on the ground moaning and made no effort to get up. I walked over to him looked down at him and asked him. "Are you okay? Why don't you get up?" He moaned again then rolled onto his side. I had to practically kneel down to hear what he was saying and at the same time was concerned that he was trying to trick me, then he said. "It's my back, for Christ sake help me up you dirty b******, what kind of way is that to fight?".

After I helped him up and walked him over to the wall, he brushed me off and pushed me away from him whilst telling me. "I'm okay, I'm alright, oh, shit. I think my nose is broken and I'm bleeding". "So am I". I groaned. He responded with. "F*** you. You dirty b******. We both walked over to the steps leading up to the pedestrian bridge over the railway lines and had a smoke. Tam was bleeding a wee bit more than I was and I thought it was mostly from his nose, so I suggested. "You should try and keep your head back". He moaned through a cough saying. "I'm smoking for Christ sake". We did eventually started walking home and all Tam appeared to be concerned about was his nose because he was convinced that I had broken it. Of course I knew that what he was really worried about was his good-looks. I suggested to him that we call into my house and let my father have a look at it because he's seen a few broken nose's in his days. If its broken, he will know what to do, if its not broken he will soon clean it up and stop the bleeding. We were both very quiet for a wee while then Tam asked me. "What are we going to say happened?". I was quick to suggest. "We will tell him that we got involved in a fight". "Ye, okay, let's do that, that sounds good and you're right, your old man will know what to do if my nose is broken".

My father was in bed, however he got up when I asked him if he could have a look at Tam's nose. It was not broken. My mother was suddenly awake and got herself into a bit of a state until my father convinced her that everything was okay and that she should go back to sleep. My mother was out of bed and fussing about whilst questioning me and Tam about why we got into a fight, why didn't any anybody stop it and where were the police. My dad lost his temper and told her. "Shst woman and go and make a pot off tea". He fixed Tam up real good and stopped the bleeding from his nose. He said that there was not much he could do about my left ear and suggested that the guy that hit me must have been wearing a ring. I glanced over at Tam as he covered his right hand with his left.

We were both at work as usual on the Saturday morning and at twelve-o-clock when we stopped, we went for our usual couple of pints of beer and a game of darts before we went home for lunch. Not once did we mention our argument, skirmish or Kathleen McAuley's name. Between us, it was as if it didn't happen. Saturday evening at six-o-clock Tam tapped on our kitchen window and we were off on our normal pup crawl. We would have a few pints of beer a couple of games of darts and eventually at ten-0-clock in the evening when the pubs closed, it was time to go to Fairlie's dance hall to sort the girls out. Tam's nose was still a bit swollen, but he knew that it would take more than a swollen nose to distract his good-looks. Hugh was no longer with us as we was going steady with his new girl-friend that he had met. I had told him about Ann, his wife being in Fairlie's dance hall but he was uninterested. I met-up and danced with Kathleen McAuley as soon as it was possible. She was already aware that something had happened on the Friday night but I told her the same as we had told my parents and everyone else that asked us what had happened and where did we get our battle scars. We told them that we had got involved in a fight with two other guys.

As I walked Kathleen home to the Cockburn Hotel that Saturday night I was of the opinion that she wanted to know a wee bit more about what had happened between Tam Leonard and myself. I was reluctant to disclose any additional information because I was of the opinion that this girl would not take kindly to the actual truth. I do believe that if she found out what had really happened, she would be so angry and ashamed that she would have nothing further to do with both myself and Tam Leonard so I deliberately and success-fully changed the subject. I suggested to her that most of the girls that worked and lived in the Lodge where my sister also worked, were Irish. She smiled at me then suggested that she had never thought about that, but now that I had mentioned it, it was true, then after a few minutes of silence she asked. "Don't you like Irish girls David Cassidy?". I immediately said. "Of course I do, I like you don't I?. "Well now, listen to yourself. Well I like you too". Kathleen went on to explain further that like herself and my younger sister, these other Irish girls come from big families and of course if they can get work that includes accommodation, a salary and meals included then the whole family will benefit. I was very impressed with this girls attitude, obvious concern and understand-ing of others and after a few minutes walking silently together holding hands, I said. "You would have been the perfect nurse". She leaned her head against my shoulder and whispered. "Oh, thank you".

When we arrived at the Cockburn Hotel, we both automatically wandered up into the very same darkened shop doorway adjacent to the hotel, only this time, I was more sure of myself. I asked Kathleen if she was on breakfast-duty and when she whispered. "No" I very gently pulled her closer to me and kissed her and suggested that there should be no rush for her to go into the hotel. We nearly chocked each other to death with our twisting tongue's in each other's mouth's and often had to stop, just to catch a breath of fresh air. Every time my hands wandered they were slapped. On the occasions that I ignored the slap and there were a few, Kathleen would just freeze and then gently pull herself free and step away from me without saying a word then I was the one that had to apolo-gise. When I had to apologised for tenth time she stepped back in close to me again and counter-apologised and whispered that she had never ever been with a boy. She didn't have to slap my hand again that night because I felt guilty and should have known better, this girl was different and of course I was indifferent! I suddenly realized that I would have to be very careful with Kathleen McAuley if I wanted to continue seeing her.

We were spending every weekend together and even started going to the movies on a Wednesday night. Then we realized that we could spend a lot more time together at the weekend if we went to the movies at seven-o-clock on a Friday night instead of meeting each other in Fairlie's dance hall at ten-o-clock at night. So we would go to the movies on a Friday evening and purchase two of the most expensive tickets that allowed us to sit at the rear and tongue twist each other all night. We both agreed that we were wasting our money because we never ever knew what the picture that was on show was all about, however, we also agreed that it was worth it. Tam Leonard was not at all pleased about the way our relationship was developing because he was now having to do the pub crawl at weekends on his own. My brother Hugh was now divorced and had already met the new love of his life and she was indeed a breath-of-fresh-air compared to his ex wife, Ann.

Indifferent: 13

Kathleen McAuley and myself had been courting now for over six months and both of our families were now aware of it. Kathleen was a regular visitor to our house and was already accepted as part of our family by both my parents. I eventually met Kathleen's parents and realized immediately that Kathleen had got her good-looks from her mother who was an extremely handsome women. Mr & Mrs McAuley were both Irish, practising Catholics and had brought their family up accordingly. They had three other daughters and a wee boy named Charlie. Two of their daughters, Mary the oldest and Rita the second oldest were both already married, each had one child and lived in Edinburgh with their respective husbands. The youngest and third daughter was working and living in Glasgow and her name was Eileen. The respective family's attended mass every Sunday morning at St Patrick's chapel in the Cowgate. Mr McAuley was a ganger in the building industry. The McAuley children were all born in Scotland except Kathleen who was born in Eire whilst her mother was on holiday in Ireland visiting her parents.

After we had been courting for nearly a year we decided to get engaged. I was shocked and felt insulted when Kathleen informed me that her parents were totally opposed to our engagement. I was unprepared for this attitude because I had never considered the religious aspect of our relationship, however when Kathleen informed me of her parents attitude, I was furious. In spite of the fact that I knew that Kathleen's parents were Irish Catholics and that the entire family were churchgoers, I couldn't understand why they would not allow me to consider marrying their daughter because I was a non-catholic. This was a very serious situation that I suddenly found myself in because I had never contemplated the religious factor. I was adamant that her parents had no right to denounce me in this way and was prepared to challenge their decision. That was until Kathleen agreed to marry me against her parents wishes and suggested that we get married in a register office. Religion was never an important issue for me or indeed for my family, whereas for Kathleen and her entire family it was sacred. I discussed it in depth with Kathleen and my parents and eventually with Kathleen parents and it was soon obvious that in order for me to get Kathleen's parents blessings, I would have to marry their daughter in a Catholic church. However, in order for me to marry Kathleen in a Catholic church, I would have to become a catholic. My parents adored Kathleen and had already accepted her as a future daughter-in-law and I also loved her deeply, therefore I agreed and so we were engaged. Mr & Mrs McAuley arranged a party in their home to celebrate our engagement and my passage into catholism. The party was a huge success in spite of the fact

139

that neither of our parents had ever met each other previously. It was just both of our families all getting together for the first time, a huge family gathering that bonded us all together and we all had a wonderful time

I eventually had to go for lessons to St. Patrick's Church to be taught the basic religious aspects of the Catholic faith. My tutor was a huge Irish priest by the name of father Gallagher and he looked more like a heavyweight boxer, than a man of God. I can only say that we tolerated each other, in the name of God !. I remember telling him one evening that I had a problem with the Virgin Mary having a baby? and Jesus walking on water and feeding all these people with only a few loafs of bread, a couple fish and turning the water into wine. He shook his head and crossed his arms over his huge chest and after a protracted silence and with a smile on his face he whispered "You have no faith, you're a heathen. Be off with you and go home, that will be enough for this evening and may God have mercy on your soul". Kathleen always accompanied me when I went to the chapel for my lessons which was twice a week in the evening. She would wait patiently inside the church probably constantly praying for me while the priest and I were isolated in a small anti room. Whilst walking Kathleen home that night as usual, I was telling her what had happened and what father Gallagher had said to me. Kathleen stopped us walking and whispered. "I have faith in you, I also have enough faith for both off us, please don't get angry". I explained that I was not angry and that I was of the opinion that father Gallagher was probably joking with me because he winked at me before he sent me away. Whilst we were kissing each other good-night, I asked Kathleen. "How on earth were all these amazing miracles performed". She touched my lips and whispered. "You're a heathen but I love you, now go home, that will be enough for this evening".

We were married on the 28th December 1957 in St Patrick's church in the Cowgate, on a freezing winter's day. We had a reception in a small hall that Kathleen's parents had rented from the church. Once more it was our immediate families, except for a few girl friends of Kathleen's and a few friends of mine including the Leonard's. We had rented a room in a house on Loganlee Road in Piershill, our land lady was a middle aged widow and we shared her lounge, kitchen and bathroom. Our very first romantic honeymoon night in our bedroom in Loganlee Road Piershill Edinburgh was ruined when early on the morning after our wedding my brother Hugh arrived to tell me that our Dad had been rushed into hospital so I leapt out of my red-hot bed. My brand new wife was insisting that she accompanies me, however I managed to convince her to remain at home and keep our bed warm. My big brother Hugh and I were soon on our way to the Edinburgh Royal Infirmary Hospital and I have to say that there was not a direct all night bus service, therefore we had to change buses several times before we reached the hospital. As it turned out it was it was a

140

temporary urinary problem. My Dad who was not a drinking man had obviously drank a few beers too many at the wedding reception and during the night he was unable to pass urine and was rushed into hospital. After this had been diagnosed and a catheter had been inserted he was eventually discharged.

Kathleen had talked me into going back to train as a Heating Engineer. So with the help of the union I was eventually employed by R. Copeland, Plumbers & Electricians who's shop was located on the Pleasance at the top of Arthur Street. The agreement was that once J & R Adams had confirmed that I had already served four years of my apprenticeship. I would be allowed to serve out the remainder of my apprenticeship with Copeland Plumbers & Electricians. However, the union insisted that I must re-commence my apprenticeship as a third year apprentice because of the lapse of time I had been active in the trade. Therefore I would have to serve a further two years apprenticeship before my credentials would be acceptable. I immediately decided that it was financially impossible and therefore unacceptable. I was a 23 years old married man and would be earning less than Four pounds a week. Kathleen who was now working for Findlay's the Chemists shop in Clark Street was earning twice as much as that, insisted and pleaded with me to accept the conditions and complete my apprenticeship. Kathleen's concept was that providing we don't have any babies for the next two years, we would manage. I agreed and I have to say that I would never have completed my apprenticeship if my wife had not convinced and supported me. During the very long two years of my apprenticeship not only did she support me financially, but with lovingly care and affection and at one time we seriously discussed the possibility of emigrating to Australia once I was qualified.

Kathleen had never drank an alcoholic drink in her entire life, unlike myself who usually drank three or four pints of beer every Friday and Saturday night. Now that I was a married man and an apprentice, I abstained and had none. We just had enough money to pay our rent, purchase our food and pay the bus fares for us both going and returning home from work. I didn't miss the beer, in fact we were so much in love we just wanted to be with each other all the time. I always felt that Kathleen deserved a lot more than what she had. She deserved to have nicer clothes for everyday use because on special occasion when she wore what she called her good clothes, she looked spectacular. However, with her natural Irish dark hair and good looks she always looked lovely. She was indeed a lovely caring person and should have been the one to complete her nursing career as opposed to me finishing my apprenticeship.

Our landlady insisted on doing all the cooking which displeased Kathleen somewhat because by the time we both got home from work she would have the evening meal for the three of us prepared and cooked. We never ever seemed to

141

be able to spend much time together on our own. The three of us dined together and also shared the living room together in the evening and if we ever left early to go to our bedroom for a wee bit of privacy, within ten minutes, there would be a tap tap on our bedroom door and it would be our landlady with a tray of tea and biscuit's. She had a small pedigree dog and one very cold and stormy evening, I made the terrible mistake off offering to take the dog for its nightly walk. That ended up being my task every night and I hated it with a passion, especially when it was wet, windy and cold. I only worked Saturday morning but Kathleen worked all day Saturday's until 1800 hours. By the time she got home on a Saturday night our Landlady as usual had cooked our meal. On a couple of occasions if the buses were running late or Kathleen had just missed her bus the landlady would insist that we had our meal and leave Kathleen's in the oven. Kathleen would be very upset, but too kind a person to object and we both failed to even attempt to make any changes in spite of the fact that it was not what we wanted. We only wanted to do our own thing and wanted to do it as much as possible together, but it was not to be.

After being married for only four months, Kathleen was pregnant and of course we were both not that surprised and should have known better because we both relied on Kathleen's full time salary. In spite of that we were both delighted and decided that we had time to work something out and we would. When Kathleen was nine weeks pregnant and at her work at Findlay's Chemist she was suddenly very unwell and was sent home. By the time I got home that evening she was in bed and looked dreadful. We were both very naive because I went to work as usual the next morning leaving Kathleen asleep in bed. As it turned out Kathleen was in a state of comatose and apparently at death's door. Thank God our intrusively inquisitive landlady phoned the emergency 999. Kathleen was rushed to Brunsfield Hospital where it was eventually confirmed that she had an Ectopic Pregnancy. Our baby was growing outside the womb. Not only did we loose the baby, Kathleen was as near to death as she would ever be. After spending two weeks in hospital and three weeks convalescent she was allowed to come home to Loganlee Road in Piershill a very sad and fragile twenty two year old lovely young girl. These were bad sad times for us because without Kathleen's salary, I was eventually unable to pay the rent for our room and our landlady very kindly allowed me to go into debt. To make matters worse, Findlay's the Chemist had been unable to keep Kathleen's job open for her and had to employ a replacement. After a week or so Kathleen applied for and was interviewed for a job in a photography shop and eventually started working in Murray Donald's on Dalry Road in the Haymarket area of Edinburgh. Murray Donald the photographer attended to weddings and other functions. Kathleen ran the shop organizing peoples portraits, the development of photographic

142

negatives and selling cameras and other photographic equipment. Ultimately we had paid our dear, caring, compassionate landlady the unpaid rent that we were in debt to her but because she was now even more involved in our every day lives, we decided we just had to make a move. Eventually through one of Kathleen's customers, Kathleen found us another room in a cottage at Rosebank Cottages in Fountainbridge. It was fantastic, we moved in immediately to our decent sized bedroom with its own coal fire and fireplace which meant that we had a lot more privacy and could make toast whenever we had the fire on. We had to share the kitchen and bathroom but at least we were left alone to get on with our own cooking, eat what we wanted and when we wanted. They were a middle aged couple with no family. Mabel, our landlady and Harry her husband both worked for Jenners the huge posh shop in Princess Street. In the evening after our meal we would sit by our fire listening to the radio and make love any time we wished without having to be concerned about someone knocking on the door to deliver a tray of tea and biscuits.

They had to administrate it into the space of Kathleen's spinal canal. This method was used to produce a loss of sensation below the waist, without affecting consciousness.

During these bad times my boss Mr Copeland, who was aware of my circumstances was extremely helpful towards me and often slipped some extra cash into my paypacket on the Friday night. It was a small business and Mr Copeland himself worked with us and also ran the office. If we got extremely busy, his disdainful wife would come in and run the office. Mr Copeland only employed two other tradesmen, Tam Gilroy and Albert Croal. Gilroy was a futile tradesman and I could never understand why Mr Copeland did not disperse of his services. Most jobs that Tam Gilroy was sent to usually ended up with the customer phoning the shop with a complaint. Copeland would either go back to the job himself, or send me. The only work that Tam Gilroy appeared to be able to fulfil successfully was the shitty jobs like blocked sewage drains and there was plenty of them, and thank the lord Tam was sent to all of them. Albert Croal was the opposite, he was a young and very competent tradesman. Albert was a few years older than me and was responsible for doing most of the electrical installation work although he was a qualified plumber. Most of our electrical installation work were in houses that were previously served by gas lighting. Mr Copeland was the only qualified Electrician and Plumber. I was responsible for doing most of the plumbing work, however, I wasn't all that keen on plumbing work in general and had always preferred the heating engineering aspects.

Albert and I eventually teamed up doing some private plumbing and electrical work in the evening. It started by accident when I answered the phone one day and It was the owner of a shop in St.Marys Street at the bottom of the Pleasance and not far away from our shop. He had water seeping in through his ceiling which he was concerned about because it was a stationery shop that sold birthday cards and all sorts of note books and calendars. I explained that it would be tomorrow morning before someone could come as It was now closing time. Albert arrived and explained that if a plumber was to come now, it would be more expensive as it would have to charged as overtime. The shop owner who was now very concerned agreed to pay whatever it cost and insisted that a plumber be sent immediately. Albert got his tools together and suggested that he may need some assistance so we should both go. Albert who had a set of keys for the shop, locked up the shop and we both rushed down the Pleasance to the shop in St. Mary's Street. Eventually we discovered that the problem was a cracked cast Iron soil pipe that served the entire tenement building. Every time one of the houses above the shop flushed their toilet the ceiling of his street level shop was being soaked with foul soiled water. We repaired it and stopped the leak and the shop owner was so pleased that he insisted on paying us immediately. Albert informed him that if he paid cash now he would not receive a receipt! In spite of this, the shop owner insisted on paying us in cash immediately. That was our first private job and certainly not our last as we started doing more private jobs after working hours at night and at weekends. It was fantastic, I was making more money doing private jobs with Albert than I was earning as an apprentice.

Kathleen was back to her normal good health and fun loving way and was enjoying her job at the photography shop and learning a great deal about photography and good quality cameras. She was now working in the dark room developing and had been taught by her boss Murray Donald how to touch up photos using a very special technique and was now earning more money than she was in the Chemist. We would occasionally go out to a posh restaurants for an evening meal in spite of the fact that I had never ever been to a posh restaurant before and never ever had the inclination or desire to. Perhaps that was because I could never afford it or was fearful of the numerous different knifes, forks and spoons spread out in front of one. Kathleen on the other hand had been trained as a silver service waitress and therefore knew all there was to know about setting out tables and the use of all the necessary cutlery. We had also started purchasing Kathleen some nice clothes so she was looking terrific again. We would also often hire a big Vauxhall Cresta car some weekend's and drive up north to Inverness and stay overnight in a hotel. Staying in a hotel was also a new experience for me, I had never ever stayed overnight in a hotel and this lovely young wife of mine was leading me astray and I was loving it.

Early March 1959, it was confirmed that Kathleen was pregnant again and we were not that surprised and very pleased. We had been advised by the doctors in 1958 to allow two years for the healing of Kathleen's loss and suffering before we should even consider having another baby. Only a year had passed, however the doctors were not too concerned and suggested that the baby would be born early November 1959. This was great news because my apprenticeship would be over. I would after nearly seven years of training be a qualified heating engineer/plumber and my salary would more than double. Albert and I were working at so many private jobs we could have stopped working for Mr Robert Copeland and started our own business. Kathleen and I started searching the Edinburgh Evening News every night looking for a house to rent and eventually found one at No 22 Blackwood Crescent in Newington that we could afford. It was a nice one bedroom flat with a large lounge with a coal fire. The lounge incorporated a kitchen and a seperate dining room area In the large hall-lobby there was two large walk in cupboards and of course for the first time in our married life we had our very own bathroom. We made the dining room area into the baby's bedroom. As I was still on my last year of my apprenticeship's salary I made a beautiful large timber cot for our baby and we decorated the dining area with baby wallpaper. We ordered and arranged a higher purchase agreement for the pram and because our flat was on the second landing in our tenement block we decided to have a medium sized pram to make it easier moving it up and down the communal staircase.

Kathleen eventually had to stop work because she was so big into her pregnancy so we were all set and waiting patiently for our baby to arrive when without warning, Kathleen suddenly became unwell. On October 1959, Kathleen was rushed into hospital, it was a truly frightening time. Kathleen was suffering from Pre-eclampsia and her blood pressure was too high. she was also going into state's of stupor and unconsciousness. Tests confirmed that she was suffering from albuminuria and her urine was contaminated. It was decided that they would save the child and a Caesarean section was to be performed. However, because of her condition and other unknown factors, an anaesthetic could not be used. On the 14 October 1959, they performed the surgery with an epidural, using a local anaesthetic. They had to administrate it into the epidural space of Kathleen's spinal canal. This was used to produce a loss of sensation below the waist, without affecting consciousness. When they discovered that there were two babies, Kate was put to sleep immediately and both baby girls were safely delivered. Kathleen herself was sedated for days and kept in a very dark room. The seven weeks premature twin babies were in incubators and weighed only three pounds each. They were no bigger than the palm of my hand and the ward sister told me that they were not just twins, they were identical twins with only one afterbirth. Kathleen was eventually allowed home nearly three weeks after their birth but without our tiny babies. It was truly amazing, because after this astonishing birth she looked slim and lovely but incredibly despondent. She spent every day at the hospital apparently sitting between the two incubators looking at our two tiny wee babies. I used to look at this lovely young girl who was my wife and wonder why she had to suffer so much and felt that I had let her down somewhat.

During the pregnancy and before she had taken ill and was rushed into hospital, my apprenticeship was over and I suddenly became a fully qualified heating engineer- plumber, thanks to my wife. Within weeks I had left Copeland's and secured a job at Grangemouth Oil Refinery as a pipe-fitter working seven days a week. This was a huge career change for me as I was now working in the Petro / Chemical Industry. This new job had taken precedence over the entire situation whilst Kathleen was in hospital. I never once visited Kathleen during the day because I was forty miles away at work in Grangemouth Oil refinery. I felt and decided that I could not afford to lose my job by taking time off work because in this business, absenteeism for any reason was instant dismissal. This type of work was temporary and casual that's why the weekly pay was so good because once the plant being built, or any modification is complete, everyone is automatically made redundant. I had to leave the house at 0530 hours every morning to catch the private construction bus to Grangemouth. This private bus left the West End of Princess Street for Grangemouth Oil Refinery at 0630 hours. It would be 1900 hours in the evening before I got home. I could only visit the hospital in the evening for an hour or so therefore I was never ever really made aware of how serious the situation was when Kathleen was in hospital giving birth to our babies. I had never been consulted by the doctors or surgeons that were looking after Kathleen because I was never around? as I said previously, I was at work forty miles away in Grangemouth Oil Refinery?

Kathleen had suggested that we should name our wee girls Lorna Theresa Cassidy and Linda Ann Cassidy and I agreed immediately. How could I disagree with this lovely girl that looked so innocent and so young to have two wee babies to look after. We were having our supper one night when she informed me. "I held wee Lorna in my arms for a wee while today". The joy of delight on her pretty face and the glow of concern in her dark eyes was so bewitching that I had too ponder for a few seconds to try and capture her concerns and feelings. Then I asked. "How do you know it was Lorna?". Without hesitation and with a huge smile she replied. "Because I named them silly. Oh Cass lets get our supper finished quickly and get the bus to the hospital to visit Linda and Lorna Cassidy". "Sure, lets go, we will wash the dishes when we get back home". Was my instant response. In the Special Care Unit at Elsie Ingles Hospital all the nurses knew and were all aware of Kathleen and her tiny wee babies. I was the odd one out, the stranger. The two wee tiny identical twins, Linda and Lorna Cassidy were still in the incubators but I could not see any difference whatsoever between them. I whispered that to Kathleen who immediately responded with. "Oh, Cass look, Lorna is bigger and her wee face is rounder and she has more hair than wee Linda". "They both look the same size to me and they are both bald". I whispered back. "Oh, Cass, they are not, you're silly but you will soon learn". As we were leaving to go home one of the nurses called after Kathleen and informed her that the doctors had decided that one of her babies can come out of the incubator tomorrow. Kathleen immediately asked the nurse which baby it was and if she could take her home. The nurse smiled, then softly told Kathleen. "No Mrs Cassidy, I'm afraid you will not be allowed to take her home yet, she will be kept with us in a in a room with a regulated temperature. She no longer requires oxygen, but we must keep her under surveillance, come I'll show you which baby it is". It was Lorna.

On the seventh of November 1959, Kathleen was allowed to take Lorna Theresa Cassidy home because she had reached the weight of five pounds and was three weeks old therefore not too delicate for Kathleen to handle and look after. I had spent every spare minute of every evening building another cot identical to the one that I had already built because I wanted the cots to be identical. I had built them to be rocking chair style and had painted them pink with large animal transfers all over them. I have to say that they were very impressive looking. On the 30th of November 1959, Linda Ann Cassidy became the fourth resident at No 22 Blackwood Crescent. There were not enough hours in the day for Kathleen, if she was not washing or feeding Linda and Lorna she was boiling soiled cotton nappies in a metal bucket, then washing them in the bath. Because Linda and Lorna were so tiny, they had to be fed every four hours, meaning they had to be fed during the night. We had two alarm clock's set for two-thirty in the morning. Kathleen would heat the milk and armed with a feeding-bottle each, we would sit up in bed with a baby each cradled in our arms, feeding them.

Working at Grangemouth as I have stated previously I had to be out off bed very early and didn't return until late in the evening and I was working seven days a week. I was therefore not around at all to assist Kathleen with our two wee babies. When we did eventually have a few minutes together, we were both too exhausted to even console each other. In spite off me having two alarm clock's on a metal tray with knives and forks scattered about on it to make as much noise as possible, we were so tired we often slept through the terrible din. I missed the works bus that left Princess Street for Grangemouth a few times and returned home to Blackwood Crescent.. The loss of the days wages was not a problem and it meant that I could spend that whole day with Kathleen and the twins. After this had happened a few times and I had been absent from work a few times the time-keeper gave me a verbal warning in the first instance then a written warning informing me that if I lost any more days off work, I would lose my job. That's the way it was in those days and in this particular industry. It was mostly American companies that we worked for and I have to say they paid well, but they were task masters and brutal. Our unions were reluctant to interfere or support us when we attempted to disagree with their conditions and harsh ethics   All I could do to save my job was immediately purchase a bigger and louder alarm clock and put a few more knives and forks on the metal tray. One evening when my parents were visiting us my Dad asked me how the job was going and I happened to mention the warning that I had just recently received. When my parents were leaving that evening my Dad asked me if we had a spare key for our flat. I asked him. "Why?". "Do you have a spare key to give me?". He replied. I looked at Kathleen who suggested. "Give your Dad your key Cass, you really don't need it and hardly ever use it". I gave my Dad the key and after putting it in his pocket he smiled and said. "You won't miss another bus son. See you in the morning". Before going to bed that night I was convinced that Kathleen and my Dad had hatched a plan.

The next morning when it was still pitch black my Dad was standing over me in our bedroom shaking me and whispering. "Get up son, come on, its time to get up. I have the kettle on but I can't find the tea. Try not to awaken Kathleen because the kids are still sound asleep". As soon as he left the bedroom I lifted one of my alarm clocks before climbing out of the bed. It was 0430. I switched off the two alarm clocks that were due to go off at 0445 and wandered through to the lounge with my clothes under my arm. The lounge / kitchen / baby's room were in darkness and my Dad was standing over the twins cots moving from one to the other with a wee torch in his hand. I switched the electric light on which startled my Dad who whispered. "Will that not wake kids up?". "No Dad, they will be too tired". I never missed another bus or lost another day off work because my Dad cycled from Middle Arthur Place to our flat at Newington every morning to make sure that I didn't.

It was my brother in law, Bill Craigens who was a plumber and married to Mary McAuley one of Kathleen's elder sisters who had suggested that I should change my job. Now we were both working at Grangemouth Oil Refinery on the construction of a new plant. Bill was an expert and had worked in this industry for many years and had worked his way into the fabrication shops where all the pipe work was constructed and made into its various different parts and sections. These extra skilled pipe-fabrication fitters were paid extra for their specialised work and Bill was already passing on all his skills to me and I was soon to join him in the fabrication shop. Travelling on the bus for over an hour every morning to Grangemouth gave me an opportunity to kick start my interest in art again. I had always been interested in Abstract Art, because I was of the opinion that this type of conceptual art with its irregular patterns shapes and colours were not only beautiful but extremely difficult to conceive and incredible once created I had asked Kathleen to get me some books on Picasso, Dali or other surrealist artists from the library and I used to get some weird looks and derisive remarks from some of the other workers as I sat reading such books. I copied a lot off their work in coloured crayon and one of my best works was an excellent copy I made off Picasso's *Guernica*. It was Picasso's response to the destruction of the Basque capital when *Franco* requested help from German bombers during the Spanish Civil War in 1937. However, Picasso and Dali's books had to be laid aside when I was able to get myself a copy of the Pipe-Fitters Fabrication Manuel which was only published in America, therefore extremely difficult to purchase in the U.K.

Our wee family were doing well until Kathleen suddenly became unwell and was eventually diagnosed as having a ruptured or broken disc on her spinal cord. The doctors were unaware of how or when this had happened. It was suggested that it could have happened during the time she was pregnant, or caused by carrying the twins up and down the staircase to and from our second floor flat at Blackwood Crescent. The twins were now six months old and no longer tiny wee babies and the only way Kathleen could get out of the flat to shop or go for walk was to carry them down to their huge twin pram which was kept in the stair-well, then eventually have carry them back up again. Ultimately, Kathleen could not walk and was rushed into the Royal Infirmary on March 1960. The proposed operation was a very serious proposition and it appeared that there was no other choice but to remove the damaged disc and replace it with a plastic one. The chances were fifty, fifty and if it went wrong, Kathleen would never ever walk again! This was so undeserving and wickedly unjust. Kathleen was devastated, but not about her own predicament, she was overwhelmed about what was going to happen to Linda and Lorna. It was eventually decided that Linda and Lorna would be taken into a private children's nursing home at Corstorphine. This was another extremely distressing, anxious and frightening time, especially for Kathleen, one would have thought that she had been through enough. Once more, I was faced with the prospect of continuing working or lose my job if I was to visit the hospital and children's nursing home every afternoon. I continued working and visited Kathleen and Linda and Lorna every evening after work. Thank God Kathleen's operation was a success and eventually she was transferred from the Royal Infirmary to the newly opened Western General Hospital. It was always late in the evening when I got home from Grangemouth and an extremely long distance between the Western General Hospital and the twins nursing home especially when having to rely on the local public bus service's. The only time that I could spend a considerable time with them was on Saturdays and Sundays when I didn't go to work. Kathleen was eventually moved from the Western General Hospital to convalescence in a small hospice near Marchment and remained there for a further three weeks. Our wee girls, Linda and Lorna remained in the children's home during this entire trying period. My Dad continued to arrive at Blackwood Crescent at 0430 every morning except the weekends to ensure that I didn't sleep-in and miss my bus to Grangemouth. If he had had not, it is unlikely that I would ever have been on that bus, or at work. Eventually, two months after Kathleen's operation and in early May 1960, we all four of us were reunited when Kathleen and the twins were all back home.

Kathleen cried a lot after she was eventually reunited with our two wee girls, especially after she had fed them and got them settled down into their cots for the night. Kathleen was of the opinion that our two wee girls Linda and Lorna no longer recognised her. They were now eight months old and they had spent an awful lot off that time parted. It was a terribly stressful time for us, especially Kathleen. I had drank too many beers in too many bars around Newington during this stressful period and had put my precious job before my young wife and family. I was now back to working seven days a week, because that was what was expected, that is why we were paid such good salaries and I have to say that I was lucky not to have lost my job. My workaholic attitude was to earn as much money as I possibly could because I wanted Kathleen and our two wee girls to have nice things and to want for nothing. We all have our problems and they never happen conveniently or sequentially to allow you to prepare for them. Kathleen's problems smashed into her and tumbled on top of her like waves crashing onto a beach and they nearly drowned her a few times. I was incapable or refused to accept the seriousness of each and every single problem that my young wife Kathleen was having to face. In the face of it all I still found the time to go for a pint of beer, especially on a Saturday and Sunday night. Kathleen was a non drinker and would never have left Linda and Lorna with baby-sitters under any circumstances, so I would go out alone for a pint. Our problems appeared to be never ending, a couple of months after we were all united and living together, the construction of the new Chemical Plant we were building at Grangemouth Oil Refinery was near completion and I was one of the first pipe-fitters to be made redundant. I was aware that this was inevitable but one can never be prepared for being without a job. I had been earning a good salary and we did have a few pounds in a bank account, however, in spite of this Kathleen had never questioned my decision to try a career change that did not guarantee continuous employment. After a week or so of being unemployed, I decided to visit Robert Copland's the plumbers at the top of the Pleasance where I had finished my apprenticeship and asked him if he had any work for me.. He smiled and asked me. "When can you start?". Kathleen was pleased to hear that I was once more going to be working for Mr Copeland and at home every night.

Nothing had changed during the time I had left Copeland's to go and work in Grangemouth Oil Refinery. Albert was still doing all the electrical installation work, smelly Tam Gilmour was still doing all the shitty work on the blocked drain's. I was immediately given the job of sorting out all the general plumbing work that Mr Copeland appeared to have been doing and he was now running the office. I had explained to Albert about how much more money one could earn whilst working in the Petro Chemical Industries but he was uninterested as he preferred the security of his job with Mr Copeland. I soon settled into working again for Mr Copeland's because he was a good man and a decent boss. I did not have to leave the house until 0730 in the morning and I was home again by 1700 hours. I was spending all my spare time with Kathleen the our wee girls and at weekends we pushed our huge twin pram along Clerk Street and nearly every second person would stop us to look and speak to the lovely identical twin girls who were now one year's old. Things were going great, we were all together every evening and every weekend.

The twins first birthday came and went, then the bombshell hit us. Our landlord gave us a months notice after informing us that he needed our flat for a relative who was now homeless. We were already aware that he was not happy once he was aware that we now had two children. This news was devastating and we could not find any other accommodation that was within our range financially. Our month's notice was up on December 1960. He reluctantly agreed to let us stay over the Christmas and the New Year period but insisted that we must vacate the flat by the end of January 1961. Eventually we had no other alliterative but to move into Kathleen's parents house. We were given her wee brothers tiny bedroom and he slept on a made up bed on a couch in the kitchen / dining / living room area. With the two cots and what remained of our personal belongings in our tiny bedroom it was an impoverished situation to be in. As usual Kathleen went about her duties under these extremely difficult circumstances without a despairing look. Her mum worked full time in a butcher and her Dad was at work all day. Her wee brother was at school therefore she did have the house to herself whilst looking after our baby girls which was a full time job. Fortunately Kathleen and her mother got on extremely well, however her Dad and I were not at all amused. Kathleen's parent's house was on the top flat at No 75 Lower Viewcraig Row. This created another huge problem for Kathleen, because if she wanted to get out of the house, she would have to carry the twins who were now 16 months old down the four landings to where the huge twin pram was padlocked to a cast-iron rain water pipe. Fortunately, Kathleen became friendly with Doreen Watson, a young married girl who lived next door who just happened to adore Linda and Lorna. Therefore when Kathleen had to go out, she not only received assistance from Doreen Watson, Doreen would assert her wish to accompany Kathleen and the twins wherever they were going.

Last thing at night I would pull the huge pram up the stairs into the lobby of the house, if not, it most certainly would have been stolen during the darkness of the night. First thing in the morning on my way to Copeland's, I would take the huge twin pram down the four landings to ground level and chain it to one of the cast iron drain pipes. Twice a week Kathleen and Doreen with the twins in the huge pram would visit the Edinburgh City Council Housing Department which was situated in the High Street in the town centre. Our name had been on their housing list ever since the day we had got married which was over three years ago. Now that we were homeless with two children, we had been moved onto the priority list. Doreen Watson, the young married girl that lived next door and Kathleen became inseparable. Young Doreen had no children of her own and spent most of her time with Kathleen and the twins. She also got herself involved in helping Kathleen to wash and dress the twins in the morning. Kathleen not only had the problem of carrying the twins up and down the four landings, she also had the extreme sloped hill of Arthur Street to push the huge twin pram up, then at the end of the day very slowly descend the very steep hill using the brakes. Arthur Street had a gradient off one in four which is a sheer slope and was indeed one of the steepest streets in Edinburgh, and Kathleen had to negotiate this extremely notorious sloping Arthur Street practically every single day.

At work one day I was reading the Daily Record and noticed that Shaw & Petrie, a Glasgow based company had a huge advertisement for Instrumentation Pipe-Fitters. I phoned them on reverse charge from a phone booth, [One could do that in those days] The project was in Motherwell in the Ravenscraig Strip Mill. They agreed to send me an application form to c/o Kathleen's parents house. I had only been back with Mr Copeland now for seven month's and here I was looking for another job in the Petro / Chemical Industry. I was happy working with Copeland and every thing was fine when we had our own flat and being at home with Kathleen and our lovely wee girls was great. However things had deteriorated drastically, we had lost our flat and could not find another one that we could afford. I just felt that I had to do something and the only thing I could think to do was to earn more money, at least enough money to rent another flat. Having to live with Kathleen's parents was the last straw. It was not that I didn't appreciate what Kathleen's parents were doing for us, I truly did, but I knew that her Dad was not exactly overjoyed with the four of us living in their house. I also knew that Kathleen was suffering in silence as usual, therefore I decided that I really did have to start earning more money than I was presently earning with my Mr Copeland.

That evening when we went to bed I told Kathleen about the job application that I had phoned for. Kathleen looked adorable in spite of the exhausted expression on her lovely face. Kathleen said nothing, then turned her back to me, but only for a few second's then turned back to face me and said. "I know how unhappy you are living here with my parents but I am doing everything I can to make it as comfortable as possible for you, believe me. I know my little brother is spoilt and it irritates you and I'm so sorry but I am doing everything I can to get us a council house, nearly every second day I go to the council with the twins and they know we are desperate and have promised to help us". In silence, I looked around the room. We were lucky if we had a two foot space on the floor, between the twins two cot's and the edge of our bed. The room was so small, the four walls appeared to be about to crush the four of us to death. I was accustomed to living in such conditions when I was young and lived with my parents. But I was a married man now and had a duty to provide for my wife and children. It was my responsibility to ensure that this should never ever have happened. I should never have allowed this to happen to us and I whispered to Kathleen. "We need the extra money that I can earn, if I get this job we may be able to rent another flat. I have to try". "You will travel back and forward to Motherwell every day?". Kathleen whispered back. "I don't think so because they will probably give me a subsistence allowance meaning I will have to live in digs during the week and come home at weekends". Without hesitation Kathleen replied. "No, I don't want you to do that, we, the twins and I need you to be home every night. We don't need more money we need you because we will be fine if we are all together". Was Kathleen's response "You may be fine Kathleen but I'm not and you're correct, I hate living here and your Dad hate's us living here, in fact everyone hates us living hear except you". Kathleen started sobbing and saying between sobs. "That's unfair and untrue. You must know how much I just want the four of us to be together and to have our own place. You must know that". I felt awful and knew that everything that she had just said was absolutely correct, I whispered. "I'm sorry Kathleen, I know you do, come here". We hugged each other until we eventually fell asleep.

Eventually the application form arrived, I filled it in and returned it. A week later I was offered a job and if I was still interested I was to phone them for further Instructions. I handed in my notice once more to Mr Copeland who had smiled and nodded his head as if in agreement. I apologised and he suggested that I had nothing to apologise for and said. "You did your work and you earned your pay. You're a good honest and reliable tradesman". It was a Friday evening and we had just been paid. Every Friday after work, Mr Copeland took the three off us, Albert, smelly Tam and myself to the local pub for a pint before he headed home. In the pub and just before he left, he asked me. "Where are you off to this time?". I told him it was Motherwell, he asked about the type of work I would be doing and after I had explained, he said to Albert and smelly Tam "Well it's just as well we don't all have the travel bug to become millionaires, someone has to stay behind to look after the rest off us". Mr Copeland finished his pint and left us after bidding us good-night and me good luck. We three normally stayed and had another round each but not to-night. I said my farewell to Albert and Tam then headed straight home to 75 Lower Viewcraig Row. On the Monday morning I was on a train to Motherwell to find digs and start work as an Instrumentation pipe fitter for Shaw Petrie at the Ravenscraig Steel Rolling Mill. I had never ever done any instrumentation work prior to this but had omitted that in my application form. I had only ever worked with large bore mild steel and stainless steel pipe. This work involved fabricating and installing ¼ inch tiny bore copper pipe for the recording of instrumentation equipment. I had spent the last few years with Copeland working with copper pipe and I knew that I had to be able to do this work because I desperately needed this job.

Indifferent: 14

Mrs Ramsey my landlady, was an unattractive fifty something year old widow who was the captain of the women's dart team in the local pub in the village on the outskirts of Motherwell near Ravenscraig where I eventually found accommodation. I was supposed to be on full board, breakfast, packed lunch and evening meal, and I was her only lodger. She was never around or available in the morning to give me any breakfast because she was probably in her bed fast asleep and still inebriated. I usually had to make myself a cup of tea and a slice of toast. Then after grabbing my sandwiches that were sitting on the kitchen table, probably there all night wrapped up in newspaper. I would run out the door to catch my transport that took me to my work. Every evening when I got home after a long twelve hour shift, the house would be full of other distasteful elderly women. These women that were as unpleasant and vulgar as Mrs Ramsey, would all be simultaneously arguing, smoking, drinking beer and throwing darts. My evening meal was always pre-cooked and sitting dried-up in the oven. It was a very unpleasant situation to be in because once I had eaten this obnoxious food in the tiny kitchen, I had no place to go except up to my diminutive bedroom. As I wandered passed all these awe-inspiring women, they would be roaring with laughter, gurgling their beer, smoking and still throwing darts.

One morning I slept late and had no time to make myself a cup of tea and realized that I would have to rush to catch the transport that took me to work. I was upset as I grabbed my appalling sandwiches and on my way out, slammed the doors behind me. When I got home that evening, there was a letter from my wife Kathleen lying in the hall. I went direct to my bedroom to read it. I had just started reading Kathleen's letter when my bedroom door burst open. It was the dreaded Mrs. Ramsey and she shouted. "What the hell do you think you were playing at this morning banging all the doors?". I laid my letter down on my lap and replied. "Listen lady, don't you ever come into this room again without knocking. Now please go. I am reading a letter from my wife and when I'm finished, I will come downstairs to the lounge and we will discuss the incident". She roared. "You will do more than that. You will get out my house and I will walk into any room in this house that pleases me. Now you can get the hell out off my house, now". With that she stormed out of my room. After reading my letter, I went down to the lounge and for the first time ever, I found it empty. She was in the kitchen so I wandered through to the kitchen and on spotting me she yelled. "Out. I told you I want you out of my house. Now". I hesitated then suggested. "Mrs Ramsey, I have already paid you a weeks rent in advance. I will leave at the end of the week, or if you wish to refund me I will leave first thing tomorrow morning". "You will leave now or I will phone the police". Was her instant reply. "You will give me a rebate, and I will leave in the morning or I leave at the weekend, you can please yourself". I left the kitchen and returned to my bedroom. About half an hour later there was a knock on my bedroom door. "Come in". Was my instant response and I have to say I was expecting my obnoxious landlady. I was therefore taken by surprise when two policemen walked into the room and immediately removed their head ware. One of them addressed me. "Good evening, the lady of the house said she wants you to leave the house". I kept my cool and replied. "Lady ?. I have paid the Lady a weeks rent in advance and I have explained to the Lady that if she refunds my money, I will go". Before I could continue, the same policeman said. "That's another matter for the courts. Now you look like a decent lad, she wants you out of her house and out you must go. Now be a good lad, pack your bag and leave or we will have no alternative but to arrest you". After a few seconds of thought, I agreed to leave. As I packed my bag the two policemen waited downstairs to escort me out of the house. As it turned out they were two decent guys because it was now very late in the evening, pitch black and very cold. They enquired as to what my intentions were and what I was intending to do. I explained that I had no idea so they offered to give me a lift to a bed and breakfast house known to them, so I accepted their offer.

I stayed in that B&B for a few nights until one of the guy's at work told me his landlady's daughter was thinking about taking in a lodger and suggested that he would check it out for me. Sure enough, next morning he gave me the address and confirmed that our works van that transports us too and from work actually passes the house. On the way home that evening I got off the van when we had reached the street and started looking for number 79. A female around thirty years old, medium size and slightly overweight opened the door. I explained that a workmate lodging with her mother had told me that she was considering taking in lodgers. "Oh, yes, my mum was around to-day and said that someone might come this evening, please come in". I was shown into a nice tidy lounge with a huge coal fire burning in the fireplace. It was so neat and tidy that I was a wee bit reluctant to sit down and disturb the cushions when I was invited to. She was explaining to me that she had never had a lodger before and she could only accommodate one person when the lounge door suddenly opened and a chubby young girl about seven years old entered. The Lady of the house introduced her as Rebecca and confirmed that the young girl was her daughter. This young girl was her mothers double, even the overweight part which I thought was sad because they were both pretty. After we discussed the cost for full board which included breakfast, packed lunch and evening meal, the three of us then inspected the tidy cosy spare room with a double bed which was adjacent to the bathroom. It was soon agreed that I could move into the spare bedroom immediately. It all looked and sounded just to good to be true and a far cry from the dart throwing bitch that stole my money. My new landlady, Mrs Robertson was charging me exactly the same weekly cost as the dart throwing alcoholic Mrs Ramsey. I moved in that night and even received an evening meal. It was during the meal that she surprised me when she told me that her husband also worked at Ravenscraig. More taken aback when I met him that evening because he was course, rough and impolite which somewhat shocked me because Mrs Robinson was so discrete and gracious. I was expecting her husband to be an insurance man or the manager of a shop. He was an arrogant, rough local rigger that also worked on the Ravenscraig construction site.

I had been working in Motherwell now for four months, at first I travelled home every weekend. Then as the job progressed they started working every Saturday and Sunday. Therefore eventually I was only going to be getting home for a long weekend every month, travelling home on the train on the Friday afternoon and back again on the Monday. During this time Kathleen had been offered three council houses and had refused all of them because they were old and located in filthy, dirty, degrading neighbourhoods. I had not seen any of them but had accepted and had agreed fully with Kathleen's decision's. We had now been on the Edinburgh Council Housing list for over three years and were homeless with two young children. We both felt that we deserved a decent house in a decent area, especially after waiting for so long. Kathleen had also been enquiring about private renting but most private renters were uninterested in renting to people with two young children and the ones that were available wanted rent that was far beyond our financial status. We decided that now that we were on the priority list for a two bedroom council house, we would save our money for the furniture that we are going to need and pray that we would eventually be offered a decent house in a decent location. Thank God that Kathleen's parents appeared to agree with Kathleen decisions. Perhaps the fact that I was no longer living permanently in their house was also a reason why they were being so considerate, we will never know. However whatever it was we were both extremely grateful to them for their compassionate act in allowing us to share their home with them, especially with two young children.

Living with the Robertson's was exceptionally good. The food was decent and the hot cooked breakfast in the morning before going to work was a luxury that I had never experienced whilst living with the dart throwing witch that had stolen my money and tried to have me arrested by the police. Packed lunch was okay and the evening meal was always interesting and beautifully served. On the other hand, my landlord Paul Robertson the rigger, was a first class arrogant twit and a man about town. Every night after work he went direct to the pub with a few of his work mates for a few beers therefore he was always very late at getting home for the evening meal. I was always washed and changed out of my working clothes long before he arrived home and would have sit in the lounge watching T.V. His wife and daughter would also be sitting around waiting for him to show up because they never knew when he would appear. Mrs Robertson at one time suggested that she would serve me if I didn't mind eating alone. Of course I pretended that it didn't bother me and graciously agreed to wait for her husband to join us. When he did eventually arrive, he would greet no one and just run straight upstairs and disappeared. At times it would be another good half hour before he would appear downstairs for the evening meal, all dressed up as if going to wedding with a suit, tie and highly polished shoes. He would jokingly shout at his wife. "Come on love, I'm loosing valuable drinking time, lets get the grub on the table". Saturdays and Sundays he went to some working man's social club and never ever got home until early morning and I know because he always disturbed my sleep as he staggered up the staircase. I would also hear them arguing, but that was not very often as his wife appeared to accept his unusual behaviour. In fact she informed me that from the day they got married, that was his routine and that was even before wee Rebecca was born. She also admitted to me that she didn't mind because Paul was younger than her and in her opinion he would eventually settle down.

I was so cold, unhappy and very angry at being addressed as,
'Hey, you with the ear-ring'.

One night while the four of us were having our evening meal and as usual Paul was dressed as if he was going to a wedding, he said to me. "You know, I think your a bit of a weirdo, why do you sit in here every night watching the T.V, don't you drink?" His wife snapped at him. "That's enough Paul". Paul the rigger glanced at her and then at me, then back at his wife again and said. "You, be quiet and keep out off this". I looked at him but didn't know what to say or what to do. Then I said to him. 'Why should that bother you?. "It doesn't. I don't give a shit". He replied. His wife threw her knife and fork down and told her wee daughter Rebecca to go to her room and as soon as their daughter left the room she asked her husband. "What on earth is the matter with you Paul?. Why are behaving like this?. He raised his voice now and said "I've told you already and I don't want to repeat myself. Shut up". I knew that this guy was a few years older than me and physically in good condition, but I also knew that he was a bully, and my Dad had taught me how to deal with bullies so I jumped to my feet causing my chair to tumble backwards onto the floor with a thud. I pointed at him and said. "Okay, Paul, if you're trying to find a reason to pick a fight with me, do it, otherwise I'm going to my room". I waited and looked fixedly at him without moving my eyes, just waiting for him to make a move. He didn't, so I excused myself and trembling with anger I went directly to my bedroom thinking that it was the only thing I could do to stop this fracas. When I heard the shouting coming from downstairs I moved out of my bedroom onto the landing because I thought he might start hitting on his wife. They were shouting at each other and without any warning wee Rebecca suddenly appeared on the landing beside me. I put my hand up as if to say stop and whispered to her that she should remain in her room until her Mum comes up to get her, thankfully she wandered back into her bedroom. Downstairs doors were opened and banged closed. I could not really hear what they were saying, until I think it was the kitchen door that opened, then I heard Paul the husband shouting. "I don't give a shit, I'm out off here, hey! why are you so concerned about him, are you f****** him, are you?". "Get out you filthy pig, that's all you ever think about, go on, go and drink with you're so called friends". The outside door banged and it was silent.

It was around nine-o-clock when I heard Mrs Robinson coming up the stairs with her young daughter Rebecca, I assumed to put her to bed. After ten minutes or so there was a very soft tap, tap, on my bedroom door. I opened it gently to find Mrs Robinson standing at the door. She whispered. "I am so, so sorry". I whispered back. "There is nothing for you to apologise for". She replied. "I am still sorry and feel ashamed. I am just going to make a pot of tea, do you care to join me?". "Sure, I'll come down in a minute". My landlady sauntered off down the stairs and I truly felt sorry for her. After five minutes or so I wandered down to the lounge and Mrs Roberson was sitting drinking a cup of tea and on the small table was the tray with the teapot with its tea cosy covering it and beside it was a plate of biscuits. She smiled at me and immediately commenced pouring me a cup of tea. After a few minutes silence she said. "I think our Paul is a bit envious of you". "Why would he be envious of me ?". Was all I could say. "Because our Paul needs people. He needs to be with a lot of other people. Do you know, its probably my fault because he often asks me what you do at night. He asks me if you ever go out. It was me that told him that you don't and that you watch T.V. for while then go to bed early. Our Paul can't do that". I felt sorry for her and eventually left her sitting watching the T.V. and went to bed. The next morning at breakfast Paul half apologised about upsetting me at dinner last night. I wanted to tell him to go f*** himself but said nothing. I did consider finding other accommodation but this place was just too good to be true except for the stupid husband, so I decided to stay until such time as he told me to get out.

Kate and I used to write to each other every Monday and Thursday so we had a sort of regular mail delivery which kept us both up to-date. One night I arrived back in my digs as usual and my letter from Kathleen was sitting on top of the electric meter in the hall, I grabbed it and dashed upstairs to read it. It was great news, Kathleen had put so much pressure on the council that she has been allocated a brand new council house in a brand new council estate in Corstorphine, a very posh area of Edinburgh. Apparently it was a ground floor two bedroom house with a large lounge, kitchen dining room, bathroom and large hall. Front and back gardens with balcony off the lounge looking out onto the back garden. Kathleen, the twins and her parents and my family and parents had already visited it because she now had the keys meaning we could move in as soon as possible. After dinner, I drafted a reply to tell Kathleen to tell her how much I loved and missed her and our two girls. I congratulated her on her excellent achievement, and told her that I would be home on Friday for the weekend to visit the house and celebrate, then ran out immediately to post it. In those days working class people had no phones in their house therefore making a phone call home was out of the question, even in an emergency.

I explained everything to my supervisor at work and hoped that it justified that I could not work over the weekend as I had to go home. I did travel home on the train on the Friday night after work and arrived at Kathleen's parents house late that evening. As soon as I arrived, Kathleen and I got the bus to our new house at Corstorphine. It was a dream come true and we were so happy we made love in our large empty bedroom. We stopped on our way home and had a meal in a restaurant in Clerk street. First thing Saturday morning we dropped the twins off at my parents house because both Kathleen's parents worked Saturday morning. We went to the Linoleum shop on the Bridges and arranged for them to meet us at the house to measure the entire flooring area and give us a price to supply, deliver and fit the Linoleum of our choice. We explained that we would be paying by opening a higher purchase account. We also ordered a double bed, two single beds and all the necessary bedding and once more we arranged a higher purchase agreement.

On the Sunday night I was sitting on a late night train to Motherwell feeling a lot better than I had felt for a long time. While I was at work in Motherwell, Kathleen was supervising the fitting of the floor Linoleum throughout the entire house. Organising the delivery of the beds and bedding. In the evening's, Kathleen and her Mum were working like beavers sewing and making curtains for the two bedrooms and lounge. The second weekend when I got home the floors were covered and the three beds were all made up. Kathleen and I shopped on the Saturday morning and selected a Gas fire for the lounge, gas cooker and electric fridge for our kitchen and on this occasion we paid cash because we still had some money in our account with Clydesdale's Bank.

I could not afford to loose my job at Motherwell now because we were paying rent to the council and two weekly higher purchase agreements for the Linoleum and beds. Paying cash for the gas fire, cooker and fridge made a gigantic hole in our savings and I was not earning as much as I normally was because I was not working weekends. In spite of the fact that we still had no table and chairs for the kitchen/ dining room and no furniture in the lounge, we moved into our new house at 22 Rannoch Road Corstorphine on a beautiful Saturday morning in July on 1961. The twins kept Kathleen very busy and when all four of us were together at weekends we spent any spare time we had in the big empty lounge with its lovely red coloured floor Linoleum. Linda and Lorna were nearly two years old now and thriving. Kathleen was looking fantastic again and thank god she had recovered from her back operation and every other problem that had been thrown at her. We were so happy and I desperately wanted to be at home every night and not just at weekends. I could not afford to leave my job and dreaded every Sunday night when I had to kiss my two wee girls and my lovely wife goodbye as I left the house to get the bus to Waverly train station and the train back to Motherwell.

One Friday night when I arrived home, Kathleen handed me an advert she had cut out of the Edinburgh Evening News. Moncure's, a large Edinburgh Engineering company based in Morningside were looking for a Heating Engineer. Early on the Saturday morning, I went to the nearest public phone and phoned them praying that they worked on a Saturday. The phone rang and was eventually answered. The gentleman that I spoke with asked me if I would come into the office immediately for an interview. I was so happy and it took me a few seconds to explain that I most certainly could but that it would take me an hour or so as I lived at the other end of the town, thankfully that was not a problem. The interview was indifferent, one of the people interviewing me was of the opinion that I was not a fully qualified heating engineer as I had only completed three years with J.& R. Adams. I pointed out that It was nearly four years with J&R Adam's and I had completed a further two years as a plumber with Robert Copeland's. I also reiterated that I now had considerable experience as a Industrial pipe fitter fabricator with Instrumentation experience and was presently fully employed. The other two gents appeared to be impressed at that. The conclusion was that they would consider my application and would inform me by post. Sunday night I was back on the train again to Motherwell and on the Monday morning my general foreman informed me that as a travelling man receiving subsistence, I was expected to work weekends and only entitled to an official long weekend every six weeks. I tried to explain to him about us moving into our new house but It was to no avail, I was to be made redundant on the Friday. I was angry and concerned and wondered if I should write to Kathleen or just wait until I get home on Friday night. I decided to wait until I got home on Friday night.

Kathleen as usual was calm and composed when I told her on the Friday night when I eventually got home that I had just lost my job. Over dinner Kathleen suggested that I should phone up the people that were looking for a Heating Engineer. I was of the opinion that if they had been interested in employing me they would have written to me by now. She then suggested that I could always get a job as a plumber which was of course very true, but I would not earn the same salary as I was receiving as a pipe-fitter. I said to Kathleen. "I could not go back and ask Mr Copeland, could I?". "Well Cass, he is a business man and I'm sure if he needed some help he would hire you again and why not, you are reliable and he does have a soft spot for you". In spite of our predicament, we both laughed and hugged each other and she whispered. "Anyway, don't worry Cass, it will be great to have you around every day for a change and our wee girls will just love it". I did not have the nerve to go back to Mr Copeland and ask him if he could give me another job again, therefore decided to go elsewhere. Within a week I was on top off a three piece extension ladder working as a plumber in a new multi storey car park that had been built at Haymarket. I was installing lengths after lengths of three inch cast iron rain water pipes. It is one of the most boring unskilled tasks any knowledgeable plumber could be asked to undertake. I had immediately requested assistance as it was heavy and unsafe work for any individual to be isolated with. I was promised that another plumber or an apprenticeship would be sent as soon as one was available. Not only was I having to move an extremely heavy three piece extension ladder around on my own, at times I was working off the top section without anyone securing the bottom off the ladder. It was winter time and very frosty and freezing cold. The working conditions were terrible and it was extremely difficult and dangerous work, especially in this freezing cold concrete newly built multi-storey car park. There appeared to be no end to this soul destroying monotonous difficult boring work and there were hundreds of lengths of this cast iron rain water pipe to be installed. I perished the thought of spending the rest of my life in this freezing building on top of this swaying extension ladder and having to hang on with frost bitten fingers. In bed one night, I was telling Kathleen how desperate I was feeling at work and how much I hated leaving the house every morning to catch the bus to Haymarket to this dreadful freezing cold car park building. She hugged me and cuddled me up very close, then whispered. "I wish I could help you, I wish the twins and I could come to work with you and help you". I knew that Kathleen actually meant it and that gave me a great deal of comfort, strength and hope that I would not be spending the rest of my life in that dreadful multi-car-park building. One morning whilst I was up the ladder, someone shouted. "Hey, you with the ear-ring. As soon as I realized that the person was shouting at me, I looked down and it was the foreman and he had another person with him. I immediately descended the ladder and as I stepped of the bottom rung the foreman was standing directly in front me. I was so cold, unhappy and very angry at being addressed as *'you with the ear-ring'.* I said to him. "I have a name and don't you ever address me in that manner again". He stepped backwards with a stunned expression on his face then stuttered. "You can't talk to me like that. Your fired, your finished". I wanted to instantly grab and punch him in the face, and perhaps I would have if we had been alone. As he was backing away he shouted. "I want you off this job right now". Then to this other person he shouted. "You, look after this job until I return" His parting words to me were. "You're finished, go back to the shop, I will arrange for you to collect whatever wages are due to you". He jumped into his tiny white van and vanished and I can only assume that the other guy was another plumber that was going to be assisting me. This other person, the stranger, didn't get involved and even when we were on our own he just wandered away towards the stacks of cast iron rain water pipes without uttering a single word. I collected my tools, bundled them up and nestled them on my right shoulder then made my way out off the concrete tomb. I looked back at the poor sole who would now be taking over my suffering and felt truly sorry for him. As usual, Kathleen was more than supportive when I arrived home and told her that I had just been dismissed from the plumbers job in the freezing cold Haymarket car park. After I had explained exactly what had happened, Kathleen was not too pleased about the circumstances in which I was dismissed, but hugged me anyway.

I had only been unemployed just over a week and had just returned from the Lauriston Street unemployment office where I had sighed-on as being unemployed. I had collected my unemployment money and had been involved in an argument with one of the civil servants because she had offered me another job as a plumber with a plumber's shop in Leith Walk. I had refused it and had explained that I was seeking a job as a heating engineer or as a pipe-fitter in the Petro-Chemical industry. The conclusion was that she threatened to sign me off from being eligible for any benefits if I continue to refuse employment as a plumber. Therefore I was so pleased that when I eventually got home and Kathleen handed me a letter from Moncure's Heating Engineers informing me that if I was still interested in employment I should contact them immediately. I phoned them from the nearest phone booth and reported for work the next morning. I passed the various tests that they had prepared for me and started work immediately on a month's trial. The month's trial soon passed and I was accepted as a full time employee and within a few months we had our lounge fully furnished complete with our first ever T.V set plus two gold fish for the twins. We also purchased a proper four seater dining table and chairs for our kitchen/dining room. I was enjoying my work as a heating engineer and was earning a decent wage because I worked every Saturday and Sunday that was available and within a few more months most off our debts were all paid up. Our first Xmas together in our very own new house was fantastic, we were doing okay and the past misfortunes were all behind us. The highlight of this time was when we had finalized all our debts, we purchase a second hand four year old Ford Popular car. We put down a deposit and signed an agreement to pay the balance off in monthly instalment's. During the summer evening's we had both cultivated our front and back gardens at our new house in 22 Rannoch Road.

Being at home every night off the week with Kathleen and the girls was a huge bonus for all off us. Another Xmas and New Year came and went and we were having such a good time that Kathleen became pregnant again and we were both delighted. A week or so before our new baby was due in 1963, Kathleen was admitted to hospital. Apparently, because of her previous problems they wanted her in hospital for observation before she went into labour. My mum moved into our house to look after the twins. As soon as Kathleen went into labour there were some problems and the doctors eventually decided the baby would have to be born by caesarean section. This was to be Kathleen's second caesarean section birth, and her last. It was decided that it was far to risky for Kathleen to become pregnant ever again. Kathleen was to have no more baby's after our son Mark McNeill Cassidy was on the 13th April 1963. Kathleen and our new born son were still in hospital when my father who was cycling home from work one day had a massive heart attack and died on the 20th April 1963, he was only sixty two years old. Kathleen and our son who was to be named Mark McNeil arrived home the day before my Dads funeral. Our wee girls, Linda and Lorna were now nearly four years old. Working for Moncure's, the heating engineers in Edinburgh suddenly became indifferent because for some unknown reason to me, all the weekend work and other overtime was stopped. Perhaps there was a recession that I was unaware off?. My weekly wage was suddenly inept. In my opinion this was not good because we now had another mouth to feed and our two wee girls were due to go to school soon, which meant school uniforms and other additional expenses. It was time for me look for another better paid job.

Indifferent: 15

The overnight ferry I was on from Glasgow to Londonderry in Northern Ireland was being thrown about like a cork by the rough waters of the North Channel of the Irish Sea. I had left my job with Moncure's as soon as I had secured myself a job as a Pipe-Fitter with Du-Pont the huge American Chemical Coy which had a massive plant on the outskirts of Londonderry. The second class steerage was crowded with Irish lads who were obviously returning home and all drinking rather heavily. We had steamed out off the port of Seamill approximately twenty five miles west off Glasgow and rounded the Isle of Arran then down the Firth of Clyde of the West Coast of Scotland and into the open waters of the North Channel of the Irish Sea. The Ferry was named *The Derry Ducker* and it was now getting battered by huge breakers that I assumed were coming down from the Atlantic and up from the Irish Sea. As I said previously, we were being battered and tossed about like a wee cork. It was impossible to sit on ones seat and I soon realized that this was going to be a long dreadful overnight crossing.

During the night the storm appeared to worsen. I was with another Pipe Fitter, a chap by the name of Jock Raeburn who also lived in Corstorphine. Most off the Irish guys that had been drinking all night were pissed out off their brains and now in the middle of the damn night whilst they were trying to sleep, they were being tipped off the benches and onto the deck and most of them were being violently sick as they skidded in their own vomit from one end of room to the other. It was indeed an incredible filthy sight to behold. This steerage sitting area was not very large, therefore there was not a great deal of space to be skidding about in. Presently the entire floor area was awash with drunk bodies swirling about in their own vomit. I honestly thought I was going to die, it was just too horrific to be true and the stench was unbearable.

Wee Jock Raeburn had got himself rolled up in a sort of ball with his head resting on his knees and he appeared to be wedged into a corner seat. Without any warning all the lights went out, they had been dimmed most of the night but now we were pitched into complete blackness. That was the last straw for me, I got myself up onto my feet and decided to get the hell out of this filthy stinking dungeon. I shuffled my feet across the wet floor while feeling with my hands and sliding them across the wooden tops of the seating stalls until there was no more seats or timber to hold onto. I headed into the darkness and the unknown hoping that I was going towards the staircase that would take me up out of this hellhole. My feet were suddenly taken away from under me and I went down like a log with both palms of my hands splashing into the wet vomit first, then my knees. As this stinking filthy ferry rolled sideways, I rolled onto my right hand side then over again onto my back and was now lying in the vomit and other stinking liquid that flooded around me. It smelled like urine. I was afraid to inhale and afraid to put my hands into the mush that was swirling all around me. In my effort to get myself up and out of this reeking putrid cesspit, I had to put the palms of my hands back into it. I did eventually manage to get myself upright just as the lights flickered back on. I was a sight to behold, my clothes were sodden and even the back of my head was soaked with the reeking putrid slops.

On deck, it was awash with sea water and the wind was howling, but the smell of the salty fresh air was life saving. I noticed an enclosed rather small lounge that was completely empty and immediately headed for it but the entrance door was locked. In my panic, I looked around frantically and was lucky to see another door at the far end. Without any hesitation I staggered around the sodden deck all the way around towards it and was delighted to discover that this door was not locked. Seeking warmth and some form of assurance, I entered and closed the door swiftly behind. A large clock on one of the timber panelled bulk heads indicated that it was ten minutes past three in the morning. All other visible signs suggested that this very stylish little lounge was *First Class*. I was the only resident as this lounge was empty. Some off the wall lights were on, therefore this was the first opportunity I had to investigate the condition of my clothes. My suit was clinging to me at places were it was soaked with the slimy liquid that covered the floor down in the steerage passenger area down below. Surprisingly, It was not as serious as I thought it would be, however I was still unaware how my back was. My suit was a dark blue raven's wing colour, therefore it did not look as bad as it would have if it was a light colour. I removed my jacket and gave it a good shake and suddenly felt nauseated and thought I was going to be sick as I watched small particles of the slop fly loose. I looked around and spotted the signs for the toilets and headed for the door with the sign of a gent in a top hat and brandishing a walking stick. After hanging my jacket on the back of one of the seats with backs and arm rests I entered one of the toilet cubicles. I could not vomit but my efforts brought tears to my eyes. I removed my tie and wiped the front of my trousers as well as was possible. I felt a bloody fool for being dressed as if I was going to a wedding or a funeral. All the drunken paddy's down below and Jock Raeburn were all dressed very casual and I promised myself that in future whilst travelling that would also be my dress mode.

Back in the lounge, I noticed that all around the timber panelled bulk heads there were long red coloured upholstered sofa seats designed to seat more than one person. I very quietly and slowly wandered around the small lounge and peered out onto the open deck through one of the large clear glass windows and there was not another single soul in sight, only the wash of the sea water swirling and churning across the deck. I hung my suit jacket on one of the large arm-chairs adjacent to one of the long red sofa seats that I had chosen to rest on. I must have fallen asleep and was suddenly startled when I heard someone ask. "Excuse me, hello, excuse me". An elderly chap was standing over me. He stood tall, very tall and muscular. He asked me. "Can I have a look at your ticket?". I very quickly sat upright and immediately started to explain to him that I was from the steerage area below deck and further explained about the drunk's being sick all over the floors. I concluded by suggesting that perhaps I could pay some additional cash, because I just could not go back down into that sloppy pit hole. He was very sympathetic and considerate and told me that we would be docking at Derry in a few hours time and suggested that I make sure that I was out of here before we docked.

After docking, Raeburn and I entered a café just outside the docks and I had a few mugs of hot tea only because I still felt a wee bit nauseated. Jock Raeburn had bacon rolls with his tea and in fact I could hardly watch Raeburn eating his rolls without feeling sick. When we asked the Café guy that had served us about possible lodging's in the town he advised us to go into one of the Garda offices because they should have that sort of information, if not they would advise us. I was surprised how large and busy Londonderry was; the guy in the Café was spot on, the first Garda station we entered gave us a list with half a dozen addresses. The first one we approached was a Mrs Leach who lived in a small terrace house and considering that it was still early morning, she made us both very welcome. The first thing that I noticed was the large crucifixion in the hallway, then the photograph of Jesus Christ in the lounge. I immediately realized this was indeed a Catholic Domain. Over a cup of tea we discussed her terms. The weekly rent was reasonable and in fact we would both be making a few shillings out of our subsistence allowance that we were to receive. We would receive a cooked breakfast, a packed lunch and an evening meal. Jock Raeburn and I would have to share a bedroom that had two single beds. Mrs Leach preferred to be paid one weeks board in advance. We agreed to arrange an advance in our salaries or collect our subsistence in advance when we get on site to-morrow morning. We were given a tour of the entire house and our landlady explained that in the evening after dinner we could share the lounge with the family. She had a seventeen year old daughter named Mary and Mrs Leach informed us that she was a widow, *rather young, I thought.* After the tour of the house it was a done deal and we both settled into our new lodging's. I changed into casual cloths as soon as was possible, then Raeburn and I went to the nearest public telephone booth. We phoned the Du-Pont site to check in and make enquiries as to the nearest Du-Pont bus pick-up point and were pleased to find out that it was very near our new digs. I had mentioned to Mrs Leach that I needed to get my suit dry cleaned and she agreed to arrange that for me.

Six-o-clock the next morning we were both up and after washing, wandered downstairs. Mrs Leach served Raeburn and I a very nice breakfast and placed neatly wrapped up parcels in front of us that contained our packed sandwiches for lunch. We were at the Do-Pont construction bus pick up point before seven-o-clock because we had been instructed the bus should arrive at that point between seven-o-clock and fifteen minutes past. The Du-Pont's gigantic chemical complex was similar to entering a military zone, every single person entered through single type turn-styles gate's and all matches or cigarette lighters were confiscated. As new recruits we were both ushered away to be photographed, lectured on procedure and the extreme strict safety regulations. Everything we were verbally told was confirmed in writing. We were issued identity cards complete with our photograph and an ID number. No type of ignition was allowed on site. Special enclosure corrals were located throughout the site and available for smoking breaks. Matches were supplied at these enclosure corrals that were under constant closed-circuit camera surveillance to discourage abusive users. When one left the site after the days ten hour shift, free matches were available for smokers wishing to light up a cigarette on the one hour bus ride back into Derry.

I got up off the floor and stood upright when this guy
leapt closer and head-butted me in the face.

We were both settling into our new lodgings and new found employment in Ireland amicably. Although Raeburn and I were both Scots and lived in the same city, in the same area in that city, we had never ever met before. As it had transpired, we were both members of the same trade union branch in Edinburgh and that is were we both met when we were being briefed about this job with Do-Pont in Derry in Northern Ireland. I have to say that I was finding this wee guy to be extremely rude and selfish. He would lie in his bed in the small bedroom we were sharing reading and smoking cigarettes until the early hours of the morning. I was also a smoker but had never ever smoked in bed and normally my first cigarette of the day would be after my ten-o-clock tea break. Our single beds only had one small bedside table separating them with one small table light between us. Therefore this bed-light that we shared was glowing until after midnight nearly every night and the smoke from his cigarettes were forever in and around my face and head. I did suggest a few times that he should consider calling it a night and put the light out but he would never respond and appeared to deliberately light up another cigarette and continue reading for at least another fifteen , twenty minutes. The last straw was when he started lighting up cigarettes in the middle of the night. He would put the bed-side light on

168

to find his lighter and cigarettes. One night we had a terrible row, I leapt out of my bed and attempted to move the bedside locker complete with light and his filthy ash tray to the opposite side of his bed. It was not possible, there was not enough space and I just lost my temper completely. I threatened him that if he did not put both his cigarette and the light out I was going to tip him and his cigarette out of bed and onto the floor. It was unfortunate that it had come to this but I have to say that after that night he never ever tried to light up a cigarette during the night and when I would suggest that he should call it a night and put the out, within a few minutes the light was out!

Jock Raeburn was a small thin guy about eight / nine years older than me and just knocking on forty years old. He had bedraggled wispy hair that matched his very dishevelled clothes. He wore glasses that had lenses like the bottom of beer bottles and he was extremely arrogant for a wee thin man. During any conversation we did have I discovered that he was very involved in the Union and never missed the monthly union meeting held at our branch office in Edinburgh at the top of Leith Walk. Apparently he spent every Friday and Saturday evening's at our Union's social club which was also situated at the top of Leith Walk in Broughton Street therefore he was well-known to our Union delegate, Brother Barrett and the committee It was people like Raeburn that always got the good jobs that were made known to our Union. These members always got first choice to the high paying jobs at home at Grangemouth Oil Refinery. In fact, I also discovered that this was Raeburn's first job away from home. Obviously that was one of the reasons that he had no experience in community living where one has to share a great deal and learn to live and let live, he was certainly not an experienced travelling man like myself.

One morning as Mrs Leach was serving us our breakfast and very casually asked. "Bye the way gentlemen, I never did ask you what denomination do you belong to?" Without hesitation, wee Jock Raeburn replied. "It's none of your business". I have to admit that I was more surprised than Mrs Leach at his response and attitude, however Mrs Leach did not respond but simply slighted her head towards me. I responded with. "I am a Catholic Mrs Leach, in fact my wife is Irish and was born in Donegal". Mrs Leach smiled and replied. "Donegal, how nice, beautiful county, beautiful". On the bus to work Raeburn questioned me and suggested that I was not a Catholic. I informed him that I was married in St Patrick's Chapel in the Cowgate in Edinburgh, then I continued. "You know my friend, you are an inconsiderate arrogant little b*******". You know that women is a devout Catholic and we are living in her house. Why on earth do you have to be such an uncouth lout. It was totally unnecessary and uncalled for the way you behaved and answered her so rudely. I hope she throws you out on your arse". I was sitting on the outside seat on the bus beside him and moved to another seat before he could reply. From that day on, we never sat together on the bus or at the same table in the cabin during our meal breaks.

Mrs Leach never ever did ask wee Jock Raeburn to leave, she had obviously decided that there was more than one way to skin a rabbit and reprimand wee Jock Raeburn and his arrogant attitude. She started off by deliberately serving smaller portions off food to him during breakfast and our evening meal. He was obviously aware of it but too stubborn and contemptuous to comment. Then the packed lunch sandwiches were suddenly very different. One day he stormed over to my table in the cabin at work and demanded to know what I had on my sandwiches. Off course I was now also very much aware of what was going on and I liked it. I opened up one off my sandwiches which was full of ham and cheese. He placed one of his sandwiches on my table which only had a slice of cheese on it. I could only smile at him but said nothing. He said nothing and stormed away back to his own table that he shared with others. That evening back in the house and after we had sat down to our evening meal, he questioned Mrs Leach about the sandwiches and she flippantly apologised and informed him that she had run out of ham after she had made my sandwiches. Wee Jock Raeburn eventually found other accommodation to move into and both Mrs Leach and I were delighted. Mrs Leach did ask me to watch-out for a nice person to share the room with me, however I was in no hurry as I now had the bedroom and practically the run of the whole house to myself because her daughter never ever seemed to be around.

One afternoon whilst I was working in the fabrication shop, wee Jock Raeburn wandered in. He was working very close to me and he put his right hand into his top overall pocket and as he was pulling his reading glasses, a cigarette lighter dropped onto the concrete floor. I was shocked. Raeburn immediately looked around and quickly returned the exposed illegal cigarette lighter back into his pocket. I'm sure Raeburn, including myself considered that that was the end off the matter. However, as wee Jock Raeburn was leaving the fabrication-shop he was apprehended by two security officers and escorted away. Within hours we heard that a body search had produced the forbidden cigarette lighter and Raeburn had been instantly dismissed. This was the beginning of a chain of events that the deceitful wee Jock Raeburn was about to get all off us involved in. At the end of that working day as we were all clocking out, wee Jock Raeburn was waiting in the car park beside the buses. He immediately singled out and approached our pipe-fitters shop-steward. I personally was uninterested, until I realized that all the buses were being delayed because our shop-steward, a local Derry man wanted to hold an impromptu meeting. All hell was suddenly let-loose because these buses carried all sorts of tradesmen including welders, riggers, mechanical fitters and various other workers and assistants. These other tradesmen just wanted to get home and were not interested in wee Jock Raeburn's problem. Eventually after some serious arguments between individuals and other shop-stewards all the buses departed.

The next morning wee Jock Raeburn was back in the site car park confronting the pipe-fitters shop-steward and his assistant. All us pipe-fitters were instructed not to clock-on as we had to have a meeting because someone had been unfairly dismissed. It was a short meeting as someone proposed that the shop steward approach the Du-Pont management to ascertain what in fact actually happened. We all checked in for work except Raeburn. We heard nothing for two day's except that the local union delegate had been on site and had a meeting with the Du-Pont management. I had assumed that wee Jock Raeburn had gone back home to Edinburgh. That was until all pipe-fitters were instructed by our shop-steward that we must not turn up for work the next day as a meeting has been arranged by our Union delegate in a church hall in Derry town at ten-o-clock tomorrow morning. We were all given a small map with specific directions.

I was shocked to find wee Jock Raeburn inside the hall and he was not sitting in the pews with the rest off us pipe-fitters. Jock Raeburn was sitting on the raised platform at a table with our shop-steward, his assistant and two other men whom I guessed must be our local union delegates. One of the delegates promptly began to explain to us how brother Raeburn had inadvertently carried his personal cigarette lighter on to the Du-Pont site and had been instantly dismissed. He continued to explain to us how brother Raeburn had freely admitted his error and had apologised profusely to the Du-Pont management for his absentmindedness. The delegate further suggested that to be dismissed for this lapse off temporary forgetfulness, is unfair and unacceptable. He continued to suggest that owing to the fact that this is a first time offence, a warning should be suffice. This delegate concluded by informing us that he had received a telephone call from the Union Delegate in Edinburgh. The Edinburgh Union delegate had confirmed that brother Raeburn is a credit to the Union and a reliable, honest and trustworthy member of our union.

Before I was aware of it I was upstanding with my arm held high up in the air and asked the Derry delegate why the Edinburgh union delegate was involved in this particular issue that is taking place in Northern Ireland. I was not surprised when he informed me that brother Raeburn had actually phoned Mr Barrett in Edinburgh, for advice! There was a protracted silence until someone in front of me pushed his arm up into the air for permission to speak and he more or less shocked the hundred or so people in the room when he suggested that Raeburn had recently been openly boasting about how dexterous he was at smuggling his personal cigarette lighter onto the Du-Pont construction site. I was shocked at this revelation, yet not too surprised. Before the delegate or anyone else on the stage could respond I raised my hand and explained that it was part and partial to all our condition of employment with Du-Pont that anyone that ignores or violates Du-Pont's security policy will be instantly dismissed. I further suggested that it now appears that brother Raeburn did not accidentally take his cigarette lighter onto the site therefore he has deliberately ignored and violated his condition of employment and he should be man enough to be responsible for his action without involving others. At least fifty percent of the people present in the hall murmured and voiced their support at my suggestion. In fact another person suggested that it was impossible to carry matches or cigarette lighters onto the Du-Pont construction site in error. He went on to explain how each and everyone of us entering the site have to pass through single-line turn-style gate's supervised by the security guards who are specifically requesting any form of ignition to be placed in the containers that or openly available. Some people in the hall became very agitated as if in support of that statement the delegate demanded some order. Raeburn denied the accusation that he had deliberately taken his lighter onto the site and once more reiterated that it was in error. Once more the hundred or so people in the hall became very rowdy and disorderly and indeed some openly expressing disagreement and at times violently. Once more the delegate demanded order however on this occasion he had some difficulty in gaining control. After a few minutes the delegate asked. "Has any member in this hall ever been told by brother Raeburn personally that he often deliberately takes his cigarette lighter into the Du-Pont compound?" The hall was now silenced and everyone was looking around them, obviously for some response. After a prolonged silence the delegate suggested that under the circumstances the rumours that brother Raeburn was boasting about doing it were nothing but hearsay. Once more some people in the hall burst into vociferous objections. The delegate once more demanded order and suggested the he arranges a further meeting with the Du-Pont management and if they refuse to reinstate brother Raeburn he would recommend that we pipe-fitters vote for strike action and seek support from all the other tradesmen on the site. There was instant grumblings of discontent from a large amount of members in the hall. Seperate groups of people were once more arguing with each other and it took a good few minutes before the delegate had control of the meeting again. I raised my right arm and the Delegate pointed at me once more. I suggested that he himself as the area union delegate for Derry must have been agreeable to Du-Pont's inflexible and strict safety policy and conditions prior to them being implemented. Therefore as we all present have also agreed to accept these terms and conditions of employment. Brother Raeburn has been caught red handed violating these inflexible and strict working conditions and acted irresponsibly. I for one have no intention off loosing time off work which will cost me financially to support his arrogant foolishness. I Proposed that we return to work without further delay and if Du-Pont refuse to give brother Raeburn a return ticket to Edinburgh, we pipe-fitters will have a collection to pay for the ticket. There was an instant uproar of whistles and people shouting. "Yes, Yes". Other people started waving their hands in the air shouting. "I second that proposal". The Delegate shouted for order and after a few minutes requested that we have a show off hands by all those in favour of my proposal. The show of hands in favour of my proposal was instant and looked uncompromising. He then requested a show off hands against the proposal. It was obvious that they were in the minority. Our shop-steward proposed that the delegate make a last and final approach to the management and ask for leniency for brother Raeburn and that he is given a final warning. There was a good fifteen minutes of heavy and serious debate and eventually it was agreed. But the final conclusion of this decision should be infiltrated to us on site by our shop steward in order to avoid further loss of time off work without pay.

The hall was soon emptied and the nearest bars were soon pulling pints of beer for over a hundred pipe-fitters. Most of the pipe-fitters were celebrating avoiding a possible strike action and obviously some were frustrated and even dissatisfied. I was sitting having a pint with a few of the local pipe-fitters from the job that I had become friendly with. A big guy walked up to our table and asked me "Hey Cass, is it true that this guy Raeburn is a mate of yours?". I looked at him and he instantly reminded me of a young *Burl Ives, the American folk singer / Actor*. I explained that we both lived in Edinburgh and that we had travelled on the ferry together. But until then we had never ever met each other. I was shocked when he further suggested that I should be the new shop steward for the pipe-fitters because the one we have presently is useless. He further suggested that If I had been the shop- steward that meeting in the hall in town would never have taken place. I gracefully rejected any possibility of me becoming a shop steward and further explained that if a job was to become available nearer home I would not hesitate in returning home. We were eventually informed that Du-Pont had refused to reinstate wee Jock Raeburn but agreed to pay for his repatriation to Edinburgh in Scotland.

Ever since Raeburn had moved out, Mrs Leach had been trying to get me to attend mass at a local chapel on a Saturday night for people like myself that had to work Sundays. I managed to keep making what must have been reasonable excuses because she informed that she would continue to pray for me. As it also turned out the big guy that looked like Burl Ives the American folk-singer also played the guitar and sang ballads and folk songs in a pub in at the weekends so that's where I used to go on Saturday nights and we become friends. I knew he was a catholic and he obviously had me down as one also then I eventually discovered that he knew Mrs Leach and that I was lodging with her and a couple of times he asked me about the Saturday night mass and hinted that he never ever met me there so I was beginning to get a wee bit concerned about this sudden interest in my ethical standards. I was still working in the fabrication shop which was a bonus because we always got paid a few pence an hour more than the ordinary pipe-fitters. I had Just returned from one of the smoking corral's where I had been for a smoke when one of the other pipe fitters told me that a couple of guys had been asking about me. When I had enquired who they were and what did the want, they suggested that they had no idea and that they had just wandered into the fabrication shop and asked if a guy named Cass worked in here and when they were told that I was away having a smoke, they just wandered away back out again. About half an hour later I was kneeling on the concrete floor in the fabrication shop marking out some angles as I was fabricating a lobster back bend when two guys walked in and one of them asked me "Are you called Cass or Fluking Cassie?" "Yes" I replied. He said. "You're the B****** that had that pipe- fitter sacked?" I got up off the floor and stood-upright when this person leapt closer and head-butted me in the face. All I remember was crashing back down onto the concrete floor. My eyes were burning and appeared to be full off huge tears. My lips trembled and my throat seized. The pain was dull, yet excruciating, I was shocked and unable to focus. After a few seconds, I made an attempt to get up off the floor but a boot was pressed on my chest and pinned me to the floor. A far away clear voice like thunder said. "You'd be well advised to stay down there were you are". I did and after another minute or so I was being helped up and onto my feet and someone was asking me. "Are you all right?. What the hell was that all that about?". It was a few of the other pipe-fitters that worked in the fab-shop that were talking to me. I was still dizzy and unable to respond. I put my hand up to my forehead and my fingers were covered in blood. I felt as if I had to sit down but there was nowhere to sit. I asked. "Who are these people?. Where are they?. Does anyone know them?". Someone said. "They've gone and I think they're *Riggers,* well, I know one off them is". I looked around and decided to go too the loo. There was a half- inch cut running directly across the top off my nose. That appeared to be all the visible damage but the thump-ing headache was invisible. I thought, a half inch lower and my nose would have been spread across my face. In the cabin at lunch, Burl Ives promised me that he would make some enquiries as to who it was that attacked me but at the moment all I wanted was to get on the bus to get home to my digs at the end of the day.

Mrs Leach noticed the cut the minute I sat down at the table for our evening meal. I lied and told her that I had an accident at work. I had a sleepless night and in the morning I knew why. I had two black eyes and a swollen nose. I decided I just couldn't go to work, I needed some treatment, some help and I felt and looked terrible. I was full off anger and hatred and was stupidly blaming wee Jock Raeburn. Mrs Leach wanted me to go and see her doctor but I was to embarrassed but agreed to her going to her chemist and getting me some pain killers. Mrs Leach fussed about like a wee mother hen so on the third day I went back to work with my black eyes, swollen nose and hurt pride. Burl Ives had collected some information about my head-butting incident. Both the guy's were rigger's, one of them was the riggers shop steward, both Orangemen, staunch trade unionist and staunch members of the Orange Order. Also the one that was the shop steward, was also the Convenor off all the shop stewards on the Du-pont construction site. He was not the one who had head-butted me, the one that had head-butted me was his assistant shop steward. Burl Ives went on to explain how the Convenor was so sorry about what had happened, because all he wanted was for me to explain the circumstances with reference to the Raeburn incident. In fact it was our own pipe-fitters shop steward who suggested that he speak with me, when the Convenor had asked him for an explanation. Burl Ives reiterated that the Convenor was shocked and sorry about the vicious attack on me by his assistant. Apparently, the guy that head-butted me was well- known for his infamous deadly head-butting techniques. Burl Ives suggested that the Convenor wants to meet with me and our own shop steward to apologise and I should let him know when that could be arranged. Burl Ives also suggested that I should let sleeping dogs lie.

It was over a week before I decided it was time for me to go with my shop steward to talk to the Convenor and if possible his head-butting assistant and Burl- Ives insisted on going with us. As we entered the cabin where we were to meet, Burl Ives pointed to the table where the convenor and his assistant were sitting playing cards with four other men. As we approached the table one off them stood up. My shop-steward introduced me to the one that was standing as the convenor. I knew immediately by his nervous and uneasy behaviour that the person sitting opposite the convenor was the person that had head-butted me. The convenor stepped away from the table and the head-butter stood upright and I immediately realized that he was slightly taller than me but very thin. The convenor stepped forward and shook my hand and immediately commenced apologising to me profusely about what had happened. He was also very nervous and kept looking at Burl Ives then he noticed that I was watching the head-butter and immediately suggested that we should go outside and I agreed until he turned around to face the head-banger and told him sit down and remain at the table. This was not what I wanted at all.

Once out-side the convenor further explained to me how shocked he was when his assistant suddenly attacked me in the fabrication-shop. He informed me that he was no longer his assistant and that the circumstances surrounding the Jock Raeburn incident had now been fully investigated and he agreed that I was correct in the action I had taken to defend our rights not to go on strike over the matter. He concluded by suggesting that the head-banger also wished to apologise to me and would I be willing to accept his apology. Without hesitation I agreed. The convenor quickly agreed to go back into the cabin and escort his ex-assistant outside to apologise. Burl Ives patted me on the back, I assumed for me being so diplomatic.

The second that the head-butter stepped out of the cabin behind the convenor I stealthily and swiftly stepped forward towards them both. Gently but firmly I nudged the convenor to one side then swiftly smashed my tightly closed right hand fist into the head-butter's face. He staggered backwards and hit the door standard with his back but remained upright. Like lightening I leapt forward and smashed my fist into his face again before he slid sideways back into the cabin. Burl Ives and the convenor looked on in utter amazement then both of them moved into the cabin after him and slammed the door shut. I waited and attempted to clean the blood off my right hand but it looked as if the blood was seeping from between the knuckles. Burl Ives appeared closing the cabin door behind him. He touched my arm and said. "Come on let's go, it's finished, it's over". I learned later that I had got myself inadvertently involved in some elaborate sectarian conflict. As it turned out, wee Jock Raeburn was friendly with the convenor and his head-butting assistant. In fact it was the head-butter that arranged for wee Jock Raeburn to move into his new digs and that was with the head-butter's mother who was also non-catholic. So at the at the end of the day, Raeburn not only attempted to create a strike, he could have been responsible for a serious sectarian disturbance on the Du-Pont construction site between Protestant and Catholic Irishmen.

Kathleen and I would write letters to each other nearly every other day and in her latest letter, especially the last chapter, she had some good news. Bill Craigens, my brother-in-law who was also a pipe-fitter had been working in London for the last year or so and was about to be transferred to a new project in Glasgow. Bill was working with a company named Humphrey's & Glasgow who had just completed the construction off a Gas Reforming Plant in London. As soon as he is transferred to Glasgow where they intend to build another Gas Reforming Plant, Bill is going to speak with the site engineer and try and get me a job beside him in the fabrication-shop. Bill Craigens was an excellent tradesman. a first class fabricator and very well known in the Industry as being reliable and dependable. Being recommended for a job by such a first-class tradesman would be an excellent reference. It's only a very small percentage of pipe fitters that are qualified enough to hold down a job in the fabrication shop therefore there are often a shortage of pipe fabricators. This was great new's and if Bill can pull it off, we would both travel to and from work in my car and be at home every evening and still be earning good money. However, if he doesn't manage to pull it off, he will have to live in digs in Glasgow as it would be extremely difficult for him to travel back and forward to Glasgow every day in public transport, so he does have an incentive to get me that job. We would both also qualify for a weekly lodging allowance and use that money to share the petrol cost. This could prove to be an excellent move for both off us because with the additional bonus of the lodging allowance and sharing the cost of petrol we would both gain financially.

I was due for my first long weekend leave back to Edinburgh as I had now been in Derry for six-weeks so I started a letter immediately asking Kathleen to inform her sister Mary to tell her husband Bill that I would be home in a weeks time on my long weekend leave. I also explained in my letter to Kathleen that I would be bringing all my personal belonging's home in preparation not to return to Derry, hoping that I could start work in Glasgow. My long weekend eventually arrived and on the Thursday night I was once more on the overnight Ferry from Londonderry to Glasgow and praying that I would not have to return. I had said nothing to Mrs Leach or anyone else about my hopes and plans because unless I get this job in Glasgow, I would be returning to Du-Pont.

As usual I was having an excellent weekend with Kathleen and the kids. It was always wonderful returning home because one was always made so welcome, so special and of course another honeymoon. Unfortunately Bill was still in London so we heard nothing about the Glasgow Project and that nearly spoilt it. I had phoned the Humphrey & Glasgow London office and they confirmed that they had a Project in Glasgow but were not yet at the recruitment stage. I mentioned Bill Craigens but it was just another name to these head office recruitment staff however they did agree to send me an application form. On the Monday morning after dropping Linda and Lorna off at school, Kathleen wee Mark and I drove into Edinburgh in our wee Ford car to visit Kathleen's sister Mary and to find out if she had any news from her husband Bill who was still in London. Her last letter from her husband Bill only confirmed that he was still waiting to be transferred to the new Project in Glasgow. As we were about leave St Mary's Street where Kathleen's sister lived, we met Albert Croal. Albert is the plumber that still works with Copeland's the plumbers where I had completed my apprenticeship. We eventually got talking about work and what I was doing and where I was working. I told him about my job in Ireland and that I was due to return. I also explained to him about my dilemma with the possibility of a job in Glasgow soon. He told me Copeland was very busy and that he was having to do lots of jobs himself. He confirmed there was still only himself, smelly Tam and a new apprentice. He explained that Mr Copeland was reluctant to take on another plumber in case this glut off work dries up and then he would have to make him redundant. Then he said. "With you Cass it's different, you two seem to have an understanding, you know what I mean". He suggested that I should explain my dilemma to Copeland and ask him to give me a job for a few weeks or until the Glasgow job starts up. I refused immediately and explained that I just could not go back to him again and then leave when it was convenient to me.

Back home as I was packing my bag in my preparation to travel through to Glasgow to get my overnight ferry back to Londonderry I reiterated that if I had to go back to plumbing I would have to find a job with some other plumber shop, because I could not ask Mr Copeland again and for the third time. We had our evening meal earlier than usual as I would have to leave around six-o-clock in the evening to get my train to Glasgow. Eventually l was on the bus from Corstorphine to Waverly Railway Station in Princess Street. I was on my way back to Du-Pont via Glasgow and then the Derry-Ducker overnight ferry to Derry in Northern Ireland. I got off the bus in Princess Street and walked down to Waverly Street Railway Station. I was standing on the platform waiting for the Glasgow train and inwardly sighed, picked up my bag and headed back home to Kathleen and our three children.

Indifferent: 16

I jumped off the bus at Surgeons Hall and headed for the Pleasance where Copeland's plumbers shop was situated on the corner at the top off Arthur Street, the very place where I was born, thirty years previously. My old boss, Mr Robert Copeland's wee Morris-Minor pick-up was not parked outside the shop which confirmed that he was not there. Albert had said they were very busy, so perhaps they are all out on job's. I tried the door handle and the door was locked so I wandered off and the sound off a car horn interrupted my train of thoughts, it was my old boss himself, Mr Copeland. He stopped his old Morris-Minor van on the other-side of the road and indicated through his open window that I should come over and when I arrived, he greeted me. "Hello stranger, so you didn't go back to Ireland, Albert was telling me that he met you and your wife. Well !, what do you think? Are we going to help each other out?". I was lost for words for a few seconds then replied. "Ye, thanks, I'm really very grateful". He held up his hand as if to interrupted me and asked me. "When can you start?". Before I could answer he continued. !Can you start to-morrow?". I nodded my head indicating yes and said. "Thank you". I was walking away when he shouted. "Eight-O-clock". I waved back in agreement and just couldn't wait to get home. Kathleen and the kids were delighted and we all hugged each other tightly.

Only Mr Copeland and smelly old Tom had beat me into the shop the next morning. Tom was his usual indifferent self when he greeted me. Albert on the other hand when he arrived greeted me so warmly. The last person to arrive that morning was the new apprentice. Mr Copeland was in the office sorting out the jobs and obviously deciding who was going where. Albert pointed to the apprentice and introduced young John to me then informed me that young John also lived in the Corstorphine area of Edinburgh. The boss, Mr Copeland interrupted the introductions when he entered the work shop and immediately chastised John the young apprentice. "Listen young man, I have told you before, Eight-O-Clock is when we all start work, okay?". The young apprentice made no response.

My first week working as a plumber again flew past and I collected my first plumbers wage packet and it was a pittance compared to what I was earning at Du-Pont in Ireland. However as much as I disliked plumbing, I was enjoying the work at Copeland's. It was so cool and relaxed working with friends and being at home every night with Kathleen and the three children was fantastic. When the application from Humphreys & Glasgow, for the pipe-fitters job in Glasgow, Kathleen was indifferent. When I was filling in the application form I suggested to her that I hope they don't offer me the Glasgow job too soon as I would have to leave Mr Copeland's immediately and he is so busy. Kathleen said. "Don't send it". The next couple of weeks past and Kathleen couldn't understand why I was taking the bus and not using our wee Ford Popular car. My excuse to Kathleen was that if I use it to go to work I may have to put dirty smelly plumbing equipment in it. But the fact was I didn't want Mr Copeland or Albert to know that we had a car.

Young John the first year apprentice spent all off his time working with Albert. It was obvious that's the way Mr Copeland wanted it to be. Albert appeared to somewhat disapprove of the young apprentice and told me that he had actually caught him stealing some of the scrap lead. We had a good laugh about that because in the past we were often guilty of helping ourselves to some of the scrap copper and lead. One day the boss sent me to a job in Marchmont, the very posh area of Edinburgh. He had previously checked the job and informed me that there was a problem with the gas cooker. He surprised me when he instructed me to take John the apprentice with me. Copeland's was a typical Plumbers business of the 60's *Plumbers, Glaziers, Gas-Fitters & Electricians.* The house in Marchmont was very large and luxurious. It was enclosed by huge stone walls that surrounded its own private grounds and circular driveway. The kitchen was as large as our living room in our house in Corstorphine. The gas cooker in question had been custom built for this kitchen with eight number gas rings of various sizes and several grills that appeared to double as barbeques. The problem was that the flames were not producing enough heat. Apparently the maid had dismantled it to clean it and after she re-assembled it, it was now unusable.

In the hall, he stopped for a few seconds to glance at the smashed glass table and pools of blood.

Not long after we had arrived the lady off the house had informed me that she had an appointment and I was to close the door behind me on leaving. Eventually I came to the conclusion that the root of the problem was an insufficient mixture of gas and air. It was a very tedious and time consuming exercise adjusting the exact mixture. Although the kitchen was huge and I was fully occupied and frustrated, I suddenly realized that John the apprentice was no longer beside me. I shouted out his name in a sort of whisper but there was no response. After looking in all the obvious places like the hall and the ground floor bathrooms, I wandered up the wide winding staircase and found him in one off the bedrooms. He was just retreating from what turned out to be a walk in wardrobe. I was shocked and furious. In all my years in this business and even during my own apprenticeship, I had never ever experienced such behaviour. Even after cross-examining him as to why he was searching around the customer's private property, I was not satisfied with his derogatory response. I ordered him out off the house and in fact pushed him down the stairway so violently that he very nearly tumbled down. He was complaining bitterly and threatened to tell his Dad about me pushing him about. At the bottom of the stairway I grabbed him by the lapels of his overalls. "Listen you little runt, I don't care about you or your Dad. Now get outside and wait there until I'm finished and when we get back to the shop I will inform Mr Copeland about this and he will have to decide what to do with you". He interrupted me before I was finished when he shouted. "My Dad knows you. You both worked together in Ireland and you got my Dad into trouble just like you are trying to do to me". I was speechless and could only stand and glare at him for a minute or so then I asked him. "You're Jock Raeburn's son?". "Yes I am and he's going to get you". He shouted. I grabbed him, dragged and pushed him towards the kitchen and the back door of the house. He broke free and away from me and stumbled into a large low standing smoky coloured glass top table. Then he appeared to slip and stumble. To my horror I watched him slowly fall backwards onto the top off the huge coloured glassed top table. As he was falling, he appeared to stretch out his right hand to steady himself and with a sudden crash and smash he fell into and through the glass table. The scream and shattering of glass echoed throughout the large white marble floor hallway. It was a few seconds before I realized the horror that had just unfolded before my very eyes. I rushed forward and started to pull the boy out of the metal frame where he appeared to be stuck fast. A large pool of blood was gathering on the white marble floor and all the shattered glass was scattered beneath him. He was hysterical and crying. The blood appeared to be pouring from his right arm and hand. I got him free and lifted him clear and was trying to assure him that he was going to be okay as I guided him into the huge Kitchen and at the same time watching the river of red blood that was following us. I knew I had to stem the flow off blood. so I got him sitting down but he refused to let me try to remove the top of his overall however but as soon as I wrapped a clean kitchen towel around his right hand it stopped the flow off blood. I still needed help so I left him sitting in the kitchen, found a phone and phoned the shop and was somewhat reassured when Mr Copeland answered the phone. He confirmed that he would be with us in five minutes and reiterated that I should stop the bleeding. The blood was now dripping steadily through the towel. I grabbed a few more from the drawer and gently removed the existing one from around the hand. Young John had stopped crying and appeared to be in a state of shock so I gently tapped his face and explained that Mr Copeland was on his way and would take him to the hospital to have his cuts attended to. The cuts appeared to be between his fingers. I very gently but swiftly wrapped the clean kitchen towel around his hand again and that's when I noticed that some blood was also dripping down his arm. When Mr Copeland arrived he had a look at the hand then lifted him into his arms and was heading out towards the front door. In the hall he stopped for a few seconds to glance at the smashed glass table and pools of blood.

We arrived at the Accident & Emergency Department of the Royal Infirmary adjacent to the meadows in a matter of minutes. The boy was taken away almost immediately. While we were sitting waiting, I explained in great detail to Mr Copeland what exactly had happened. He said nothing except assure me that the boy would be okay and that I was not to worry because he would take care of everything. After a half an hour or so a staff nurse called us and the three of us went into went into a small office. The boy was fine, stitches had been inserted into three of his fingers and his thumb on his right hand. He was still recovering. Then she dropped the bombshell. She informed us that when they had cut his jacket sleeve some jewellery had fallen out off the pocket. She held up what looked like a ladies silver bracelet with at least a dozen little trinkets hanging from it and a pair of ear-rings. After a few minutes silence, Mr Copeland suggested that the jewellery could be the property off one off his customers. He eventually signed for and took possession of the jewellery, phoned the customer from the hospital and explained what had happened and assured her that his insurance would replace / repair everything that had been damaged. After the boy had been discharged he drove us both to Corstorphine. Apparently he met with the boys mother, discussed the incident, the accident and the jewellery. It was soon confirmed that the jewellery was owned by the customer and had been removed by the boy from the bedroom. Mr Copeland managed to convince his customer not to press charges as the jewellery was safely returned. His insurance took care off the cleaning and the replacement of the glass table top etc. As the days passed I was expecting Raeburn senior to seek me out and accuse me of being responsible for his stupid boy loosing his apprenticeship job and most probably for his son's accident. It never happened. Eventually Bill Craigens was transferred from London to Glasgow and convinced the site engineer that I was the right man to be offered a job in the fabrication shop. I informed Mr Copeland that I had got the job in Glasgow and that it was once more time for me to move on. As was usual, on the Friday night after he had paid us he took us to the local pub for a pint off beer. Mr Copeland wished me well on my new job and thanked me for helping him out. I suggested that it was my pleasure and that once more he had done me and my family an enormous favour. He finished his pint and bid Albert, smelly Tom and myself goodnight and left. That man had thrown me a life line a few times and I wondered if I would ever see him again?

Hansen, Cass, Falconer – Trieste 1953

Falconer, Cass, Hansen
– Trieste 1953

Falconer, Cass, two colleagues
– Trieste 1954

Colleague and Cass – Trieste 1954

Nurse Kathleen – 1953

Nurse Kathleen and colleague – 1953

Tam Leonard and Cass – 1955

Kathleen – 1956

Cass – 1956

iv

Kathleen and Cass – 1956

Kathleen – 1956

Kathleen and Cass engagement – 1956. Left:
Kathleen's parents. Right: Cass' parents.

Kathleen and Cass
engagement – 1956.

Kathleen and Cass wedding – 28 December 1957.

Kathleen and Cass wedding – 28 December 1957.

Kathleen and Cass – 1958

Cass – 1958

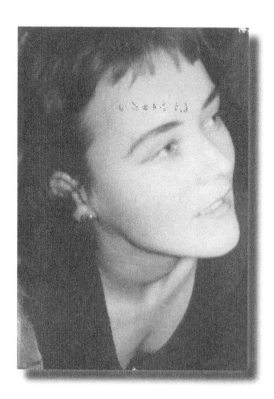

Kathleen – 1958

Cass' elder sister
Cathie's wedding, with
Kathleen – 1958

Linda and Lorna– 1959

Linda and Lorna– 1959

Cass and Bill Craigens. Proven Mill Glasgow Project – 1962

Bill Craigens and Cass with colleagues. Proven Mill Glasgow
Project – 1962

Lorna, Mark and Linda – 1963

Lorna, Cass and Linda – 1963

Lorna, Linda and Mark – 1963

Linda, Mark, Cass and Lorna – 1964

Kathleen – 1968

Indifferent: 17

Bill Craigens and I were now both working for Humphrey's & Glasgow on the construction of a new Gas Reforming Plant as pipe-fitter fabricators on the Proven Mill site on the outskirts of Glasgow city. We were travelling back and forward every day seven days a week in my wee Ford Popular car. It was mostly Glasgow pipe fitters and welders that had been recruited on the job therefore Bill and I were the only two Edinburgh guy's. Because of this and the fact that we almost always worked together as a team in the fabrication shop, the Glasgow guy's nicknamed us, simmet & drawers [Vest & Underpants]

Proven Mill Glasgow was a terribly wicked, treacherous and very dangerous council housing area. The construction site itself was the old Gas Works where the original old Coke Gas Plant was on the outskirt of the local housing estate. This entire Proven Mill estate was defunct and a no-go area even for the police. The majority of the council houses were all empty and boarded up. Apparently most of the ex tenants were in prison or had managed to escape to another safer area. According to the guys on the site, even the infamous Gorbals council housing estate was a paradise compared to Proven Mill. It was believed that the baths in the bathrooms in these houses that had still had tenants living in them in were ever only used as coal bins. Coal stolen from the rail wagons that rumbled ever so slowly up the steep gradient that ran past the estate. When the huge train wagons laden with coal slowed down whilst climbing the steep grade, the residents still living in the boarded-up houses in the Proven-Mill estate would jump up onto the slow moving wagons and throw off the coal, while their wives or children collected it in their prams. The coal board eventually fenced in the entire area and had guard's with huge ferocious Alsatian dogs patrolling the area twenty four hour's, seven days a week. The tenants from the Proven Mill council housing estate would take bitch dogs that were in heat up to the fences and when the Alsatian dogs put their heads through the wire to smell the bitch, they killed the Alsatian dogs with one blow of a hammer and the dog handlers ran for their lives.

We had discovered that these Glasgow drunks and ruffian's that we shared accommodation with, could be extremely violent.

Our construction project had Porto cabins situated strategically throughout the entire site that housed a half a dozen security men in each one working twenty four seven. That did not stop the thief men during the night stealing all the welder's heavy duty copper welding and earth cables. The stories go that the gangs from the Proven Mill estate would arrive during the night armed with hatchets, knifes and iron bars and inform the security guy's that as long as they did not call the police and remained in their cabins they would be safe. If they did phone the police they would eventually return, lock them in their cabins, set fire to their cabins and burn them to death. It was surreal. One morning we all arrived on site just after all the welders heavy duty welding and earth cables had been stolen during the night and it was chaotic. The security team had told their story to the resident engineer who immediately phoned the police. The police eventually arrived and after interviewing all the security men arrested them all. Our resident engineer phoned the manager of the security company to inform him what had happened and demanded that he gets himself to the site without further delay. The police bundled all the security men into vans and whisked them all away off the site. It was madness. Eventually new security teams arrived on site to take over. Thousands and thousands of pounds of new welding and earth cable would have to be replaced that day to allow the work to proceed and during this time our construction site was practically at a stand still until such time as new cables arrived. A few weeks later all the cables and all the security guards were gone again and so it went on and on and on.

Bill Craigens and I had to play a very low key existence on this Proven mill construction site being the only two Edinburgh men. We got on quite well with some of the local Glasgow tradesmen because we knew them whilst working with them at Grangemouth Oil Refinery. However quite a few of the labourers employed on the site were from the area around the Proven Mill council estate, therefore one had to be careful because some them were impertinent and daring individuals. Because we were both making good money and being at home in our own beds every single night eliminated any thought of resigning. It was complex at times but worth it. We were leaving Edinburgh at 0600 hours in the morning and not getting home again until after six-thirty in the evening and that was seven days a week. Bill was fortunate in that he could fall asleep at times on the way to work in the morning and most definitely every night on the drive home.

When it was getting near the end of the job, Bill and I were selected to be members of the commissioning team and there were nights when we had to work until after midnight. Instead of driving back to Edinburgh we decided that when that happened we would stay overnight in the local Salvation Army working men's club's. These place's in the 60's was where the homeless and down and out's also stayed. They were clean and cheap but most of the residents were drunk's, alcoholics, ruffian's, thugs, and thief's. We were of the opinion that we were capable of looking after ourselves but I was always concerned about my wee Ford car and if it would still be there in the morning and if it was, would it still have four wheels. When we did have to work these long shifts and that was often during commissioning, the company was responsible for supplying food and it was normally from the fish and chip shops and it was a choice of black pudding and chips, haggis and chips or fish and chips. If we had prior warning, we would make arrangements to take a couple of litre bottles of Buck- Fast local wine back to our local Salvation Army lodgings after work. It was the only way we could get some sleep because some of the drunk's and wino's used to stagger back during the early hours of the morning and would start shouting and fighting. Often because they were so inebriated they didn't know where their rooms were and a few times would often try to knock or smash our door open. Bill and I always made sure we had a double room with two single beds because we felt it was necessary for security reasons and in order to help to defend each other. We had discovered that these Glasgow drunks and ruffian's that we were sharing accommodation with could be extremely violent. When we had finished drinking our wine we always placed our two empty bottles on the floor a few inches away from the door, then in the event that anyone during the night did get access to our room they would knock the bottles over which would give us a warning. However, that never ever happened and we never ever had to defend ourselves and my wee Ford car was always there waiting patiently for us in the morning and it still had its four wheels.

We were actually working on the Proven Mill project in Glasgow during the 1962 Cubin ballistic missiles deployment know as the 13 day confrontation [14th October - 28th October 1962] between J.F Kennedy of the U.S. and Nikita Khrushchev of Russia. Khrushchev had sent ships from Russia to place it's cargo off ballistic missile's on Cuba just ninety miles from the shores of America. J.F. Kennedy, president of America threatened Khrushchev that if he didn't turn his ships back to Russia, he would blow them out of the water. This could have been the start of a nuclear war, however Khrushchev did eventually turn his ships around and back to Russia. I do remember that period because Bill and myself started a betting syndicate on who would back-down first and we kept a day to day report by writing our report in chalk on the side of a huge metal heat-exchanger.

The day finally arrived when the Gas Reforming Plant at Proven Mill Glasgow was complete. Because Bill and I were involved with the plant commissioning team, we were both fully employed until the very last day and even then, the company had decided that they wanted to offer both of us further employment on the construction of another Gas Reforming Plant. Further employment meant that we were both made redundant and once we reported to the site of the new project, we would then be re-employed.

We both decided that we would have a couple of weeks off work to spend with our families, then once more we would get back on the road again. Our wee boy Mark was now over a year old and Linda and Lorna were now nearly five and would be going to school soon. We had a fantastic two weeks together at home and Kathleen was looking radiant again in spite of being run ragged at times with the three children and I have to say that during that two weeks after we had put the children to bed, I was exhausted and often dozed of to sleep whilst Kathleen and I were watching the T.V.

Indifferent: 18

Leeds in England was the location where the other Gas Reformer Plant was about to be built and that's where Bill Craigens and I were offered further employment and eventually, we travelled down to Leeds overnight in my wee reliable Ford Popular car and eventually found the project site the next morning which was practically in Leeds town centre. Once more the site for the new Gas Reformer Plant was in the old existing Coke Coal Gas Works in a place named Meadow Lane.

We found digs not far from the site in a large house adjacent to a cemetery with a huge weeping willow tree in the front garden and It looked a very bleak house indeed. Mrs Benn was the name of our landlady and her husband Dee was a gentle giant who worked in a factory that made copper pipe fittings. They were a very pleasant couple with one young daughter who's name was Rebecca and they also had a wee horrible horny dog. Like her mum, wee Rebecca was slightly overweight. Mrs Benn had explained to us that she had never had lodgers before and had only recently decided to take in lodgers after one of the local news papers had reported the construction of the new Gas Plant and that the town would soon have to cater for a sudden influx of specialized tradesmen that would be employed in the construction the new Gas Plant. Therefore, Bill Craigens and I were their first lodgers.

The civil Engineers that were already on the job were in the process of demolishing and removing the old Gas Coke Works and levelling out the new construction site. They were also erecting the temporary cabins, stores and canteen facilities for the hundred or so craftsmen that would soon be employed. This was the to be the third Gas Reformer Plant Construction that Bill had been on and my second one and we were once more employed by Humphreys & Glasgow. We were both aware that this plant would take between eighteen months and two years to complete and that we were the first two skilled workers to arrive on site. The Trade Union agreements and normal procedure was at that time the first tradesmen employed, were the last tradesmen to be made redundant, that was of course, all things being equal. Therefore we were both more or less guaranteed steady employment for the next eighteen months at least.

Bill Craigens was well known in this Industry as *The Burglar*, it was his nickname because he was so consciences and keen to get on with his work that he would furtively take tools and other equipment away from others, rather than wait until they were available for him to use. This Industry was made up of a close bunch of individual tradesmen that would meet up with each other on many other jobs in many other parts of the country. There were many characters, famous and infamous and Bill Craigens was one of it's famous and colourful characters. Thomas Ray, a Glaswegian pipe-fitter was nicknamed *Sheets Ray,* because he always referred to a sterling one pound note as a Sheet. When he needed to borrow a few pounds from someone, he would ask. "Could you let me have a few sheets until Friday?". Rumour had it that at one time he was a script writer for some Glaswegian comedians. He was a larger than life agreeable middle aged unmarried man. A gambling man who loved the atmosphere of the typical pub with the smoke, the conversation and the tinkling of the drink glasses. No matter how much money *Sheets* had picked up in his paypacket on the Friday night, on the Monday morning he had nothing and that is when he would ask. "Could you let me have a few Sheets until Friday?". In desperation, he would write himself a letter from his mother requesting him to send her some money because she was in financial trouble and despairing. Before inserting the letter into an envelope addressed to himself he would sprinkle a small drop of water over the letter. Then finish the letter off with his mother apologising for the tear-drops on the paper. He would then make an appointment to see the Site Engineer to request an advance in his wages and produce the so called letter from his mother requesting financial assistance from her beloved Son.

Thomas Ray [Sheets] arrived on this construction site in Meadow Lane Leeds with another Glasgow pipe fitter nicknamed *The Bear,* because of his immense size and cranky personality. They were an awesome and impressive pair. *The Bear* like *Sheets* was also unmarried and like *Sheets* was larger than life. However *The Bear* unlike *Sheets* was ungraceful, awkward and fearsome looking. The story goes that during the very first week that both arrived in Leeds, *Sheets* was sitting having a quiet drink in a pub in the centre of Leeds one Friday evening waiting patiently for his friend, *The Bear.* He very casually commenced a conversation with two middle aged women that were sitting together at a table adjacent to himself. To *Sheets* delight he realized that these two members of the opposite sex were suddenly interested in his reserved and composed conversation. As the evening progressed *Sheets* became aware that things were going so well that he was now in a position to choose which one of these two females he was going to spend the night with. In fact things were going so well that he could be spending the night with both off them. Without warning, *The Bear* entered the bar and joined them and according to *Sheets* and the story. Within half an hour of *The Bear* joining them, *Sheets* said. "*The Bear had* scattered the herd".

Most of these charming characters were Glaswegians. Bobby Durham, another colourful character from Glasgow was nicknamed the *Rope.* Unlike *Sheets* or *The Bear,* the *Rope* was a wee wiry thin guy and an ex fly weight boxer that never made the grade, therefore would remain a pipe-fitter for the rest of his life. The *Rope* was a married man with a couple kids and hailed from Paisley. He was nicknamed the *Rope* because of his ability and expertise in using the ropes in the boxing rings to avoid and confuse his opponent's when boxing. Apparently during his boxing career he was never off the ropes as he would continually spring from rope to rope around the ring. He was a wee contentious and precarious little guy. After drinking a few beers he could become very disruptive and without warning could lash out at any one of us in the company without justification and the innocent recipient being unaware of such a pugnacious assault could suffer gravely. All off these guys were aware of their nicknames but never ever raised any form of objections, perhaps that was because they were aware that it would have been pointless anyway.

Within weeks of us moving into Mrs Benn's *Bleak House* it was full to capacity. *Bleak House* now had four lodgers, thanks to Bill and myself. Mrs Benn had requested us to try and find another two trusty and reliable lodgers for her. So when Bobby Durham [*The Rope*] arrived on site with another pipe fitter from Glasgow, we sent them both to Mrs Benn's, *Bleak House.* Bill and I had occupied the only two small single rooms and now *The Rope* and his friend were sharing the large double room with its two single beds. We were indeed a Mutley Crew. We were not concerned about the *Ropes* often anti-social behaviour, as that would only happen after he had drank a few beers and the atmosphere was raucous, which undoubtedly reminded him of his boxing days in the ring and why he would suddenly lash out and floor the poor innocent exposed individual nearest him.

Gas Reformer Plants were being built in the Sixties to convert liquid natural gas that was being shipped in huge tankers to Britain from the Middle East. This Natural gas had no odour, therefore extremely dangerous because it was impossible to detect any accidental escape until there was the almighty explosion. Gas Reformer Plants not only converted the liquid back to a gas it also impregnated the gas with an odour.

Whilst working in Leeds I reluctantly became involved in the union. We had such an incompetent depraved shop steward that I master minded a Ben-Bella and had him voted out of office. However I was not prepared to find myself being overwhelmingly being voted into office to replace him. It appeared that I was so popular as the shop-steward representing the pipe-fitters that within months I was elected the convenor off all the shop-stewards and being nicknamed El-Cid, after the Spanish Castilian military leader. It turned out to be a huge mistake on my part to get involved with the union. Prior to this shop-steward / convenor El-Cid period of my career, I had a very good reputation as a first class technician. During my El-Cid period and because of my desire to represent the workers, my challenging manner and absolute insistence on proper procedure, I was to become very unpopular with the management. I was eventually to become a serious threat and enemy to the very management that had previously appreciated me and had transferred me from the Glasgow project to the Leeds project.

Two, then four dark figures appeared like ghosts
from the darkness behind us.

I had now played the roll as El-Cid for over a year and now that the construction site was nearing completion, it was time for the first redundancies. I was shocked and saddened to find myself being one of the first pipe-fitters that was being made redundant because this was a grave mistake on behalf of the management. I did everything I possibility could to persuade them that they were making a huge error and that it could result in many tradesmen walking out the gate on an unofficial strike. I explained that my works number was number 2 and under the normal terms and conditions of employment on the site I would or should be one of the last pipe-fitters to be made redundant. I also explained that my standards as a tradesman were unquestionable therefore by making me redundant at this time they were discriminating against me because I was a shop-steward and convenor. I also warned them that not only will the pipe-fitters not accept their decision, the possibility exists that every tradesman on the site will withdraw their labour. The management were still adamant and I was made redundant.

I had to call a meeting off the pipe-fitters to explain the dilemma. Under the circumstances I had to resign as their shop-steward. My assistant was immediately voted the new shop steward and the pipe fitters voted to go on strike immediately on the grounds off my wrongful dismissal. We went on strike and I suggested to our new shop-steward that he informs all other shop-stewards that they all remain at work on site and give the management some time to consider their options. Within two days I was reinstated as a pipe fitter. On the second day back to work the pipe-fitters called a meeting and I was overwhelmingly voted and reinstated as the pipe-fitters shop-steward. In spite of the emotionally overpowering support I had received and the fact that the management must have been aware that they were guilty of wrongful dismissal on my part, this was to happen four more times.

One of the time's while we were on strike I was approached by a local news reporter whilst we were in a pub in Meadow Lane directly opposite our construction site. He wanted to interview me about the strike. I refused to make any comment until he agreed to purchase a few pints of beer for the guys from the site that were with me at the time inside the pub. My interview was printed the in the local newspaper the next day because the site management had refused to make any comment. My interview highlighted the fact that the management had already been proved wrong in the past and was about to be proved wrong again. However I also highlighted the fact that this unreasonable determined attitude by the management was delaying the commissioning of the plant and procrastinating the much needed natural gas from being piped onto the British customers. I soon realized that I personally was becoming infamous with not only the site management but with the company Humphreys & Glasgow and perhaps other companies. However within a few days we were all back at work and I was once more playing my roll as El-Cid.

Bill Craigens received a letter from his wife complete with a letter from William Press, offering him a job on a new project about to commence at Wilton I.C.I. Middlesbrough. As our project in Leeds was coming to an end Bill made a phone call to William Press to confirm that he would accept the offer of employment and commence employment as soon as it was possible. He resigned immediately and went home to Edinburgh then took up his new post in Middlesbrough at the huge I.C.I complex at Wilton on the outskirts of the industrial town of Middlesbrough.

I had no choice but to continue working on the Leeds project which was now entering the Commissioning Stages and the majority of the labour force had now been made redundant. It was now obvious that I was going to be kept on as part of the commissioning team in spite off all the strike action that had taken place by the pipe-fitters and masterminded by myself. However the management were aware of the fact that I did have previous experience of the construction and commissioning of these Gas Reformer Plants. I have to admit that I sadly missed Bill Craigens and all my other friends and colleagues that had been made redundant, including, *Sheets, The Bear* and the *Rope.*

I had become very friendly with a local Leeds pipe fitter named *Tinsdale* who was also still employed on site and an Irish guy who was a rigger named *Martin.* *Martin* like many others of his kin had moved and had settled in Leeds a few years previously. *Tinsdale* was a young pipe-fitter who lived very near Bleak-House in Meadow Lane. *Martin* lived at the other side of Leeds and nearer the town centre. *Tinsdale* had become a troublesome young guy, which did not surprise me considering that he had spent the previous eighteen months drinking with half a dozen of us Scots nearly every weekend. I could never understand his reasons because he was at least perhaps eight / nine years younger than most off us and he was a Non - Scot. Bill Craigens and I first met him when the project first started. He was the fourth pipe- fitter to be employed on the site and apparently had only recently got married. He was a very inexperienced pipe-fitter but a decent young man therefore Bill and I sort of took him under our wings and kept him right and perhaps that was one of the reasons he had taken to us Scot's. When the other Scot's began arriving on site young *Tinsdale* became a member off our group. He had spent all his life in Leeds and we introduced him to the Yates Wine Lodge that was situated in the Leeds town centre. We also introduced him to characters like *Sheets Ray, The Bear* and the *Rope*. Although *young Tinsdale* only lived ten minutes away from the project on Meadow Lane he started bringing a packed lunch with him and I'm sure it was only because he wanted to be involved in the witty banter then went on every day at our tables during the lunch break. We all eventually met his young wife because he made the mistake of introducing her to the Wine Lodge one Friday night to meet us. She was a very pretty middle class girl. *Tinsdale* himself was from a similar middle-class family background as opposed to us lot. His decision to bring his young attractive middle-class naïve wife into the Yates wine lodge and the company of characters like *Sheets Ray, The Bear and the Rope* was indeed a grave error on his part. Without any malice or indeed intentions to embarrass his young wife *Karin,* the onslaught of the Glasgow banter at the table was powerful. Young *Karin, Tinsdale's* young wife was completely mesmerized. I could see that at one time she was undecided as whether to smile, cry or scream. She was continuously attempting to acquire her young husband *Tinsdale* attention, but he was too interested in the banter and teasing stories that were unfolding endlessly. I also imagined that at times she was torn between remaining in our company or running. However, her husband young *Tinsdale*, was enjoying every second off every word whilst ignoring the turmoil and anxiety that his young wife *Karin* was experiencing. For reasons unknown to me someone suggested that *Sheets Ray* was apparently at onetime a potential ballroom dancer. Well the others at the table including myself were more than surprised at this innovation, especially when *Sheets Ray,* confirmed it. Amusing and teasing remarks suddenly erupted from almost everyone at the table, *Sheets* Ray eventually pushes his chair away from underneath him and for a large man, he was very fast and agile on his feet. We were all silenced as he sauntered around the table to where young *Karin* was sitting and he very politely held out his left hand and invited young *Karin* to dance with him. Well, once more the people at our table erupted into a laughing banter and the clapping of hands. Young *Karin* looked terrified and nervously shook her head indicating 'No'. The now boisterous lads including *Karin's* husband *Tinsdale* were encouraging *Sheets* and young *Karin* to dance. I felt truly sorry for this young girl because this was a Yates wine lodge not a dance hall. The poor girl appeared to be terrified because *Sheets* was still standing by her seat as if insisting that she gets up and dances with him. With the same agile approach that *Sheets* had made towards *Karin's* seat, he returned to his seat with thunderous roar of approval from the guys at our table. We were all drinking large glasses of white Australian wine, except young *Karin* who was drinking orange The wine was very potent, however I doubt if any off us were inebriated

192

yet, because the night was still young and unfortunately so was young *Karin*. I could not help but notice that *Karin* had indicated to her husband a few times that she wished to leave but he appeared to take no notice of her. Eventually she pushed her chair very gently away from the table and with what appeared to me to be tears in her eyes, she walked out of the wine bar. *Tinsdale* remained unconcerned, as he only appeared to be interested in listening to the amusing banter. We were all well known to the management and staff off the Yates wine lodge. Ever since the early days of the project the half-dozen off us were there nearly every Friday night. On the Saturday afternoon at lunch time we would drive to the wine lodge in a couple of cars and we would all order a bowl of the thick soup with bread. Because the soup was so hot and we only had a half hour lunch break we would pour a glass of white Australian wine into it, quickly sup it up then dash back to work.

Tinsdale, unlike us was not a travelling-man or an enigma or a misfit. That was about to change and for some reason it was only after he had met us that he became a very angry young man without a cause and a bit of a trouble maker. One Friday night when most of all the other pipe-fitters had gone because they had been made redundant, *Martin,* the Irish rigger invited young *Tinsdale* and myself to his Irish Club. *Tinsdale* had been drinking far too much that evening and had become exceptionally loud and sarcastic, especially when some members of the club were singing Irish rebel songs. In fact I do believe that if *Martin* who was a member of the private club had not been at our table and in our company, *Tinsdale* would have been unceremoniously removed from the premises, and me with him.

At the end of the evening and after we had left the club, although *Martin* lived in the opposite direction from myself and *Tinsdale* he decided to assist me escorting the young inebriated *Tinsdale* home. In the darkness under the railway bridge that the three of us were walking and supporting *Tinsdale* the silence was suddenly broken by a single voice that asked. "And where the Fluck did you pick him up Martin?" Two, then four dark figures appeared like ghosts from the darkness behind us. It was a few seconds before I could focus on the shadowy figures in the darkness in the tunnel. The four shadowy figures remained silent and two of them appeared to be stepping forward and nearer towards us. One of them was small and thickset looking, and the other taller one that was behind him broke the silence with a wheezing soft laughter. We three had stopped dead in our track's. I glanced towards *Martin* and silently breathed a sigh of relief when he enquired. "Is that you *Corley*?" "Time enough *Martin*, sure, now let's be having that scaly-wag that you have there with you *Martin*". Was the response. *Tinsdale* started staggering towards the four figures until I grabbed and stopped him. *Martin* slowly and stealthily manoeuvred himself in front of *Tinsdale* and myself. I noticed that two of the figures had now moved into a position on the road but still in front of us therefore completing a half circle around us. *Martin* was now explaining that we were both workmates and friends of his and that the young guy had far to much to drink and that he meant no harm and was no threat and even apologised for *Tinsdale's* behaviour inside the club. In spite of this, there was no response and everyone remained silent. The one nearest to me in front of us who was standing on the road had moved even closer to me and that concerned and worried me. An approaching vehicles headlights highlighted him and the other guy confirming that they were both middle-aged. As the vehicle continued to approach, it appeared to be slowing down as its headlights highlighted all seven of us. The four people standing on the road in a half circle around us had to move forward to allow the vehicle to pass. We three on the pavement immediately moved back against the wall of the tunnel. The on coming vehicle that had slowed down stopped. It was a police car, and two policemen climbed out of the vehicle with what looked like batons in their right hand. I was personally glad to see these cops and they appeared to know immediately that something was afoot. They interrogated the seven off us and after a while they appeared to think that it was the five Irish guys against *Tinsdale* and myself. As they were attempting to split us up into the two groups I confirmed that *Martin* was with us. This was turning out to be more complicated than it should have been because they started questioning why *Martin* was going in the opposite direction to where he had said he lived, which of course was absolutely correct. I informed them that he was assisting me getting the young inebriated *Tinsdale* home which they eventually accepted. We three were then instructed by the two policemen to get on our way towards Meadow Lane and *Tinsdale's* house. The four Irish men were ushered in the opposite direction and away towards the town centre. After the police car had gone *Martin* insisted on running back to speak to four the Irish guys. I was okay with that, because after all he did appear to have known them, well at least to know *Corley* their spokesman and if by *Martin* going back to speak with them, it could avoid them coming after us again, therefore I was all in favour off *Martin* going back to speak to them. *Tinsdale* and I continued walking towards Meadow Lane, *Tinsdale's* house and my *Bleak House*. After about fifteen / twenty minutes *Martin* caught up with us again. Apparently the four Irish guys had been on their way to confront us again but *Martin* had convinced them otherwise, but only just.

It was after midnight when we eventually arrived at *Tinsdale's* house. *Karin* his wife was either not at home or she was refusing to answer or open the door. *Tinsdale* had forgotten, or lost his house key because he did not have one so he started banging and kicking the door until we stopped him. He then decided

194

that he was going to break one of the street level windows and climb in. That was all we needed to have the cops on us again. I insisted that he comes home to *Bleak House* with me and stays the night and suggested to *Martin* that he does likewise. It was eventually agreed and the three of us were soon wandering up the hill towards *Bleak House*. As we were walking past the graveyard adjacent to *Bleak House,* young *Tinsdale* suddenly stopped and in due course said. "I bet you that I'm not afraid to sleep all night on one of the flat gravestones". It was early August and a warm evening, or rather a very early warm morning. *Martin* and I looked at each other in silence until I replied. "Come on *Tinsdale*, we have work to go to in the morning and it's already very late". *Martin* and I walked on and after a few steps we both stopped and looked back to find *Tinsdale* walking through the gates into the grave-yard. I was about to go after him until *Martin* grabbed my right arm. He didn't say anything but his face was serious and expressionless so we both walked on in complete silence. As we walked up the path in the front garden of *Bleak House,* Irish *Martin* stopped and as I was walking behind him I also had to stop. There was a protracted eerie silence until I asked. "What's wrong *Martin?*" He answered me with another question. "Is that a Willow Tree in front of the house?" Of course I knew it was but I still looked at the house and the huge sprawling Willow Tree and replied. "Yes". *Martin* sort of moaned making a low sound as if expressing pain and said. "Oh Jesus, oh I cant stay in that house, I can't be staying in this house. Oh Jesus no surely now I can't stay". Was his eerie plea. He moved backwards to be level with me and even in the darkness his face was pale and white. He gripped my right hand as if to shake it but didn't. He turned about and swiftly vanished out of sight leaving me standing alone staring at the Willow Tree as it stretched it's huge branches out towards the front entrance door to *Bleak House.* I never did find out why *Martin* had suddenly ran away from the Willow Tree and *Bleak House,* or if *Tinsdale* had slept all night in the grave-yard because next morning at work, both of them refused to discuss what had happened that night.

Indifferent: 19

The only thing that we Petro-Chemical construction workers all had in common was that we were all tradesmen and technicians Some off us were satisfied with our lot and perhaps others were unsatisfied with their status. Bobby Durnham [*The Rope*] would have preferred to have been a Feather Weight Champion boxer. Thomas Ray [*Sheets*] should have been a script writer for stand-up-comedian's or perhaps a ballroom dancer. [*The Bear*] should have been a professional wrestler and myself [*El-Cid*] was always interested in the arts and wanted to be an artist and eventually after retiring did become a writer of some sort. My brother-in- law and very good friend Bill Craigens [*The Burglar*] had visions at one time of being a Middle Weight Boxer, which brings me to a tale about us both whilst we were working in a town named Fleetwood.

We made our way home with only our socks on our feet as
the torrential rain lashed around and over our sodden bodies.

We were working on the construction of a Petro-Chemical Plant on the huge I.C.I complex on the outskirts of Fleetwood the fishing harbour town near Blackpool. One day just after noon and because off the continuous torrential rain the site was shut down and we were all sent home. The project buses dropped us all off at our normal pick up / drop off points in and around Fleetwood. I do believe that most off us travelling people headed directly for the nearest pub rather than go back to our usually indifferent lodging houses. Bill and I nursed our pints as we watched some of the other lads playing dominoes and darts. Even when we had to leave the bar at the three-o-clock closing time, it was still raining extremely heavy. Bill and I were still dressed in our bright yellow coloured project issued inclement weather jackets, complete with matching yellow wellington rubber boots. On our way back to our little one bedroom flat that we had rented, we spotted a sign on a very private looking posh door that said *Private Club*. We had had a few beers and It was still early afternoon. If we went back to our apartment we would be using gas and electricity, and that would inflate our monthly bills. We still had a few pounds in our pockets so we very quickly decided, why not!! After we had rang the bell a few times and were just about to walk away, the door was opened by a an elderly well dressed gent that appeared to be a wee bit inebriated. We explained to him that we were working in the town on an extremely important project and had just been rained off. We then suggested to him that it would be an honour if we were allowed entrance to have a few pints of beer in his Private Club. He was aware of the project that we were referring too but went on to explain that the club was very Private and further suggested that it would be impossible to allow us entrance dressed in the manner in which we were. Without a single word, Bill commenced removing his bright yellow plastic inclement weather coat and then his huge yellow rubber wellington boots. The slightly inebriated elderly gent smiled and suggested that he must leave the dripping wet coat and rubber wellington boots at the door. I immediately did likewise and eventually we both very humbly entered this very Private Club.

It was indeed a very reserved and secretive looking place. The elderly gent guided us into a large room with a large coal fire burning brightly in a large ornamental fireplace. Opposite the huge fireplace with the welcoming coal fire there was a small bar. Not another single person appeared to be present in this very old school looking private club. It was a possibility that the only reason we were allowed entrance was because our host, being without companionship appreciated our company. Our slightly inebriated host turned out to be a member of this Conservative Club, committee. He pulled the pints of beer that we ordered and spilled some of it's contents on the posh carpeted floor as he carried them over to the fire where he insisted that we sit down and warm ourselves. The three off us sat at this huge coal fire with our pints of beer and chatted about the I.C.I. the project and Fleetwood in general. When he eventually became aware that we were both Scots he immediately explained to us that when Queen Victoria was on her way to visit Scotland in 1847 she stopped and stayed overnight in Fleetwood. He then went on to emphasize that Fleetwood from that time on was known as the Victorian town. After a protracted silence. He pointed to Bill Craigens who had removed his scrawny old cap revealing his jet black wavy head off hair and said. "You know, I thought I recognised you. You remind me of that Scottish boxer Peter Keenan". The boxer that he was referring to was indeed a young Glasgow bantamweight European champion and renown for having kept his handsome good-looks in spite of being a professional pugilist. Bill Craigens smiled and with a sudden swiftness threw his old cap into the fire. His cap was so impregnated with oil and hair cream that it instantly burst into flames with such ferocity that the three off us had to lean backwards and away from the flaming pile of Bill's cap.

After an hour or so of enjoyable conversation and the fact that our host had been led to believe that he was conversing with the famous boxer Peter Keenan, we eventually had to leave the club because we were now insolvent. Because our host was now lacking the ability to detach himself up and out of his comfortable seat, we had to let ourselves out of the Conservative's private club. The first thing that we immediately noticed was that the rain was still falling heavily from the sky. The second thing we were soon aware of was that both off our company issue yellow wellington rubber boots and the bright yellow water resistant jackets were gone! They had obviously been taken by others that clearly had more need of them than we had. We made our way home with only our socks on our feet and the torrential rain lashing around and over our sodden bodies. To make matters worse, poor Bills head was now exposed to these dreadful elements because his faithful and long time companion, his cap had gone up in flames in the coal fire in the Conservative clubs fireplace.

Normally when working away from home we usually live in full-board accommodation but in this instance we had both travelled in my car from Edinburgh to Fleetwood and had decided during the trip that we could both save some money from our living allowance if we rented a flat and cooked for ourselves. This particular flat was supposed to be temporary as it only had a double bed in the one bedroom. We were not that fussy about having separate bedrooms because we knew that would be more expensive but we both agreed that we really needed single beds. However this temporary arrangement had lasted longer than we had anticipated. We were working seven days a week and normally ten hours a day. Therefore it was difficult if not impossible to find an alternative apartment unless we were to take some time off work, which was unthinkable. We were both in bed very early that evening or perhaps it was still very late that afternoon. During the night I was awakened when the small low area of my back felt warm and wet. It was pitch black outside and I could not put the bed lamp on because it was sitting on the only bedside table which was at the side of the bed were Bill was sleeping. I pushed Bill awake and asked him to put the table light ON. He moaned and sort off screamed silently to himself and without another single murmur he appeared to leap out off the bed leaving me to feel and fumble about for the bed light. The light from the bed light confirmed that our bed was wet and that obviously my best friend had been lying their pissing up my back. I looked around the bedroom but Bill had vanished. I climbed out of bed and quickly removed my wet vest and underpants. I was standing naked when Bill sauntered back into the bedroom also naked now. We looked at each other but said nothing. We both looked at the bed but still said nothing. Bill started stripping off all the bedclothes and lifted up the mattress as if looking for something. I asked him what he was looking for. He didn't reply but looked at me surreptitiously. After some silence I suggested. "Oh, I see Bill it wasn't you! It was a wee boy that did it then ran away. Where the hell is he Bill? He's not in the bathroom as you have already looked in there. He's not under the mattress, so where has the wee guy gone Bill?" He closed one eye expressively as if in answer and then looked under the bed. I suppose it was a shade of mockery to relieve the seriousness of the situation. I headed for the bathroom to have a shower. After we both showered and made some tea it was still only five o-clock in the morning. Bill suggested that he should take the day off work and take the sheets to the laundry and do something to get the mattress dry. I asked him what he was going to use for money and suggested that we still both go to work and borrow some cash from our fellow workers, or get a sub from the site agent. Then instead of working overtime we would come home early and replace the soiled goods. As we were eventually preparing to leave for work and catch our project courtesy bus, Bill was searching all over the flat looking under the chairs cushions, under the chairs and in the cupboards. I was standing holding the outside door open and eventually shouted to him. "Come on, we are going to miss our bus. Are you still looking for the wee boy that pissed on our bed and ran away?". "No smart Ass, I'm looking for my Cap". Was Bills instant reply!!!

The Gas Reformer Plant in Leeds was eventually commissioned. I left Leeds, Meadow Lane, *Bleak-house, Martin* and *Tinsdale* and everything else in Leeds. I never ever had any reason to return to Leeds and as young *Tinsdale* was not a travelling man like the rest of us, I never ever met up with him again.

Indifferent: 20

On returning home, I eventually had to take another job as a plumber because that's all that was available. I didn't have the nerve to ask Mr Copeland for another job so I just approached the unemployment office at Tollcross and they had given me a choice of half a dozen plumbers jobs that were available so I selected the plumbers shop that was the nearest to where we lived in Corstorphine. I disliked plumbing work immensely, I found most of the work demeaning and wages compared to pipe-fitting were poor therefore I found it extremely difficult to accept this type of employment as being permanent.

I eventually found a job as a pipe-fitter with Costain's International on a project that they were involved in down in South Wales. The job was in Newport in one of the huge sheet steel rolling mills. However I had only been on the job a few weeks when I received a message that one of our wee girls was seriously ill in the Sick Children's Hospital in Edinburgh. The Site Agent had just driven me in his car from my accommodation in Newport to the railway station in Cardiff. He had received an urgent phone call from the London office and had turned up at the house where I was lodging around 0900 hours in the evening with the bad news and a travel warrant for the overnight train from Cardiff to Edinburgh. After he had assisted me in checking in for the overnight train he eventually left me sitting in the waiting room in Cardiff railway station. I was suffering and was in a state of shock with huge tears swelling up in my eyes so I decided to go for a walk as the waiting room was crowded. I walked about the dark eerie railway station aimlessly like a zombie. I remember being unsure as to where the ticket collector had told me where I had to change trains as the train that I was about to board did not go to Edinburgh direct therefore I was concerned about missing my train connection The train that I was about to catch was due any minute and I didn't want to miss it by wandering off to find the ticket collector to ask him again which station I had to change at to catch my connection to Edinburgh. I remembered that it was an overnight train therefore I had all night to get it sorted. I also remember thinking if only I could speak to Kathleen and find out if she was okay because I knew she would be extremely upset and that once more I was not there for her. I didn't even know which one off our wee girls it was that was seriously ill and what the serious illness was and exactly how serious it was.

As I touched my wifes arm the huge tears that were
swelled-up in her eyes burst like a dam and flooded her beautiful tired face.

The train journey was a nightmare. I do remember having to sit with other people but they did not exist. I knew they were there but could not see or hear them. I must have dozed off to sleep and when I tried to open my eyes again they appeared not too want to be opened. Perhaps my tears had glued them together. It appears that even in my sleep huge tear-drops were escaping from my closed eyes. I was crying for a wee girl with no name because I was unaware if it was *Linda* or *Lorna* that was so ill. Tears also for my lonely wife who I knew would be suffering unimaginable agony. My uncontrollable tear drops were also because once more I was not there for them. I was aware that the other passengers sitting around me were anxious and perhaps uncomfortable at my distress. An elderly lady did to talk to me but I was so distressed and troubled I just could not speak and decided that I must try and find a carriage were I could suffer in silence. I wandered up and down the train like a robot that was mechanically programmed until I eventually found an empty first class carriage. I was totally unconcerned of the consequences of my behaviour if and when I was discovered by the ticket collector. I slid into the empty first-class carriage and ultimately cried myself to sleep.

Without having been disturbed in my first class carriage by the ticket collector I did change trains in Leeds early next morning and eventually arriving in the Waverly railway station in Edinburgh and went directly to the Sick Children's Hospital in Sciences Road. Kathleen my dear wife smiled at me as I entered the room where one of our wee girl's was lying in a bed. It was wee Linda and she was attached to various plastic bags that were hanging off a metal stand above her wee head. Linda was asleep. As I touched my wifes arm the huge tears that were swelled- up in her eyes burst like a dam and flooded her beautiful tired face. We hugged each other but could not speak as we were both crying. In due course through sobs and tears Kathleen told me in huge gulps. *"She, she Is going to be okay".*

Wee Linda had an unusual blood disorder that nearly took her from us. Kathleen eventually explained to me that wee Linda was in a Coma when she was rushed into hospital and remained in a Coma while they ran all sorts off tests. In time they eventually discovered that she was suffering from *Hypoglycaemia*. A serious lack of sugar in her blood cells. After a good few hours and when Linda was awake, we both fussed over her and just wanted to cuddle and hug her. Some time later, the doctors and nurses persuaded Kathleen that nobody was going to kidnap wee Linda and that she must get out off the hospital and go home and get some rest. We went directly to my mother's house as she was looking after Lorna and Mark. That afternoon Kathleen, Lorna, Mark and myself went home to our own house in Corstorphine. After a few more day's Linda was eventually discharged from the hospital and was smothered in loving kindness and care.

I had registered myself unemployed at the Tollcross unemployment office. However after a few weeks and owing to the fact that there were plenty of jobs available for plumbers, I was eventually forced to take a job as a plumber with a shop in Leith. I did not have the nerve to return to Copeland's. The job as a plumber with the plumber shop in Leith lasted about a month. I was sent to a house to repair a lead cold water pipe that was leaking at the sink in the kitchen. Whilst I was using the paraffin blow-lamp to make a new lead joint, the flame from my blow-lamp touched the edge of the flimsy window curtains and they instantly went up in flames and disintegrated within seconds and disappeared. The friendly elderly women who had just given me a lovely cup of tea and biscuits was so shocked that she remained silent. I explained to the elderly lady that she should not be concerned as by boss's insurance would have to replace the window curtains. My boss did have to replace the window curtains that turned out to be the most expensive curtains available in Edinburgh because apparently the elderly lady produced a receipt for window curtains purchased from Jenners in Princess Street. Not long after that incident I was made redundant.

I immediately went to work for another plumber shop directly across the road from the Tollcross unemployment department. I remember thinking that this could be very handy because If I get paid-off again, I wouldn't have very far to go to look for another job. I was sent to a roof job, not just an ordinary roof job but a church roof job. Not just an ordinary church roof job, this church was located at the *Holy Corner* in Morningside in the centre of Edinburgh. *Holy Corner* is a cross-roads and on each and every corner there is a church, and all four churches are all facing each other as if in combat for parishioners

I have no idea if it was the spiritual awe that frightened me or if it was the fact that this was an old zinc roof dome that was being replaced by copper. There were three off us on this job. One really elderly guy who was in charge. In fact he was the only one who knew what the hell was going on. He was the only one with real knowledge on how to go about covering this dome-roof in copper. Laying copper sheets on a flat roof was a bit off a specialist job. Covering a dome-roof with copper requires the skills of an expert who has to be a very creative technician. I had worked previously on laying Zinc roofs and found that was a wee bit difficult, but nothing compared to covering a dome-roof in copper because this was a first for me and the other plumber. The wee elderly plumber in charge looked more like a retired professor. The way he went about his business was overwhelming. Another aspect of this daunting task was the location. Nearly everywhere you looked it was nothing but domes and church pinnacles. It was as if God might strike you stone dead if you uttered an unkind or foul word.

The elderly plumber, the professor had a very long nose which highlighted his pious and reverent appearance. I always thought that the synagogue would have been more appropriate for him. His chin was also longer than the norm, perhaps that was because he would continually stop to ponder a thought and stroke the long portion of his lower jaw. As I have said previously, this was an extremely specialised technical assignment and he had no one that he could consult, except himself He was also a veritable peace-maker. When ever the other plumber and I would disagree about some procedure in reference to a particular task he had given us, he always succeeded in making us both, correct. The professor always appeared to work alone unless he needed assistance in moving the heavy bundles of copper. He would give us tasks that required us to work together as a team. He was such a nice guy, he would rather allow us to make mistakes and then show us where we had went wrong. He was not one for smiling or laughing, perhaps that was because he had nothing to laugh about because he had a couple of unreliable incompetent copper roofer's working with him.

One evening after the three kids had gone to bed I confided in Kathleen how inadequate I felt working on this copper dome-roof job. Because neither of us wanted me to work away from home again as a pipe-fitter, Kathleen suggested. "Why don't you try doing something else. I know how you dislike plumbing, but you're so clever and smart, so why not do something else?".

Eventually I left the copper dome-roof job, the good professor and the plumb-ing. I had applied for a job as a salesman selling insurance. After an interview and a two week's intense course with the Prudential Insurance Company, I was out and about collecting the weekly payments for existing insurance premiums and attempting to sell additional insurance cover. I was using my own car and was being paid a measly car allowance. No one had explained to me that the previous salesman in this area had just recently resigned and I very soon learned why. It was an area in Granton that was sordid and immoral. It involved me having to work in the evening because most of the customers would see you coming to their doors during the normal nine to five hours and they would not answer the door. It involved trying to get payments for existing insurance premiums from people that did not have any money or would rather spend the money on alcohol or cigarettes. It involved dealing with people that had no moral ethical virtues. I was instructed by the Prudential Insurance Company who employed me to go for the Friday- night pay-night's. These Friday nights were a nightmare. Inebriated males were more interested in giving me a thrash-ing, as opposed to making any payments. Females, old and young were more interested in offering me their bodies as an alternative to giving me cash for the payments. I was soon to realize that I should have remained with the professor on the copper dome roof and learn a great deal. I could have been looking at the spectacle of the completion of the masterfully copper shining dome. I very quickly escaped from the nightmarish Friday nights, the drunken men and poor desperate women and immediately returned to the boring plumbing. I eventually managed to talk my wife and children into leaving the beautiful city of Edinburgh with its Castle, Palace, Royal Mile, Princess Street and not forgetting its stunning green coloured copper roof-domes. I persuaded them to move to the North East of England where I was offered a permanent job as a pipe-fitter supervisor with the Imperial Chemical Industry [I.C.I] The exact location was Middlesbrough.

Lightning Source UK Ltd.
Milton Keynes UK
UKOW06f1651240416

272802UK00001B/58/P